CASSANDRA EASON

A complete guide to
Psychic
Development

PIATKUS

PIATKUS

First published in Great Britain in 1997 by Piatkus Books
This paperback edition published in 2002 by Piatkus Books

Copyright © Cassandra Eason

Reprinted in 2004, 2005, 2007

The moral right of the author has been asserted

A CIP catalgue record for this book
is available from the British Library

ISBN 978-0-7499-2323-5

Typeset by Action Typesetting Limited, Gloucester
Printed in the UK by CPI Bookmarque, Croydon, CR0 4TD

Piatkus Books
An imprint of
Little, Brown Book Group
100 Victoria Embankment
London EC4Y 0DY

A Hachette Livre UK Company

Contents

Section One

Developing
Your Psychic Powers

Introduction

Tracie's mother had been dead for thirteen years when she appeared beside her daughter's bed one night. 'I've got something to tell you,' she said. 'Don't be frightened because you will be all right. It is not the time for you to come to me. But you are in danger. You are going to meet your friend Kate and she will drive carelessly on the motorway, so you have got to be her other pair of eyes. I want you to put on the cross and chain Dad and I gave you and wear it all the time.'

When Tracie awoke from what she described as something 'more vivid than a dream' she told her husband about the warning. But he dismissed it. Nevertheless, when Tracie left her home on the Isle of Wight to meet her friend, she took the cross.

They went to Maidstone in Kent to see Tracie's brother:

On the way back, we were chatting and singing along with the radio on the motorway when suddenly I touched the cross and saw my mother's face, saying, 'You've got to look round now. The danger is here.'

I turned just as Kate accelerated to 70 miles per hour. She was just about to pull out into the fast lane when I screamed out to stop. I spotted a car that was coming through fast out of nowhere and we just clipped him. Had she not pulled back we would have smashed into him, as she had not seen him. We were trembling and shaking. We went on slowly to the next services and I told Kate about my mother.

Of course, my husband dismissed the incident as coincidence but I know that my mother made me look round at that moment and saved our lives.

Tracie recounted her experience at a psychic development class I was teaching at our local college. Unlike her husband I did not dismiss her experience, although I cannot explain it. Could it be that the ghost of Tracie's mother, like so many deceased mothers and grandmothers whose cases I have researched, acted as her daughter's guardian angel? Or was it that, during her dream, Tracie somehow tapped into the future? Predictive dreams have a long history – take the story of Joseph in the Bible for example.

Creative dreaming, precognition and seeing ghosts are all discussed in this book and techniques are suggested to refine and focus these natural abilities. But there are also many other forms of psychic power, some of which appear quite spontaneously in times of crisis and others of which can be practised and developed. A number are described in the following pages.

We all have these intuitive powers and may find that an experience such as Tracie's can not only trigger an interest in the paranormal but awaken powers that may have been dormant since childhood.

What Are Psychic Powers?

At their simplest, psychic powers are the natural, powerful instincts and intuitions we all possess. These manifest themselves quite automatically in everyday life and may only seem remarkable on careful consideration. Here are some common examples:

1. You frequently phone your mother to find her number is engaged. She is trying to phone you at the same moment.
2. You meet someone new who is wearing a smart city suit and appears to possess impeccable credentials. Nevertheless you instantly distrust him or her. You find, days or even weeks later, that your initial reservations were justified.
3. You wake minutes or seconds before your baby, even though the infant is in a different room, has no regular waking pattern and you are so tired you could sleep through an earthquake.
4. You decide, apparently on impulse, to change your route to work one morning. Later you hear on the radio that there was a motorway accident or an unusual traffic problem on your customary road.

5. You 'know' instinctively that someone you are meeting will be early and, to their amazement, meet an earlier train or plane which he/she had unexpectedly caught.

6. You phone your best friend on impulse to ask what is wrong. He/she tells you that there has been a disaster in their love life or an unexpected financial or health problem, but he/she had not wanted to worry you.

7. You visit an old castle or abbey, touch one of the walls and instantly see in your mind's eye an event which the guide confirms or you may see a person who appears in a portrait in another room.

8 You book into a hotel room but feel a bad atmosphere and cannot sleep. On making discreet enquiries you discover that long ago a person died tragically in that room.

9. When you are distressed, you can smell your deceased grandmother's perfume.

10. When you were a child you had an invisible friend who told you things that later turned out to be true.

11. Sometimes your dreams are so vivid that you feel they are real. Next day you find that part of your dream comes true in a totally unpredictable way.

12. You suddenly think of someone you have not seen or heard from in years and the next day you receive a letter or phone call from him or her.

13. You have a special outfit or charm that always seems to bring you luck.

14. You have a mother or grandma who was psychic.

15. Your family call you a witch because you always know who is calling as soon as the phone rings.

16. You are fascinated by a particular period in history and, when you are just drifting off to sleep or just waking, you seem to have strange memories of another life.

17. You go abroad to a place for the first time and instantly feel totally at home and can identify landmarks and find places without a map.

18. You have seen lights and colours around people's heads since you were a child and were surprised to discover that not everyone could do this.

19. Animals and children trust you instantly and your pets are always in the hall waiting whenever you come home.

20. You have always possessed the ability to make people feel

better and can detect a warmth coming from your hands as you rub a child's hurt knee or soothe a partner's headache.

21. You know about people's lives before they tell you and find that strangers treat you as a psychic agony aunt.

If you recognise eight or more of these experiences your psychic powers are already well-tuned. Even if you only relate to three or four, psychic ability is still present, although more dormant. Perhaps your natural psychic powers as a child were not encourged and you have come to rely on your five senses and logic alone. In psychic development, logic is just as important as the more intuitive side of your nature, for real 'magic' is rooted in the everyday world and relies on planning, consistency and action rather than airy-fairy spells on windswept moors. Intuition (the ability to obtain information from the sixth sense) unfolds and develops quite naturally the more you rely on it. This book therefore includes a wide range of divinatory forms, magical rituals and suggestions for finding the right way to become more aware of other dimensions.

Magic evolves, and the practices of the Ancient Egyptians or Vikings, for example, must be adapted to meet the needs of today's world. Above all, psychic development is a personal path. Following the rules of others blindly as I used to do, no matter how expert these established rituals may seem, stifles personal creativity. What is more, it reduces a process as natural as smiling, appreciating a beautiful sunset or marvelling at a newborn child or animal, to a series of learned steps to achieve a prescribed solution. This rigid approach has spread from medicine, psychology and technology to magic and so we have learned to distrust our innate wisdom. Yet we all know the right way for ourselves if we trust our inner voice and instincts.

Throughout this book you are encouraged to experiment, substituting your preferred substances or rituals where the ones in the book do not quite fit. Until the Industrial Revolution in Victorian times, and even later in remote parts, magic belonged to ordinary people and was based on the countryside, on the seasons, on flowers, trees and herbs. People tried to make sense of life, love and death by using natural forces as a focus for their own needs. Until shortly before the Second World War, grandmothers read tea leaves or looked into bowls of water lit by a candle and offered a source of wisdom to their families. Mothers sat by the bedside of a sick child and gazed into the candle flame at the visions that naturally flickered through the exhaustion, anxiety and love. Women washing clothes in huge old coppers, in the brewhouses that were a part of my own childhood in the back streets of Birmingham, saw pictures in the suds as they worked and used these to interpret the present and perhaps the future. They paused to read the clouds scudding overhead as they pegged out the laundry in the bleak backyards. Leave the pages of this and any other book as soon as possible and follow your natural instincts.

How to Use This Book

You will need a notebook or ring binder so that you can make your own book of rituals, keep the results of your divination work, create your own symbol system and make notes of special dreams, talismans that prove useful or any past or future life recall. Witches traditionally had a Book of Shadows containing all their spells and healing remedies. Such books are often thought to be dark tomes containing weird ceremonies and demonic incantations, but most would bear more resemblance to a herbal recipe book and personal journal. Because not many people could write before the Victorian era, few of them kept such books. Much of the lore of ordinary people followed an oral tradition.

A Book, not of Shadows but of Wisdom, can be a personal record of important aspects of your life – a spiritual CV. You can hand on this healing wisdom to your children when they reach adulthood, much as you would hand on a family photograph album. It may even include family psychic experiences, such as children's invisible friends, examples of occasions when a child reads a mother's mind or of a man's or a woman's telepathic links with a partner, moments of positive precognition or dates when you sensed a grandma's perfume. We always think we will remember these precious examples of love but it is very easy to forget the details over the years. Also, you may like to record bits of family folklore, remedies, tales of a great-grandfather who perhaps walked 50 miles from the countryside to the city or Romany family links. These legends, embellished over time, are the folk memory of tomorrow. As we tell fewer stories of family myth and wisdom to our children so the personal spiritual culture is lost.

Most of the items you will need are obtainable from any food store, supermarket or department store. I believe that we should use everyday items for magic. Magic and divination should always be rooted in the everyday world both to ground the energies in the real world and to prevent the tendency inherent in many of us, myself especially, to dress up and play-act, to use the psychic world as a substitute for (rather than a supplement to) reality.

Begin reading the book and trying out different forms of divination. If any section does not interest you skim through it very quickly or miss it out. However, if you see an area that fascinates you, begin with that. There are many entry points into the psychic. Many of the sections are linked and the more you experiment, the further your psychic powers will unfold and evolve. In this way, all the different forms of psychic development become strands of a unified increased awareness and inspiration in all aspects of your life. Magic is closely linked with psychic development because, once the boundaries of possibility are expanded, you can reach other dimensions, and use natural forces outside your own psyche or soul, to improve your own life and the lives of others.

What Is Magic?

At the most basic level, magic is an ability to make connections between apparrently disconnected elements and to use the natural energies of the earth and the sky to amplify our own innate abilities both psychic and worldly. Magic, said one clairvoyant, is giving a project, wish or idea 'a dynamic kick-start to get it off the tarmac of thought into actuality and then following the initial impetus with action in the everyday world'. Magic is therefore the accumulation of inner and outer energies, focused on a particular goal expressed in an actual or visualised symbol, and the release of those energies into the cosmos so that they echo in other lives and perhaps touch others in a positive way.

Where Do Magical Powers Originate?

The Aborigines of Australia, the Maoris, Native American Indians and Africans of many tribes are influenced by the wisdom of their forebears. Some people in our technological world still believe that they have spirit ancestors who guide them in similar though less manifest and direct ways. Others, like the psychologist Jung, think that there is a two-million-year-old man in each of us and that we can reach him via the collective well of unconscious wisdom from all ages and places. Indeed, in other belief systems, such as Theosophy, it has been suggested that we can access the future through the same pool of knowledge, remembering that we all have choice and that we alone can decide our future path. I am more comfortable with these ideas than with those involving spirit ancestors, but have met many people who put up a powerful case for benign influences from beyond.

Is It Possible to Foretell the Future?

Some people do have powerful foreknowledge of specific future events. This tends to come spontaneously through dreams or visions and it is hard to explain away such instances as coincidences. What is interesting is that foreknowledge can actually change the future. For example, Dolores who lives in California had a vision of her son riding his motor bike and having a bad fall. Two weeks later, at work in the local police department, Dolores 'saw' – as if on a television screen – Greg falling off his moped and his head hitting the cement. Cars were running over him as in the dream. Dolores began clapping because she believed that by performing a different action, however bizarre, she could change the ending of the dream. Minutes later news came that Greg had just hit the cement but a van had stopped inches from his head and protected him from the traffic. Greg survived.

However, conscious fortune telling through scrying, looking into a surface such as a mirror, crystal or bowl of water, tends to capture potential futures (that is, given our personal heritage and unique talents, the destinies we are likely to fulfil). Through exploring them we can again change them by seeing alternatives, and psychic development can enable us to tune this natural faculty to a high degree of precision.

How Far Can You Develop Your Psychic Powers?

Some people find it easier to acknowledge and develop their psychic powers than others; just as some people go on to become great concert pianists, while others are content to bang out a tune on social occasions. On the other hand, some of the most gifted mediums and psychics I have met have used their talents privately for their friends and family and the strangers who seem to recognise a wise soul instinctively rather than on the public platform.

We all have psychic powers and can develop them to enrich our personal lives and to help others either personally or professionally. However, psychic powers always operate best when concerned with human needs and emotions and are actually diminished when the desire for gain or prestige replace the desire to learn and serve. With the psychic, what you give out you get back, perhaps not in financial terms but in happiness, peace of mind and the joy your positive gifts impart to others.

In a later section there are suggestions for working in groups and also bodies that can offer training. However, spiritual work is very tiring and can be quite heart-rending when dealing with some of the sorrows that make people turn to you for a psychic reading or advice. If you do become a professional clairvoyant or medium, you will find it is work to which you must always give 100 per cent. For every Mystic Meg or Doris Stokes there are thousands of gifted healers, clairvoyants and healers who can barely cover their overheads.

The ideas in the book come from a variety of traditions and have all been tried in a variety of situations and with people I have met in my magic classes at the local college, at work and at home. In this book are ideas I suggested in previous books which have been developed, modified or sometimes completely turned around by the feedback I have received from readers and those who have worked with me. For example, I was giving a class in wax divination – a method of seeing pictures in the melted wax from a candle – and my students were drawing deeply spiritual meanings from it. Then we came to Ian, an operating theatre nurse. 'What do you see?' I asked. 'It looks like the kidney operation we were doing this afternoon,' he replied.

Under such conditions, ego has to take a back seat. I welcome any feedback from readers and do eventually reply to letters, given the limitations of a full working day, five children and five cats, plus assorted kittens according to the mating season.

1

Psychic Exploration

Psychic powers can be used on many levels, for personal development, to help others through psychic readings and healing and to attain what it is we really need. Mary, a healer from Cork, described how, through focusing on her special crystal, her wish came true – not for wealth beyond her wildest dreams or an exotic holiday but simply a floor for her home.

I believe that in every crystal there is a special spirit or angel who can, if you can learn to communicate with him or her, help you with any problems. I have a special clear quartz crystal containing a wonderful spirit who helps me with my healing work and to whom I talk when I am in trouble or unhappy. Some years ago, my husband and I built our own house on some land in Ireland. However, when we had finished there was no money left to finish the floors. We had to make do with rough cement which was cold and damp in the winter months and very uncomfortable for the sick people who came for healing. At last I decided to ask my crystal if he would give me a floor, for there was no other way I could afford one. A few days later, totally unexpectedly, a well-dressed man came to the door. He had injured his left leg but was desperate to run in the London marathon and had heard that I was a healer. I used my special crystal to ask for healing for him. His leg recovered very quickly and he ran the marathon.

Not long afterwards, he turned up again at my door, this time asking for urgent advice about a deal that could make him a great deal of money. I consulted my crystal, but refused to take any money for giving the answer, as I do not charge for healing or advice.

About a month later, a woman who said she was his wife knocked on the door. She pressed an envelope into my hand and begged me to accept the enclosed money as a gift because the deal had made them both very rich. I refused to accept, but she insisted that such an amount was only pocket money to them and that her husband would be very offended if I did not take it. When I opened it, the cheque was, I thought, for a modest amount and so I accepted. However, when I showed my husband, he told me to put on my glasses. The cheque was for £2,500 – enough to pay for all the floors in the exact material I wanted. I still have the cheque as a memento.

Many people have discovered that, as they become more spiritually aware and able to tune into information that comes from no known source, urgent needs are met and difficulties are more easily overcome. This seems to occur through the conjunction of seemingly unconnected normal and paranormal factors (what Jung calls synchronicity or meaningful coincidences). For example, you might find yourself in a particular place totally unexpectedly because of a transport hitch and meet someone important, a new love or business partner. Or a stranger, given your name months or even years earlier, may turn up for the first time exactly at the moment when he or she can fulfil some wish that you have secretly made and consigned to the candle flame or scratched on a stone and cast in a flowing river.

Or you may need a computer or fax but be unable to afford one. Having changed your plans owing to a cancelled appointment, you meet a new acquaintance and he or she just happens to mention an old but perfectly serviceable machine gathering dust at home. Then again, you might be homeless temporarily. A friend of a friend is sent to work abroad with only a few days' notice and urgently needs a flat sitter in return for looking after the cat. Or you are searching for an obscure book or record and suddenly see it in the window of a shop in a strange town you are only in because you took the wrong turning on a journey.

These are all actual instances I have encountered and they all began with the needy person asking the cosmos, an angel or chosen deity for help. No one fully understands this process, but it would seem that, by pushing back the boundaries of possibility, our own efforts are amplified by creative powers within ourselves and others. The key factors are a specific urgent need and a strong belief that the request or wish will be granted.

'Psychic bargaining' can begin quite early in psychic development. Keep a note of any seeming coincidences when the right person is in the right place at the right time, almost as though our paranormal magnetism is attracting others to a web of mutual advantage. The only proviso is that we are receptive to the unspoken needs of others.

Where to Begin

Creating a Psychic Place

As children, many of us had treasure boxes, filled with gold and pearl buttons, sequins, glittery ribbons and tiny silver figures from the top of birthday cakes. We spent hours weaving magical worlds around our treasures. In return we could skip in and out of the other dimensions at will, playing with fairies, seeing angels, magic animals or people invisible to the adult eye.

To rekindle those early psychic powers, it can be helpful to create a magical place – whether a table top, a dressing table or even a piece of slate propped on two bricks – not for expensive magical tools but for personal symbols. There you could have a few special crystals, bought during a happy holiday or given to you by friends or family, two or three basic essential oils such as lavender for tranquillity, lemon (kept away from sunlight) for energy and eucalyptus for health.

There could be a small circular tray on which to keep a herb pouch created for a current need (see p. 213–4) or a talisman (see Chapter 22) or lucky charm, etched with special words of power or healing, perhaps written in a magical alphabet (see Section Six). You will also need two candlesticks. I have one with a sun design and another in a moon shape, but you can choose whatever kind you consider magical. The first will hold a candle in your personal astrological colour and the second a candle in a colour to represent your present special wish or need (see p. 86).

You may want a central focus for your magical space, a pottery or glass animal representing a species that has significance for you, a figure of a deity that for you represents wisdom and goodness, or a carved wooden abstract sculpture, perhaps created from a piece of wood you found in a forest. Decorate your special place with a natural symbol according to the time of year: a corn dolly at harvest; greenery with red berries at Christmas; the first buds of springtime. Finally, make a circle of small crystals to mark the boundaries.

Spend a few minutes each morning or evening in your magic area and let it gradually accumulate your personal essence so that it becomes a repository of energy or calm.

You can use psychic powers anywhere – on a crowded train, in a noisy office or factory. But it is good to have a warm comfortable place, where you can keep your treasures and be quiet, perhaps sitting on cushions or your bed. There you can enjoy the most precious commodity of all – time for yourself to be yourself and widen the bounds of possibility by staring into a candle flame or watching inks make patterns as they drift over water (see Scrying, p. 59).

Making a Magical Treasure Box

Have a square container of wood or some other natural substance such as raffia, to hold items you will need for your initial explorations. You can add to your treasure box as you read the book and try new techniques, so make your container large enough to keep a store of essentials. However, you may like to buy a few basic supplies to begin with. These include:

1. Small jars or pouches of dried herbs, especially those associated with divination: parsley, sage, rosemary and thyme.
2. Candles of different colours, especially red, gold, silver, white and green and, if possible, an undyed beeswax candle that can be used in any kind of ritual.
3. A small selection of essential oils: jasmine for the intuition of the Moon; frankincense for the joy of the Sun; patchouli for the communicative powers of Mercury; geranium for the empathy of Venus; peppermint for the impetus to action of Mars; bergamot (keep out of direct sunlight) for the wisdom of Jupiter; and tea tree oil for Saturn's acceptance of change.
4. Incense sticks or cones and a small burner: pine for energy

and money; rose for love and healing; and sandalwood for both psychic insight and protection.
5. A long pointed crystal of clear quartz for energy and a rounded black crystal for protection.
6. An uncut and unpolished piece of amethyst or rose quartz large enough to use as a focus.
7. A plain white china bowl for water scrying (looking for pictures in water).

I used to think that such preparations were pretentious but, after years of having my magical things scattered by my children and used as playthings, I now have my own special place where they can touch my magical items but must not remove them. This has been an important step for me emotionally as well as spiritually for, before I began psychic development seriously, I regarded myself as part of my children and so did not have a definite centre. Now, however, I am developing a stronger sense of myself.

When to Begin

Before the invention of clocks as we know them, sand, candle clocks and sundials were used to measure the regular divisions of the day by the movements of the Sun. And these pivotal times, coming as they did at natural marker points in the agricultural day, accumulated the energy of human desires and concerns over the centuries. When most people lived in villages, the day was regulated by the chiming of the church clock. So the so-called chime hours – 3.00, 6.00, 9.00, 12.00, 15.00, 18.00, 21.00, 24.00 – were said to be very magical. You can use the chime hours, each of which has a special focus, based on the old country timetables where people rose and went to bed by the sun. The most powerful time is on the actual hour and the five minutes after:

* 6am – For new beginnings and fertility both of humans and of projects
* 9am – Money problems and money-making ideas.
* 12pm – Career and overcoming seemingly impossible odds.
* 3pm – Change and travel.
* 6pm – Family matters, marriage and partnerships.

* 9pm – Love, friendship and learning.
* 12am – Healing, mending quarrels and the psychic.
* 3am – Peace, elderly relations and quiet sleep.

The Celtic day began at sunset and for this reason Halloween (the eve of All Hallows) and May Eve became more significant than the following days for magical rituals. Dawn, noon and sunset were also regarded as significant times:

* Dawn is good for magic involving new beginnings, change and attracting magic.
* Noon, when the sun is overhead, is for action, power and success.
* Dusk is for love, healing and banishing magic.

When dawn or dusk fall on a chime hour the energies are especially strong. For this reason noon is always a peak time.

How to Begin

Some of the finest psychics neither consciously relax nor meditate before giving a reading or carrying out a ritual. With experience, we can all learn to read 'cold' and trust our intuitions when faced with a sudden dilemma or opportunity that demands an instant decision.

However, may people find that, especially if psychic work is unfamiliar or decisions are more complex, a more gentle transition between the everyday bustle of the physical world and divination or magic enables them to leave behind conscious worries and influences that may block unconscious insights.

Informal Preparations

In practice, much psychic work takes place in the evening when there is time and quiet, but shift workers can easily work in the early morning. Eat a simple meal, as light-headedness can induce dizziness and actually blur focused inspiration. Have a leisurely bath, using about ten drops of essential oils that encourage psychic awareness. Place the oils in the water after the bath has been filled so that they float on the surface. Either mix three drops each of oils such as bergamot, geranium, neroli and ylang-ylang (see Oils for Happiness, p. 197) or use 10 drops of a single oil and afterwards slip on something warm, but loose and light.

Light a candle in soft pink or lilac (colours of the spirit) and hold a large uncut piece of amethyst or rose quartz – these are gentler than crystal quartz. Let light from the candle and shadows from the wall reflect on the crystal. Do not try to induce visions but visualise within the crystal a multi-petalled pink or lilac flower slowly unfolding so that it fills the whole room with soft light and encloses you within it.

We can all visualise quite spontaneously. However, like a camera that is out of focus, we may need to readjust our perspective. As infants we visualised our needs and desires and made sense of our universe through pictures not words, using our imagination as a powerful tool of creativity and psychic energy. Children's psychic powers operate entirely through the imagination and begin where the imagination ends. Imagination is not regarded highly in today's world and so we may need to bring imagination, daydreaming and fantasy back into our lives. These are the first stages in reawakening our latent psychic abilities.

You can also use a technique such as going backwards through the alphabet and seeing all the letters from Z to A falling behind you; or counting down from 100 to 0, visualising the numbers as coloured butterflies fluttering just out of reach.

For outdoor psychic work, such as past or future life recall or place psychometry, walk along a long straight road or track through a field or forest, looking ahead so that the scenery blurs into colours and images. Walking so that your body moves rhythmically is an excellent way to free the unconscious and to induce visions of past or future lives.

Swimming too can grant access to a deeper level of awareness. Swim – outdoors if it's sunny – early in the morning when the pool is fairly empty or in the evening under the lights. Go home to a ready-prepared tray of dark inks and a bowl of clear water, for you will be particularly receptive to any form of scrying involving water.

Alternatively, you could read pictures in the clouds or stop at a wood or park and listen to the messages rustling in the leaves. There are few limits to the kinds of natural stimuli you can use for creating magical pictures. This book touches on only a small sample of stimuli that go back to the beginning of conscious awareness.

A More Formal Approach

Relaxation works on the principle that you begin by consciously tensing your body. Then, as you relax, you become receptive to a world of images and awareness that bubble beneath the constraints of conscious concerns. You can sit cross-legged on the floor if this is a naturally comfortable position, or sit in a chair that supports your back and arms well with your feet resting gently on the floor. For many people a hard chair, without arms, creates discomfort that can intrude on a relaxed state.

Conventional methods of relaxation begin with either closing your eyes or fixing your gaze on a point on the wall. Block out your immediate worries, such as the shopping list, report or speech you are mentally composing, and become aware of your body and yourself inside the body – safe and protected.

You may wish to play a pre-recorded tape, giving step-by-step instructions on relaxation, allowing about a minutes to tense and relax each limb. Experiment. Some people take much longer, but others prefer to progress rapidly. You should ask a friend to record a tape for you and make one for him or her. Or you can work together, taking it in turns to guide each other. Often I find, when I am trying to relax other people, I almost send myself to sleep. So, in time, you will be able to share the experience.

Begin with either the top or bottom of your body and move slowly to the other extremity:

* Starting at your toes, press your right foot against the floor, tighten your toes and then relax them, visualising them resting on a soft pillow.
* Press the left foot against the floor, again tightening the toes and relaxing gradually.
* Next, clench your lower legs as though you were going to kick out. Begin by tensing the right, then relaxing it. Now do this with the left and let go, so that each leg is resting against an unseen bank of cushions.
* Tense your thighs, pressing them together and relaxing (once

again, right followed by left), then your buttocks, lower back, stomach, arms (right and left), hands (clenched to make a fist and unclenched in turn, right and left), your upper spine, neck, jaw, face. Screw your eyes up and relax them and finally press your head upwards as though against a hard car roof and let it fall again. See your whole body cushioned and supported gently so that you need make no effort to keep it taut.

* Listen to your breathing and gradually and quite naturally let the breaths get deeper and slower. If your leg itches scratch it and return to the state. Let the outer irritations drop away, one by one, and do not fight them.

* Allow your mind to wander where it will, moving away gently from any worldly worries. Have a dark box in a corner of your mind in which you can visualise these worries being locked away to rest until you have time to deal with them.

* Follow any images or paths to their conclusion and do not attempt to direct yourself or to analyse your thoughts.

The aim is not to control or direct the experience. That is a different technique to be developed when you are trying to visualise a particular goal or achievement.

After the initial instructions you can leave the tape blank and then, after twenty minues, add the words, 'When you are ready, open your eyes slowly'. However you may find that ten minutes is quite enough and you will be aware quite spontaneously that the outer world is beginning to intrude. Let it come slowly and naturally. You may even fall asleep if you are in a chair. Try to spend some quiet time, either talking to a friend or writing or drawing some of the images that emerged. If you can do this before psychic work you may find it easier to scry or see images from other dimensions, but in time you will find it easier to reach deeper levels of awareness almost instantly.

Drawing In the Light

Forms of psychic breathing are also used to harness what is called pranic energy to reach altered states of consciousness. Simple breathing techniques can give you quite fast access to psychic levels but do not worry about 'getting the technique right'. Find the right way for you. Once ideas of right and wrong enter the psychic field natural barriers arise, and some meditation classes fail for this reason by making members feel inadequate. Some Eastern techniques involve visualising drawing in coloured light with each deep breath – pink light for harmony and quiet thought, and white or gold for spiritual energy – and slowly breathing out black mist or smoke light as all the negative energies leave your body.

Prana is a term from Hindu philosophy and is widely used to represent the life force. Western spiritual healers regard prana as the healing energy that emanates from their hands and flows from their fingers to their patients, and see prana as the vital energy that allows our etheric or soul bodies to travel astrally. One pranic breathing technique is as follows:

1. Sit comfortably tense by placing your hands behind your head, pulling, then releasing and stretching, like a cat awaking from a sleep.
2. Breathe in slowly, hold for a count of three and exhale through the mouth with a sigh. Do this five or six times. As you inhale, visualise the air as pure white or golden light radiating through your body.
3. As you exhale, see black mist being released, leaving your body lighter and more harmonious.
4. Breathe in slowly again (one and two and three) and see that lovely golden or white light entering. Hold your breath for three seconds (and one and two and three). Breathe out slowly (one and two and three), so that the dark breath leaves. Then wait for three seconds (one and two and three) and breathe in, repeating the pattern about half a dozen times at first. In your mind's eye, the exhaled breath should become paler and paler until all the negativity has gone.

Chakra Magic

Chakra is Sanskrit for wheel and its form of magic belongs to the Hindu and Buddhist yogic tradition. Yoga comes from the Sanskrit word *yui*, 'to harness horses to a chariot', and refers to a search for the mystery of the universe through finding one's own self. Some psychics believe that you must open these chakras and raise the bodily energies to the level of the spirit before psychic awareness is possible. Opening the chakras and closing them after psychic work is another, but not the only nor necessarily the best, way of preparing for psychic work. As with all these methods, the aim is to move away from the conscious physical world and become attuned to your inner spiritual level and psychic abilities. Generally people are happier with one technique, but you can experiment and use them all at different times if they help you. The seven chakras, which vary in name and function according to different systems, are seen as whirling lotus petals of various colours. They form symbolic energy centres based at the cardinal points of the body.

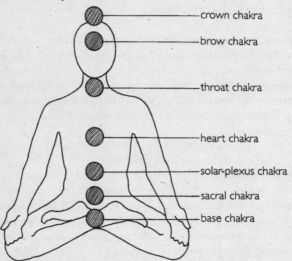

- crown chakra
- brow chakra
- throat chakra
- heart chakra
- solar-plexus chakra
- sacral chakra
- base chakra

Your body and the chakras

You cannot see chakras physically. The universal life force is said to enter through the Crown chakra at the top of the head and is filtered down through the other chakras, each of which transforms the energy into usable form for the function it governs. Energy also passes in the opposite direction from the Root chakra situated at the base of the spine.

Kundalini means snake or serpent power in Sanskrit. It is the basic energy that drives the chakras from within and is pictured as a coiled snake sleeping at the base of the spine. It travels up the body on a spiralling psychic pathway, activating the various energy centres and changing colour, eventually becoming pure white light at the Crown. You can visualise each of your chakras opening, whirling and the light rising within and changing through the colours of the rainbow. Make the path as simple or as complex as you wish, so long as the energies reach all parts of your body. There are no absolutes and many different theories as to the nature of these connections and even the number and sites of chakras. This is just one concept and you should follow your own instincts or draw your chakra path using a pendulum held about 5 cm (2 inches) from your body. You may wish a friend or partner to help you. Concentrate especially on the purple and white circles of light rising from the brow (Third Eye) to the top of the head and falling again.

Each chakra involves a different area of the body (see Crystal Chakra Healing, p. 260) and also different concerns. Therefore it can be helpful to summon the energies of a particular chakra symbolically if you are carrying out a ritual for a particular need. You can either focus directly on the specific chakra or build energies up from the root and see the colours changing to the appropriate one.

Chakra Colours

The Root or Base Chakra

This is the red chakra and is rooted at the base of the spine. It is the energy centre of the physical level of existence and survival. You can summon this chakra when you need courage and physical strength.

The Desire or Sacral Chakra

The orange chakra, centred around the genitals and reproductive system, focuses on all aspects of physical satisfaction, such as eating and drinking. This is the energy centre of earthly happiness and is the home of the five senses. You can use this chakra not only when you need to invoke fertility in the biological sense but also when you need schemes, relationships and projects to be fruitful.

The Power or Solar Plexus Chakra

The yellow chakra is situated just below the navel around the solar plexus. This is the energy centre of assimilating experiences, building confidence and focusing on achievement. You can use this chakra when you want to achieve an ambition or when you are planning a career move.

The Heart Chakra

The green chakra is situated centrally or slightly to the left of the chest, close to the heart. This is the centre for love, emotions and sympathy. You can use this chakra for matters of love and friendship and understanding others.

The Throat Chakra

The blue chakra is situated close to the vocal cords in the centre of the neck. This is the centre for ideas, ideals and clear communication. You can use this chakra when truth and principles are at stake or to protect you from those who would mislead or betray you.

The Third Eye or Brow Chakra

The purple chakra is in the middle of the brow, just above the eyes. This is the centre of inspiration and the doorway to other dimensions. You can use this chakra for psychic awareness, prophetic dreams and harmony.

The Crown Chakra

This is the white chakra. White, the source of pure light (all the other colours combined), pours upwards and outwards into the cosmos and downwards and inwards from the cosmos back into the Crown and so is the seat of light and enlightenment from within and beyond. The Crown chakra is situated at the top of the head, in the middle. This is the centre of creative and spiritual energy and represents either spiritual awareness or a striving for happiness through unity with one's higher self or a deity if you worship one. You can use this chakra when striving for perfection, wisdom and understanding of past, present and future.

Creative Visualisation

Visualisation involves using an internal focus rather than an external object to represent an urgent need, desire or wish. For example, if you need a new(er) car so that you can get the children to school or get to work, you could focus on the car you desire. Be specific and realistic, for creative and magical energies work best when their object is not beyond your wildest dreams but just out of your grasp. For every magical leap and lottery win there are a hundred thousand smaller steps that make life happier. Use one of the above techniques to relax or find a place where there are plenty of external stimuli to match your inner desire. If you want a car, go to a service station or a garage or sit in a coffee shop overlooking a car park or busy road. Look for a car within your normal price range or a little above it.

Now draw the image slowly into your mind and try to visualise small details so that the car becomes yours. See yourself opening the door, adjusting the seat and the mirror and pulling out of the location where the real car was situated. Drive it home in your mind's eye. Smell the material of the seats, hear the radio on your favourite channel, wind down the window and take in the smells of oil or fresh air if you are driving through the countryside. This is a magic spell or a psychological empowerment ritual, depending on how you want to see it.

Imagine parking your car and getting out, remembering to lock the door. Then let the car go out of focus and draw back to the present. Enjoy the sense of happiness and then begin, point by point, to find ways of getting the car in actuality. Visualise each step before you attempt to focus your energies. You can visualise any legitimate aim, whether for love, happiness or a specific need. You may find that your visualisation processes are assisted by following the sympathetic rituals described in Chapter 18.

Developing your psychic awareness will not only help to make your present life more fulfilling but also to use your intuitive processes and tap the unconscious wisdom that will give you more control over your destiny. The first step is to activate your latent inner psychic powers or to develop them further, if you have already started your psychic explorations. Even the most experienced clairvoyants and mediums can benefit from new ideas and perhaps a different approach. For magic constantly evolves, and each time a person attempts an unfamiliar form of scrying or divination and makes fleeting contact with another dimension, past or future, he or she adds to an ever-changing, developing art. Use the suggestions and methods in this book to build on your own natural abilities and feel free to change what does not fit with your life or aims. The magic lies not in the artefacts or even the techniques but within each one of us.

2

Protective Magic
and Rituals

As with learning to drive a car, the first vital knowledge, as your intuitive abilities begin to unfold, is psychic protection. Because they are so receptive and often deal with the problems and fears of others, healers and those who do psychic work may absorb negative feelings that can, if not checked, spill over into their own lives. What is more, some people can unintentionally become emotional and psychic vampires, draining energy from others. We all have a colleague or friend who comes to visit, invariably full of woes, resentments and negativity. And when he or she leaves, feeling refreshed, we are left feeling drained and depressed.

Protective magic is of great value as, even with the most positive rituals or readings, you may be affected by the negativity of others or the overwhelming feelings that contact with the inner self and natural energies can awaken.

However, no protection, however powerful, can be effective if people dabble with black magic or try to summon up unearthly entities, whether psychological or psychic, over which they may have no control.

Ivan, who lives in Texas, sent this account of how his dabbling with magic went seriously wrong:

This incident took place in Denver, Colorado, in late 1979. I was stationed at Lowry AFB for training at the Air Force Air Intelligence Training Center. I consider myself a very objective person but this incident shook me up. My roommate at the time was an older guy, twenty-six or so, from Kentucky. I was eighteen and had only been in the Air Force three or four months. Like many people, I was interested in paranormal activity and began reading some books on this subject. One of these books mentioned a ritual on how to summon a demon. My friends and I were contemplating a trip to a reportedly haunted old hotel, The Peck House, in Empire, approximately an hour or so away, so this kind of subject was often on my mind at the time.

One evening in our room on base my roommate and I were 'playing' around and tried to summon a certain demon by name. I don't recall where I got the name from but I wouldn't give it out anyway. At one point we both began to feel a 'coldness' that I refer to as an ion wind coming from the corner of the room where my bed was located. After some time we attributed it to a draught, as it was winter in Denver. We then got ready for bed. We each had a twin-size bed in the same room.

After lying down on my bed I noticed that it was vibrating pretty violently, almost like those old magic fingers beds in motels. This scared me pretty badly, to the point that I jumped across the room into my roommate's bed, vowing that I would not sleep in mine.

Of course, like young guys do, he ridiculed me pretty badly and laughed. He said he'd sleep in my bed. Almost as soon as his head hit the pillow his eyes got wide as saucers and he jumped up from the bed, bellowing that the whole thing was moving. This guy was not the type of person to be intimidated easily and I was nearly as frightened by his reaction as I was by the incident itself.

After seventeen years I don't really remember how we passed the night but I do recall that after this incident we both started losing things. I don't believe my roommate had anything to do with this, since we were both required to be in classes all day without much opportunity to get back to the room for mischief. Specifically I remember one case where I was missing one of my combat boots from a pair I often wore. Our room consisted of one main living/bedroom area about 12 feet by 15 feet, a small bathroom, and two closets. Not many places to lose things in such a small place. I looked everywhere for that boot but was not able to find it. Then, one day, I came home from class and there was my boot in the middle of the floor where I couldn't have missed it with my eyes closed. Just a few days after all of this we both relocated to different rooms with different roomates and I never heard any reports of strange happenings in that room. I was just glad to be out of there. I take this type of occurrence much more seriously than before.

The golden rule is: do not try to harness powers other than those of the natural world and your own inner energies. Do not use a ouija board. Do not call down spirits into the candle flame or hold seances in which you summon the dead. Talking in a positive gentle way to a beloved mother or grandfather who has departed is very different from trying to invoke ghosts or spirits as a way of demonstrating or testing psychic ability. Mediumship involving contacting the deceased on behalf of others should only be attempted in a controlled situation with the help of a trained medium and addresses are given at the back of the book for initial contacts of training circles. This is not a game and I have known very gifted psychics to be driven insane by thinking that they can control spirits, send demons against enemies or manipulate magical powers.

Innate abilities are quite safe. Magic is safe, but if you ever feel that you are becoming obsessed with it, to the exclusion of the everyday world, that your mind is being controlled by outside forces, earthly or otherwise, or that you cannot close down your energies, this is the time to stop and perhaps seek advice from an experienced healer and medium. Like all gifts, psychic powers are not intrinsically good or evil but can be used either positively or negatively. You may instantly sense whether a psychic group or individual has darkness all around them. Avoid them and contact one of the reputable organisations, whether Christian or pagan, for reliable and benign contacts.

Protective Rituals

Invoking Protection

Some people invoke four archangels to stand in each corner of the room: Michael, the Archangel of the Sun; the warrior, Gabriel; the messenger Raphael, the traveller with his pilgrim's staff; and Zadkiel, the Angel of Wisdom. Others ask their personal guides,

God, the Goddess or a named chosen deity for protection or invoke the blessing of Light and Benevolence before beginning psychic work.

Remember also to thank your psychic guardians, and feed the wild birds, make a small offering of a few seeds scattered in an unloved area of land, make a friendly phone call, write an encouraging letter or even make a small donation to a favourite charity after your wishes have been granted.

Protective Crystals

Certain crystals have natural protective powers that have been used from the time of the Ancient Egyptians. You could buy one or two to add to your magical collection and you can place them either in the corners of the room or on the four corners of the table where you are working. Or you could carry one with you to place on the table or floor directly in front of you whenever you give a reading or carry out a magical ritual, to act as a psychic shield from negativity (see Charging and Cleansing Healing Crystals, p. 259). Protective crystals traditionally include: black agate, amethysts, bloodstones, carnelians, garnets, black and red jasper, lapis lazuli, tiger's eye, topaz and turquoise.

Remember to wash your protective crystals in running water frequently. If you have been in touch with a particularly negative influence, after you have washed them sprinkle them with salt, pass over them an incense stick or oil burner in a fragrance such as lavender, pine or rose and the flame of a purple, silver or pink candle (for the power of the other three elements, earth, air and fire), and wrap them for a few days in a dark cloth.

Making a Protective Energy Field

In ritual magic an actual or visualised circle is drawn around the area of work both to concentrate the magical energies and to give protection against any negative forces. However, whether you are carrying out a psychic reading, practising personal projection into different dimensions or feel hostile or negative vibes during psychic work or at any time, you can keep yourself safe by strengthening the natural protective aura we all have.

Many people are aware of a spiritual energy field around our bodies that makes us feel uncomfortable if someone intrudes mentally or physically on what is currently called, in psychological terms, 'our personal space'. This energy field is our aura.

In your mind's eye create around yourself a golden protective ellipse, drawn clockwise from the top of your head and under the soles of your feet, joining at the top. You can trace with your pointed energising crystal or a pointed golden energising citrine, or draw a representative figure on a circle of paper and crayon round it clockwise in gold pen or yellow crayon, an oval from above your head right round. After you have done this place the paper, anchored by a crystal quartz, on a window ledge where it may receive energies from sunlight or moonlight while you are doing your psychic work.

If you can feel that someone or even some identifiable energy is not friendly, make the ellipse more jagged in your mind's eye, crackling with protective energy, so that it forms an electric fence. This is not meant to hurt anyone, merely to keep out those who would intrude in a hostile way. When you have finished, remember to un-draw the circle, either with the crystal or crayon or in your mind's eye, beginning at the top but this time travelling anti-clockwise. Keep your psychic figure in your folder as part of your psychic record.

Moving Back into the World

It is important to draw a boundary after special psychic activity, whether closing a magical circle you have visualised anti-clockwise in your mind (see Section Five on Ritual Magic), extinguishing candles, tidying up and putting away equipment you have created, washing out bowls you may have used for scrying, sweeping up any ash or herbs you have scattered, running tired crystals under water. Carry out quiet worldly activities, such as serving a simple meal or drink with friends who have shared psychic work. Gardening or tidying up the garden after outdoor rituals can also be an important way of marking your psychic work as a special time. Of course you do not need to make special preparations when you give a friend a quick reading or make a decision using intuition at work or wherever the need arises. Spontaneous psychic work is and must be a part of everyday life and, the more practised you become, the fewer demarcations you will need.

Closing Down Your Psychic Energies

Using Crystals

After your psychic work, arrange a circle of seven small crystals anti-clockwise on the table or on the floor in front of you, beginning in the true north or the representative twelve o'clock position (with yourself sitting in the south) with a black crystal, such as an obsidian (or Apache Tear) or a soft black pebble, representing the boundary between other dimensions and the everyday world. Accept that there is a right time for every purpose. Place a soft purple crystal, such as sodalite or amethyst, on its left, feeling all the magical energies passing into the cosmos and leaving your inner spirit at peace.

Next comes a pale blue crystal, such as blue lace agate or a moonstone, for healing of all negativity and a realisation that some of the things that seem so important today may have paled into insignificance by tomorrow.

A subtle green crystal, such as jade or moss agate, fills your heart with love and sympathy even for those who wrong you and prevents you wasting time on regrets. A gentle yellow crystal, yellow calcite or rutilated quartz, placed next in the circle encourages you to listen to your inner voice and let the demands of the outer world fade. A soft pink, such as rose quartz, banishes unresolved anger or bitterness. Finally, to the immediate right of the black crystal, a brown pebble brings you back to the earth plane and to the familiar world of home.

Closing the Chakras

You can do this either by visualisation or by using crystals. If you are using crystals, use each stone from the circle and then return it to its bag or box so that when you have closed all your chakras the circle will be empty:

* First take the black stone from the circle and place it on the crown of your head, gently closing your crown and seeing the pure white energy filtering downwards to your third eye in the centre of your brow, transforming as it does so into purple.
* Place your soft purple crystal on your third eye and gently close it, letting the purple move downwards to your throat chakra, as it does so merging into a soft misty blue.
* Next place the pale blue crystal on your throat chakra, seeing this gently closing and the blue light moving down to the region of your heart, becoming turquoise as it merges with the green.
* Use the green crystal to slow down and close the throat chakra, so that the green moves downwards to merge with the yellow of your solar plexus, just below the navel.
* The light will become orange as it moves down to the Desire chakra close to your reproductive system. Holding your pink crystal here will close this chakra. The light will become a pale transparent red and return to the root chakra at the base of your spine. Use the brown crystal to quieten the natural red energies so that they will sleep at the base of your spine until you need their power again.
* The rising power of the energising crystals is thus reversed and you can feel the buzzing in your head slowly descend until you have a slight warm heaviness at the base of your spine.

Alternatively you can lie on a bed or a pile of cushions and, one by one, beginning with the Crown, visualise the whirling lotus petals moving more slowly until they are turning slowly and regularly like a charging battery and their contact with other worlds has closed down.

Section Two

Developing Your Existing Powers

3

Extending Your Senses

In childhood many people have psychic experiences that are channelled through their existing senses. The five basic senses in
pre-school children extend beyond the material world and can pick
up information that is not accessible by means of conscious reasoning. They can also fleetingly touch other dimensions where they
may link into both the past and the future. As we grow older, our
developing rational processes blunt our extra-sensory perceptions
so that our normal senses are less receptive to sixth sense messages,
except from those with whom we are emotionally close or when we
are experiencing times of crisis.

While inner powers mainly operate spontaneously, it is possible
to regain access to them so that we can use them in real life both to
expand the horizons of possibility and to tap into areas of knowledge that cannot be reached through normal sensory channels.

This section explores the major powers that begin in and transmit through our five physical senses. They are the first and most
important steps to developing psychic awareness. These powers
include telepathy (mind-to-mind communication), clairaudience
(hearing what is not physically present), clairsentience (sensing
what is not accessible by normal channels), clairvoyance (seeing
both places and people far off, especially in other dimensions), and
psychometry (gaining information by touch). Psychometry
involves all the other arts and so is a good starting point for ESP
exploration.

Psychometry – the Magic of Touch

Psychometry means using an object to pick up psychic impressions either about the history of the artefact itself or the past, present and future of the person who is holding or owns the object. The item used may be something very personal, such as a family ring or necklace, an old photograph or family treasure (in a sentimental rather than a monetary sense) – for example, a teapot that has been used by different generations.

Most people sense impressions from the past or strong emotions that are not connected with their own immediate feelings if they handle a family treasure or touch the stone walls of a ruined castle or ancient monument.

Both forms of psychometry are closely linked and may operate in tandem. There are two theories about how psychometry operates, neither of which excludes the other. Indeed, the most powerful and accurate psychometric impressions may occur when both channels are open.

The first theory explains the ability to pick up the history of an item and impressions from stones or pottery that may reveal their history even when examined hundreds of miles from their origin. If an article has remained in the same family for generations, it can retain a whole family history, just as a gramophone record holds music or words within its grooves.

Objects from ancient sites seem to absorb physical and emotional imprints from those who have lived in the place, trodden its paths or halls and visited over the years. The strongest impressions from place psychometry come from dramatic or violent events – such as murders or battles – or from long periods of unbroken tranquillity (for example, an abbey where monks may have lived the same way for hundreds of years, so that their individual lifespans ran into one).

The most powerful impressions transmitted are emotions transferred to the article from the people or place. For example many people have sensed great fear and pain when holding a stone from the site of a great battle, such as Culloden Moor (see Culloden Ghosts on p. 120). Clairsentience, sensing an atmosphere, is very much akin to psychometry, as is clairaudience, hearing voices from the past. Clairvoyance, seeing figures or scenes from the past, can also be triggered by a psychometric experience.

Clairvoyance may be experienced either as a picture in your

mind's eye or as a two- or three-dimensional image beyond you. Neither is better and the mind's eye can be just as accurate as external manifestations.

Even experienced mediums may find that they work best clairvoyantly when they hold an object belonging to a deceased person or visit a historic site. Jenny Bright, a professional medium and skilled psychometrist, described how her mediumistic powers manifested themselves through psychometry.

> I am always very much at home in abbeys and churches and have a oneness with them. In Rievaulx Abbey in Yorkshire, I was instantly at home. As I went inside, I heard and sensed the voice of an old monk, 'You will like this place. Put your hands on here.' As I placed my hands on the old stones, as if on a smoky-black transparency or negative, I saw how the abbey used to be, the old library full of medieval manuscripts. I could make out the building housing the information centre in its old form – I walked round the old buildings, now sometimes just part of a wall, and saw the life inside them through the misty greyness, the monks working, silently praying or eating their simple food in silence in the old refectory. I could see without a plan how everything was, and when I read the notices and guide book it was all where I had pictured it.

Place psychometry is perhaps the easiest to try initially and may have already occurred spontaneously in your life, perhaps during childhood. However, an article can also be used to transmit information not just about its own history but also about the past, present and future of the person holding the artefact who may or may not be the owner. Here the object is acting as a crystal ball or Tarot pack does, providing a channel for the intuitive impressions.

Often both forms of psychometry will occur but usually one predominates, according to the nature of the item and the purpose of the reading. So if you visit an old site and touch the stones you will probably learn more about the stones than about your present dilemmas or those of anyone else present, although this can be a valid method of accessing past lives.

However, if you are holding a friend's grandmother's ring, you will sense not only the story of the ring but unvoiced concerns from your friend about her own life, transmitted from her psyche to yours via the ring. The newer the object and the less personal, the more you will pick up about the enquirer rather than the artefact.

Psychometry at an Ancient Site

Begin at a place of recognised antiquity, an old stone circle, a burial mound or a ruined castle, where you can pick up stones or old pottery and hold them. Psychometry may be easier in a site which has been stripped back to its bones than in an elaborately furnished stately home which may have artefacts taken from many different places that have not shared the life of the house. Sometimes, too, a very detailed reconstruction of a period that centres on the lives of the noble and famous can obscure the richer vein composed of the lives of ordinary people who worked there as servants over centuries. If a location has been used for many purposes – and many religious centres were built on old pagan temples – you may see images from several distinct eras either in your mind's eye or as external visions, as sounds, smells or even tastes: the taste of tar in an area of former industry or the smell of baking bread on the spot where a kitchen once stood.

To practise place psychometry:

* Choose your transmitter object before you read a guide book or take a tour.
* Sit in a quiet corner and hold the object between your hands. Close your eyes and run first your fingers, then your palms over the surface, cradling the stone or pot, putting it close to your face, to allow it to penetrate all your senses.
* Allow impressions to emerge through the sense most strongly stimulated. Do not be impatient.
* Do not try to imagine the former scene on a conscious level. If the picture is unexpected, accept it and you may find that it makes sense when you learn more of the legends and history of the place.
* If you sense nothing, stand up and let the stone or piece of pottery take you back to the spot where it originally stood in the house or grounds. This may be quite a way from where you found it. Pause here and try again.
* Afterwards look round the immediate area to put your

impressions in context. You may discover the oldest wing of a house or in the garden a well, choked with weeds or rusted over. There may be a wall with the remains of a door or rings on it or a grave hidden in the grass. Before the nineteenth century many people were not buried in graveyards, and suicides and witches were often placed at a crossroads or near a former pagan site.

Psychometry with an Object

It is easiest to begin with an artefact that has belonged to a family for many years. One of the best objects is a cup from an old tea set or a teapot that has been used for generations and has witnessed countless gatherings over the years. Births, marriages, arguments, reconciliations, joys and worries may have been recorded while tea was poured. Faded family photographs can also reveal, not only the scenes shown in those carefully posed images, but the lives hidden behind the sepia smiles of yesterday.

To practise object psychometry:

* Close your eyes and run your fingers and hands over the surface, letting colours, sounds, even fragrances come into your mind.
* Keep holding the object as you talk, to maintain the connection. Do not pause to ask if you are correct. Use a tape recorder so that your impressions can be checked afterwards. Do not worry if the scenes you describe seem unfamiliar to the owner. When he or she checks with older relatives they may well understand the incidents you mentioned.
* If impressions are hazy, picture the teapot being used for the first time and tell its story. See a ring being placed on a finger by the first owner. Again, pursue these images. Gradually widen your range of focus. Keep moving further and further from the object. Look all around for clues as you would if you were in an actual room.

Practice is the key. Go to an antiques fair or even a junk shop where you can wander freely, hold items and let yourself be drawn to any that attract you – an old medal, a picture of a scene that seems familiar, a lace shawl, a piece of furniture. It need not be valuable in monetary terms.

Scribble down your impressions and then gradually begin using objects belonging to people you do not know. At first, hold the object casually, admire a book, run your fingers along a fine piece of furniture. Gradually insert your psychic information into the conversation.

Personal Psychometry

For this, you need a personal object such as a ring or necklace belonging to or connected with someone with whom you are at ease. Ask him or her to give you an unfamiliar object whose past you do not know or something personal such as car keys. The age of the item is less important than the personal connection.

With all forms of personal psychometry you will usually progress from the past through the present and future concerns of a person. Childhood scenes are most common, perhaps because at that time the psychic world is at its strongest. Impressions gained then stay imprinted like flashbulb memories and do not get tidied up or changed by normal psychological processes.

To practise personal psychometry:

* Ask the person for whom you are reading to hold the item for a few moments while concentrating on any questions he or she may wish to ask.
* Hold the article between you so that the psychic vibes from you and the other person mingle within the artefact. Experienced readers can pick up personal impressions without doing this, but it is helpful in the early stages of your work to establish a physical link between the reader and the enquirer through the article. Hold the object yourself with your eyes closed and run both your fingers and your palms over the surface for a few minutes so that you become almost part of the object temporarily, just as some clairvoyants will enter a crystal ball by projection.
* Until you are more confident, begin talking and do not keep stopping for confirmation.
* As you become more practised you will be able to tell auto-

matically whether a picture relates to the distant or more recent past. Having gained confidence, you will learn to trust your first impressions and they will become more accurate as you lose the fear of being wrong which awakens conscious thought processes that block natural intuitions.

Reading the future is the most important aspect of any personal psychic reading, as it is usually his or her concern about the future that prompts the enquirer to seek a reading. You are seeing potential paths that he or she could take. The key to becoming a good reader is to present these possibilities as positive options so that the enquirer feels totally in control of his or her destiny.

Flower Psychometry

Flowers are traditionally a good focus for personal psychometry as they quickly absorb psychic impressions from a person. The person for whom you are reading should bring a flower he or she has chosen from a whole bunch or picked from a bush. Just as Tarot cards or runes are selected apparently at random, the person may well have 'just picked' or even found a certain flower that mirrors aspects of themselves.

To practise flower psychometry:

* Roses, irises and carnations are especially potent, perhaps because they are associated with the emotions. If you decide to organise a group, you can get all the members to bring favourite flowers and read for each other (see Chapter 29 on Forming a Psychic Development Group). The initial stages are the same as those used in personal psychometry to establish the link between enquirer and reader.
* In flower psychometry, you can also take into account the stalk, which deals with the life path of the subject, with the childhood being at the base. You may find marks or discolorations indicating important changes and smooth bright patches indicating periods of stability.
* Take the first third as the past, the middle third as the present, and the top third as the next ten years. Run your fingers over each section and pause at any knots as you are talking.

* Any leaves and other stalks where smaller separate flowers branch off the main stem can be seen as present external factors which are influencing future paths – for example, friends, family, work, friendships or love affairs. Where there are buds, plans in material matters have not yet come to fruition. Many leaves suggest commitments, friends and family. Holes in leaves can indicate partings that have occurred that are still painful.
* A solitary bloom may indicate that a person is alone either through choice or through necessity.
* Discoloration on subsidiary stalks and leaves can suggest conflicting interests, choices, even opposition. Pause on them to sense how these blockages can be removed.
* If the flower rises high above the leaves and other buds then the person may be ambitious and independent. If it is immersed in foliage then happiness is found through others and through working in caring professions.
* The flower itself is indicative of the person's characteristics both in the world and in their dreams. Shape is the first consideration. If the bloom is tall and stately, this denotes a love of travel and restlessness. A small and multi-petalled flower reflects a love of the familiar and of home; symmetrical imply a sense of order; profuse, a lover of luxury; oval, a degree of self-containment; large with rounded petals, a natural giver; or, with bells, a keeper of secrets. Tiny single flowers often mean that the inner world and personal happiness are more important than material success.
* If the main flower is still budding then it is not yet time for dreams to be fulfilled; half-closed suggests hesitance and a lack of confidence; open means affectionate and generous; full-blown indicates wisdom; and a fading bloom that present life is clouded with regrets.
* Finally look at the colour of the chosen flower. Red indicates passion and also anger; yellow a desire to be loved and natural optimism; blue a logical but just person; white unworldly and easily hurt; pink gentle and conciliatory; purple mysterious and secretive depths; brown materialistic or practical; orange confident and independent. More than one colour indicates versatility but also changeability. Look at the colours nearest the centre for the true self.

4

Clairsentience

Clairsentience is frequently defined as the ability, close to intuition, to sense psychical manifestations that cannot be perceived in any other manner. The most common example is an ability to sense a strange atmosphere in a house as soon as one enters it. This ability is akin to psychometry and can show itself as a general uneasiness, prickling of hairs on the back of the neck or a distinct feeling of coldness. Some people can actually see former inhabitants either in the mind's eye or externally.

Joyce and her husband Bill were house-hunting in Edinburgh and were sent to view a property that seemed to fit their requirements perfectly. However, as soon as Joyce entered the house, she started to feel very light-headed and strange. She told Bill and the estate agent accompanying them that she wanted to leave the place immediately.

Bill told her not to be silly as they had not even viewed the house. Joyce tried to pull herself together but still felt very ill at ease. As soon as she reached the basement where the kitchen was located, she felt extremely ill and was on the verge of fainting. Joyce could sense something dreadful had once occurred in this area and, as she neared the cooker, began shaking uncontrollably. As the estate agent opened the oven, Joyce ran out of the house. Her husband took her to a nearby café for a cup of tea to help her regain her composure.

A few weeks later Joyce mentioned the incident to her mother who had a friend who lived in the same street as the house they had viewed. Her mother discovered that, years before, a single man had shared the house with his elderly mother whom he had killed. Then he gassed himself in the oven.

However, the majority of clairsentience experiences are far more positive. Houses can retain happy atmospheres of former inhabitants, living as well as dead. Some exude a sense of peace. After a family member has died, relatives often sense the deceased person's presence around their former home; on anniversaries or at times of sadness, a calm, loving presence. By far the majority of family ghosts are experienced in this way.

Jan, who lives in Essex, told me:

My sister-in-law, Carol, was killed at twenty-three and her favourite food in the world was my ex-mother-in-law's chocolate cake. Carol had given me the recipe, and after her death when I was living in her flat, I made the cake several times. Each time I felt I had someone with me. Eventually this annoyed me so much, I said, "Carol will you please let me make this cake in peace."

'Soon afterwards I lost the recipe. I now regret my action in that I lost the recipe for the best chocolate cake ever and also my sister-in-law.'

Such experiences are usually spontaneous, but it is quite possible to tune into places, and into the essence of people we have loved, who have died, by visiting places where we shared happy memories with them. Psychometry is a natural way of receiving impressions, but from my own research I have discovered that the sense of smell is a good entry point into clairsentience and indeed is often the primary way people sense either the deceased or the history of a place. Smelling a deceased grandmother's favourite perfume or baking or a grandfather's tobacco is a universal paranormal phenomenon and a strong smell of a certain flower is often associated with a particular ghost.

For example, one of the most frequently reported ghosts at Billingham Manor in Chillerton on the Isle of Wight is the Grey Lady, whose appearance is accompanied by a strong scent of Madonna lilies, not to mention the shaking of furniture and ornaments, even in the calmest of weather. The Grey Lady, known only as the former Miss Leigh, lived in the house in the early eighteenth century. She had been forced to marry one of the very powerful Worsley family who took up residence at Billingham after its rebuilding in 1722. Miss Leigh was passionately in love with a French nobleman and the affair continued after her marriage. Eventually her husband confronted the lovers in the garden. Some accounts say that this was near a bank of Madonna lilies; others say that the nobleman was wearing a Madonna lily given him by his love when he was killed in the ensuing duel. Henceforward the wife was confined to the grounds of the manor and died of a broken heart; in some more romanticised versions, clutching a Madonna lily, the symbol of her lost love.

How to Become Psychically Attuned to Atmospheres

Your psychic antennae are already present. Few of us have not felt at some time that a place is spooky or unfriendly or that we feel irritable or afraid for no apparent reason. Often there is, on investigation, a reason – perhaps an unhappy incident at the place in times past.

Clairsentience is a very important skill to develop because it offers protection, not only against bad vibrations from the past but also against present dangers or potential hostility. The intuitive response that tells us a stranger is untrustworthy, even though his or her outer appearance or actions offer no apparent justification for this distrust, is inbuilt in us all, but too often we do not recognise our natural warning system. Dogs will growl at some strangers but not others, while a normally confident child will sometimes instinctively back away from a friendly smile and outstretched hand. In both cases, the person usually proves to be unreliable or to have negative intentions behind the smile and soft words.

This is the same intuitive ability that makes us instantly like or dislike a place. And a person who readily senses an atmosphere in a place usually has the same knack when summing up people. 'He [or she] didn't smell right' is one expression used by children.

Tuning into Places

Old battle sites are especially evocative of all who have fought and triumphed or perhaps died there. When visiting Gettysburg in Pennsylvania more than twenty years ago (when I dismissed all forms of the paranormal as imagination) I can recall being overwhelmed by a sense of mingled fear, anger, pride and triumph. I did not understand what was happening and, being with my first husband who was entirely devoid of imagination, I responded with a total feeling of panic and a desire to get away from the site. This annoyed him intensely, as he loved the names and dates but not the flesh-and-blood people who were the essence of the battle.

People will argue that you sense fear at a battleground precisely because you know it is a place of suffering and respond according to your expectations. However, I have discovered time and again that people have experienced raw emotions when they knew nothing of the origins of the location. A Down's Syndrome teenager being driven across Culloden complained that she could see lots of people dying and refused to get out of the car because she was afraid. The family had not mentioned the place or its history for fear of upsetting her (see also Culloden Ghosts, p. 120). Another woman, who was working for the War Office during the Second World War in London, was walking with her bosses through the Imperial War Museum when she felt tremendous fear and panic. She later discovered the building was on the site of the former Bethlehem Hospital, the notorious Bedlam.

To test your clairsentient abilities:

* Visit a reconstructed village, workshop or street in a museum or leisure park, where the buildings and artefacts are genuine. Walk from building to building, preferably alone, and concentrate on what you feel, rather than what you see or hear. You may find that you also see and hear sights and sounds from the past, either within you or externally.
* On this occasion, do not use psychometry but rely on your impressions. Note down the prevalent images or feelings – perhaps happiness, fear or anger.
* Return to the same place at the same time of day with a sensitive friend or member of your family. Let him or her go in alone at first so that you are not transmitting your own feelings telepathically. You will find that you both experience many of the same feelings.
* At this stage find out what you can about the origins of each building and revisit each building together, building up the jigsaw of information.

Using Earthly Scents as a Catalyst for ESP

It is very easy, in a world of air conditioning and deodorisers, to become desensitised to specific scents. However, there are several ways of learning to isolate and then amplify a single smell that will carry you to another place – your childhood or even a more distant past. It's best to use common trigger scents from your childhood or from far-off places. You may also find that fragrances, like sounds, can help to trigger astral projection and out-of-body experiences (see Chapter 16). We can all experience places and lives beyond our own if we open our extra senses far enough, and developing this particular sense channel ability can increase your responsiveness in many forms of divination and magical ritual as well as telepathy and precognition and channels traditionally regarded as mediumistic.

In mediumship, a scent from another dimension can often help a medium identify a person from the enquirer's distant past whose memory is instantly evoked. And in reading, a subtle fragrance or smell can have an association for the enquirer that can offer a clue to the meaning. For example, when I was reading for Jane, a legal executive, I could suddenly smell engine oil and car fumes. When I mentioned it she said that her father had run a small garage and she had grown up in the workshops. She had been wondering whether to return to her home area at the risk of losing face or struggle on alone in London. Her long-term relationship had ended abruptly when her partner had begun an office affair. She decided that right now she needed at least a few weeks in an environment where she felt secure. Apparently she did return home and started a relationship with the owner of her father's former garage but I never heard the end of the story.

The following smells are, in my experience, most likely not only to evoke impressions of the past, but also to offer access to the past and present worlds of others associated with them.

Bread

Visit either an in-store bakery or specialist bread shop at a time when bread is being taken out of the ovens. Close your eyes and slowly inhale the fragrance, letting your mind evoke the first time you smelled fresh bread. Recreate the different senses related to this experience, the feel of a wooden table, a splash of colour from a yellow milk jug, perhaps the sound of birds singing or cows mooing or the rush of traffic past a window, the taste of salty butter on warm crumbly bread.

You may also receive impressions of an unfamiliar place or earlier era. Note them in your record book. You may find that the scenes reappear when you attempt past life recall. Lesley, who works as a home help, says that many mediums comment on the smell of freshly baked bread that accompanies her. She associates this with her grandmother's presence.

Coffee

Go to a shop or coffee house where many different brews and beans are mingled so that your senses are overwhelmed by the fragrance. Try to isolate one particular blend and, if possible, order a cup or buy some beans and brew the coffee at home. Absorb the steam and let the smell fill you. In your mind's eye, go back to its source. You may see, hear or taste not only a half-forgotten memory from your own past, but a different place, blue skies, a brilliant sun, worlds through which, if you enter them, carried along by the fragrance, you can interpret your own challenges and questions.

Flowers

A flower show is, of course, a multi-sensory experience and fragrance is naturally the most powerful trigger for extra-sensory experiences. If you cannot attend a flower show, go to a hot-house in a botanical garden or a garden centre where a variety of blooms are clustered together. Let the different colours blur through your half-closed eyes and take on separate fragrances. You may identify one particular scent that you associate with a place or person. Use this to move back in your own past or to more distant places in your mind's eye. Record any strong impressions. Try to buy some of these flowers to take home so that you can place them in a room in which you spend time, to heighten the impressions.

Furniture Polish

There are still many furniture polishes on the market that date back many years, especially lavender ones. Sprays do not evoke the same smell as polish worked into a piece of furniture or an area of floor, and many deceased grandmothers use the fragrance of furniture polish to announce their presence.

Choose a sunny day and place the item you are going to polish so that the warmth of the sun falls on it. Work the polish with a soft cloth into the wood grain and let the scent gradually pervade your movements. You may well recall your childhood or a special person who has died, or link into the worlds of others who have dreamed as they polished.

Other fragrances

Perfume, soap, spices, starch and tobacco are also evocative fragrances. A deceased relation's favourite perfume can instantly recall former laughter and love and a sense of being protected and cherished. If you are feeling sad and lonely, placing a little of your loved one's scent on the pillow can bring positive reassuring dreams of them and perhaps wise advice. Grandfathers often announce their presence by the smell of a well-starched shirt or a favourite tobacco. It may be that future generations will tell a different story and grannies will return in a flourish of Spray and Shine! But these scents recall more than the dead, important though this may be to some people. They are a passage through which the conscious mind can travel to a world accessible only on a far deeper level.

5

Clairaudience

Both psychometry and clairsentience can trigger clairaudience, the ability to hear words or sounds that are not part of the material world. The majority of clairaudient experiences occur quite spontaneously.

In the early summer of 1996, newspapers throughout the world reported disembodied voices speaking in unknown tongues in the Council offices in São Paulo in Brazil. They had been heard by workers for several years but were not taken seriously until they were heard by a senior official. Councillor Paulo Roberto Faria Lima had disregarded stories of the ghostly voices until, in May 1996, he stayed late with his wife to update his computer files. 'At 12.30 am we wanted to leave but couldn't open the door. It was weird because it can only be locked from the inside,' Mr Faria Lima recalled. 'Then we started hearing voices speaking in an unidentifiable tongue and heard furniture moving around. I phoned security and a guard came up and opened the door with no problem. He told me that we were the only ones in the twelve-storey building.'

The City Council is located in a district known as Vale do Anhangabau – a Tupi-Guarani Indian name meaning Valley of the Spirits.

Ghostly or discarnate voices are usually heard either because a person's auditory channels are tuned into an extra-sensory wavelength or because the person is at a place which has such strong vocal imprints from previous occupants that the sounds of the past are triggered by the slightest stimulus. In the latter case several people may hear the voices or ghostly sounds. The fact that not everyone hears them would suggest that clairaudience is naturally more developed in some people than others. However, a considerable number of people are naturally clairaudient. After clairsentience, clairaudience seems to be the most common channel of contact with other dimensions.

As you become increasingly psychically aware, it becomes easier to pick up different frequencies, much as an experienced radio operator can tune a radio more accurately. This means you may hear extra-sensory sounds in a variety of settings. Andy, who lives in Scotland, heard ghostly voices that were attached to a place. They did not attempt to communicate with him and indeed seemed disturbed by his presence. Andy explained that he was sitting in his car with his girlfriend near Wymms Caves in Scotland. It was after midnight and the spot was deserted. Suddenly they were aware of many voices in the darkness, although they could not hear the actual words. Andy turned on the headlights of the car. Immediately the voices ceased, but the couple could see no one. As soon as Andy turned the lights out, the voices resumed. Again Andy turned on the lights and the chattering abruptly stopped. At this point his girlfriend became afraid and they fled the area. Voices have been heard by many people near ancient standing stones at night in many parts of the world. They may be imprinted on the area but heard only by those sensitive to such phenomena. The unanswered question is whether the voices need a receiver to be activated. Do they chatter when no one is present?

Equally common is a single voice heard by only one person. In this case the voice is linked to the person who hears the message rather than attached to a location. This personalised voice may be that of a deceased relative, a warning voice from another dimension, perhaps from a guardian angel, or our own inner voice that can instinctively guide us on the right path. The concept of being guided by disembodied voices can seem worrying, especially as certain mental illnesses are characterised by voices suggesting bizarre or dangerous actions. However, the true inner voice is heard only at important times and offers advice that we instinctively know is a guide to right action.

Such a voice can also be a lifesaver. Sometimes it is hard to distinguish whether the warning voice is that of a guardian spirit or angel or an inner precognitive message that is heard as an external voice, but the result is always positive. Indeed the source may be a matter of interpretation. One woman suddenly heard a voice saying: 'The children are on the railway line.' She rushed to the railway line and found a gap in the fence through which her children had squeezed. She had never heard the voice before or since and it was the first time that the children had wandered near the railway.

Another frequently reported clairaudient experience is that of footsteps heard by a person in an otherwise empty house. As with disembodied voices, they can exist independently of the hearer and may be heard by several people with developed clairaudient faculties, although, frequently, one member of a family will not mention the incident until years later. It is usually possible to identify the footsteps as those of a former owner of the house who is still following a routine established during life.

Wendy, who lives in New York State, wrote:

When I was fourteen, my family moved to a new town in upstate New York. The house we moved into wasn't a classic haunted variety at all, but a fifteen-year-old ranch house. Some months after we moved in, however, I started hearing footsteps in the dead of night. I would hear them walk through the basement, climb the stairs into the dining room, and enter the kitchen. There they would always stop. No amount of arguing with myself would make those footsteps go away. Night after night I would lie awake in the dark with my heart pounding, praying those steps wouldn't continue out of the kitchen and down the hallway to my bedroom.

I finally told my mother what I was experiencing so that she would allow me to keep the hall light on all night. Mom was very impatient with me. She told me I had a hyperactive imagination, and that I must not mention these steps to my brothers and sister, because the last thing she needed to deal with was four children who were terrified of ghosts. However, I was allowed to put on the light.

Two years after I moved out and married, Mom told me she owed me an apology for her reaction. It seems my brother, two years my junior, had been hearing the steps, too, and on more than one night he had climbed out of bed with a knife and gone to find out who had broken into the house.

This brother brought his wife to live in the basement for a couple of years while he finished graduate school. One night during that time, my youngest brother was sitting on the patio outside the dining room in the evening. No one at all was home. But he heard footsteps on the basement stairs and thought my older brother and his wife had come home. He went inside to check and found no one there.

A guest, who slept in the basement, early one morning felt someone grab his leg and tug gently, trying to wake him. No one was there and no one had told him about our ghostly steps.

Eventually, the steps began to pass beyond the kitchen and down the hallway to the bedroom area. I was long gone, living elsewhere, but my poor mother watched all her children grow up and leave, and then, when my dad was out of town on business, would retire to her bedroom at sunset and keep the door closed, too scared to be out where the ghost roamed.

One afternoon when Mom came home from work, she found the sugar bowl upended in the middle of the kitchen floor, a good 4 feet from the counter. She got so mad when she saw the mess, that she yelled at the ghost, by this time called George by the entire family, 'You can live here if you want to, but don't you dare make another mess!'

My folks moved away from there fifteen years ago, but we all still talk about it from time to time.

Wendy's family did not discover the identity of the ghost they heard. However, Mary, who lives on the Isle of Wight, was in no doubt about the name of her noisy resident ghost. Mary was fond of a particular cottage owned by a man called Charlie and often said that she would like to live there if Charlie ever moved. Some years later Charlie died and Mary and her husband Mick bought the empty cottage. They renovated it and moved in. On the first evening they were in the sitting room when they heard the tread of heavy boots upstairs although no one else was in the house. Mick jumped up in alarm but Mary was not worried. 'Oh, that's just old Charlie checking we are all right,' she told him.

Mick rushed upstairs but found no one and the house instantly fell silent. As soon as Mick returned downstairs the footsteps started up again and Mick complained, 'I'm not living in a haunted house.' Mary called up the stairs, 'I know it's you, Charlie, and you are very welcome to stay. Just don't make a noise when Mick is around, as you are scaring the living daylights out of him.'

After that Charlie never made a sound when Mick was in the house.

Developing Clairaudience by Using Sounds

Cymatics is the study of the relationship between sound waves and matter, a two-way reaction between free vibration and the solid state. The first experiments were carried out during the eighteenth century when Ernest Chaldni demonstrated that sound made patterns in sand that had been spread on thin metal plates.

More recently Hans Jenny created a tonoscope, to be used with the human voice as the source of sound. Spherical patterns resulted from the sound 'O' being spoken into the microphone.

However the idea of sound affecting matter is a very ancient one. The sound OM is considered in Eastern religions to be the source of everything, the sound of the universe vibrating. The Mandukya Upanishad says: 'All that is past, present and future is truly OM. That which is beyond the triple dimension of time is also OM.'

In Africa and the East chants and songs have long been used in healing rituals. In the West, technology has produced two methods of using sound to combat disease using both low-frequency and high-frequency sounds. You may have noticed in a really loud disco how the low notes seem to pulse right through your body. Rather than reduce your ears and entrails to jelly, these low notes can be used by a small loudspeaker, placed on an affected area, to soothe painful conditions of the bones and joints. At the other end of the scale, ultrasonic frequencies, too high for the human ear to hear, can be pulsed through tissues that have been strained to produce a soothing warmth.

These physical effects extend into psychic spheres and, through clairaudience, sounds from the non-material world can expand the horizons of possibility attainable by the human mind. As with clairsentience, one way of fine-tuning clairaudience is to isolate a single stimulus from many and amplify it so that it acts as a vehicle to reach other dimensions. If you become sensitive to your clairaudient faculties, you will gradually learn to distinguish between natural anxieties or wishful thinking and a true precognitive warning or extra-sensory knowledge.

Many New Age meditation tapes are based on natural sounds such as birdsong, children laughing and playing, dolphins calling, rain, the sea or the wind in trees. They all have a timelessness and universality that can stimulate early memories and perhaps help you link into other times and places. Man-made sounds, like church bells, fairground organs, old machinery in an industrial museum, horses' hooves, or music from flutes and brass bands, can also awaken deep responses.

Begin with a single sound, either naturally occurring or on a tape, and let it form pictures in your mind so that the sound becomes colours, images, memories. Note down the different impressions the sounds create.

Next, practise isolating one sound. Stand in a noisy place, like a market or a fairground, and let the sounds wash over you. Select one sound. Allow the others to recede, at the same time amplifying your chosen sound in your mind's ear and letting it carry you to a childhood memory. See, feel, taste and touch the impressions flooding from your mind's ear.

Finally choose a time of silence – late at night or early in the morning. Remove all clocks and electrical machines and turn off the central heating. If you live in a place where traffic roars day and night, drive to a deserted country place before dawn and birdsong, or after dusk, and listen to the void. Then create within you a voice you have known and loved, perhaps someone who has moved away or died. Hear the words they would have spoken, the tone, the emphasis on words, the accent. One woman heard her young daughter singing in her Welsh grandmother's voice for a few moments.

Try to spend a quiet time every evening, and if you have children, turn down the ringer on the telephone, switch off any machinery, light some candles and encourage them to love, not fear, silence. Clairaudient abilities have declined in the modern, noisy world but it is easy to restore them as a natural faculty. At these quiet times you may hear your inner voice quite clearly or enter into a creative reverie. When earthly voices cease, there is space for the sounds of other dimensions.

Magical Sounds

As children we have all made the rhythmic sound of train wheels into words or rhymes. Indeed the late Reverend W. Awdry, in his famous children's books about Thomas the Tank Engine, made his engines and carriages repeat rhymes such as 'Got to make it, got to make it' from the wheel sounds as mantras of encouragement. Using sounds to reach deeper levels of awareness, and perhaps other dimensions, is a very important aspect of clairaudient experience, and our childhood ability to hear words in water, wind and wheels can easily be rekindled with practice.

Many native peoples use sound to call up spirits and also to renew their own magical energies. For example, the Aborigines in Australia use a bullroarer, a musical instrument consisting of a piece of wood or stone on a cord. Whirled around the head to make a sound, it is a very important object painted with sacred symbols and given to a boy at his initiation. At the Kunapipi earth mother sacred sex rite to make the rains come, those who are to be initiated enter a crescent-shaped trench which symbolises Kunapipi's womb from which they emerge ritually reborn. While in the womb, each boy is given a wooden bullroarer to swing. His spirit double enters the instrument and remains in the trench with the bullroarer when he is born again.

An Aboriginal bullroarer

As the bullroarer disintegrates, the spirit double is released and goes to the Place of Shadows where it will await the death of its owner, who will then reunite with it and await rebirth. The wind whirling through the holes creates a mesmeric sound that can lead to out-of-the-body experiences and visions of the Dreamtime – the hero-gods and animals who first roamed and created the earth and who still exist, it is believed, in this altered state.

Making a Rain Stick

A gentler alternative to the bullroarer is the rain stick which is used in many societies, including Africa, New Zealand, India, and Central and South America. Originally created to encourage rain by imitating its sound, the rain stick is also used in healing and meditation to open channels to unconscious powers and also to link with the creative and healing energies of the earth. You can buy rain sticks in many shops where ethnic goods are sold but, as with the bullroarer (which is fashioned by a relation or the owner himself), a rain stick is most potent as a psychic tool if made by the person who uses it.

Rain sticks are 30–60 cm (1–2 feet) long, made of hollowed-out wood or bamboo, the thickness of a circle made by the thumb and first finger of an adult. They are filled with shells, tiny stones or small dried beans, and sealed at each end. They can be decorated with magical symbols or the name of the owner written in a magical alphabet (see Chapter 20 on Runic Writing and Chapter 22 on Talismans and Amulets), astrological signs or natural symbols according to the contents – shells, leaves, spirals, stars or serpents, signs that have been used for the adornment of sacred objects since Palaeolithic times. You can get large pieces of bamboo at garden centres or craft shops or you might, if you are skilled with tools, choose a special branch from a forest and hollow it out.

Close your eyes and gently swing your rain stick until you are carried away, by the sound of gentle rain or the swish of gentle waves on shingle, to a half-dream state where you may see magical animals, birds or just soft colours and perhaps hear your inner voice telling you the answers to questions you have not voiced. Some people feel as though they have left their body and risen above it, while others feel the sound penetrating their whole body, driving away tension and fatigue.

Talking Stones

Talking stones are a very ancient magical tradition going back to the groves of Dodona which were sacred to the Greek Father God Zeus. Here the prophetesses would hear the answers to their suppliants' questions in the rush of the water and the chattering of the stones beneath the water. You may know a place where a stream runs over pebbles. If so, you have a natural source of wisdom that can be reached by sound.

If not, you can let a hose or cold tap run slowly into a large tin bath or metal bucket with a layer of pebbles at the bottom. Scratch your question or a symbol of it on to a pure white stone and cast it into the running water. If you are using a tin bath or bucket you may need to stir your stones gently with a stick. Close your eyes and let the water give you the answer.

Talking Trees

This is another art practised in Zeus's oak grove, especially his own sacred oracular oak. Wood from there was said to have been used in Jason's legendary ship the *Argo* and to have acted as an oracle to the Argonauts as they voyaged in search of the Golden Fleece.

You need not use an oak grove, although the oak tree was also regarded as especially divinatory by the Druids. Any thickly leaved forest or wood will do. Pine trees, sacred to Cybele the Phrygian Mother of the Gods, are also very evocative in a strong wind.

Using a knife (black-handled ones are said to be magical in the formal ritual tradition but any kind will do), carve the first letter of each word of your question on a fallen branch without leaves. Wait until the wind pauses and cast it as far as you can. The wind will answer very shortly. Close your eyes and listen to the words made by the leaves as they rustle.

Finding Your Inner Voice

The more you trust your inner voice, the more accurately you will hear it. This is one aspect of psychic development that works best in response to an actual spontaneous need. It is very different from free-floating anxiety or logic. If you hear an argument in your head or the message is preceded by 'I wonder if?' or 'It might be better …' it is not your inner voice but your doubts and reasoning powers at work.

Begin with a decision where, if you are wrong, the consequences will not be dire but where the matter is of immediate concern. With each success you will gain confidence so that, when you have a crucial decision to make instantly, you will have learned to trust the clear voice within.

When you have a question or need to make a decision, first clear the clutter in your mind by seeing it as a cobweb that you are sweeping away. Now you have a clear space.

Ask the question either silently or out loud if you are alone. Listen to the first answer that comes – almost instantly. It is usually clear, unhesitating and often seems to be coming from a great distance. You may find that your inner voice becomes easily recognisable after a while. Mine is a cross between a school teacher and a BBC Radio 3 announcer.

I sometimes ignore my inner voice to my peril. However, recently I was due to meet Richie, a TV producer in Portsmouth, about some work he was offering me as a researcher. Since I knew Richie well, I was not at all anxious about being late and I checked that the ferries were running on time.

The question was quite simple: 'Should I travel on the early or later ferry from the Isle of Wight to Portsmouth?'

Logic dictated that I had three choices: to catch the early ferry and do some shopping on the mainland before my meeting as I needed a particular book urgently; to shop at the ferry port town on the Isle of Wight where there was a good bookshop and catch a later ferry; or leave home, catch an even later ferry and go straight to the meeting place. I would then shop afterwards.

'Catch the early ferry' was the answer from my inner voice. When I reached Portsmouth I was surprised to hear my inner voice saying, quite unprompted, 'Go straight to the hotel. Richie is waiting.'

I knew I would be well over an hour early but my inner voice is rarely wrong. As I walked through the doors Richie was waiting. He had told the researcher who had come with him that he 'knew' I would be there, although he had not tried to contact me on my mobile phone. Had I arrived at the appointed time, we would not have had the opportunity to discuss the ideas fully, since Richie had to leave earlier than expected to go on to Brighton. As a result, I was offered even more work.

Had Richie contacted me telepathically via my inner voice? All the extra senses are linked and, as one develops, so do the others. The only drawback was that I was concentrating so hard on the synchronicity, I forgot to buy the book!

6

Clairvoyance

Clairvoyance means clear- or far-seeing. Second sight, regarded in Eastern philosophy as being seated in the third eye or sixth brow chakra, can take many forms. It is popularly associated with seeing the future rather than visions of a distant place, although remote viewing (the ability to describe a scene that is taking place miles away) is one of the easier forms of clairvoyance to test scientifically.

This book will not concentrate on fairground fortune-telling, although this occasionally has remarkable results, but on using different ways of focusing to explore future possibilities in either our own lives or those of others. The clairvoyant ability to see those who have died is described in Section Seven which covers ghosts and mediumship.

The Nexus Effect

It can be very dangerous, as well as misleading, when unscrupulous clairvoyants predict disasters or death or even such a golden future that the enquirer ceases to make any effort in the real world. I have received many phone calls on radio programmes because a fortune-teller has foretold a death in the family or a road accident. This can trigger great anxiety and, in the case of a car accident, actually make it more likely because the person warned is concentrating on avoiding green cars rather than the usual dangers of the road. For this reason, traffic collisions do increase on Friday 13th.

The nexus effect, rather than focusing on a fixed unchangeable future, sees the future as a web. This follows the Nordic tradition in which Yggdrasil, the world tree, formed the axis of the nine worlds and had three roots. One was sunk into Asgard, the home of the gods. Under this root was the Well of Urd of Wyrd, guarded by the three Norns, the Goddesses of Destiny. The three sisters (Macbeth's 'weird sisters') wove the web of destiny, both that of the world and of individual beings, mortal and divine. They wove, not according to their own desires but according to Orlog, the eternal law of the universe.

The first Norn, Urdhr, the oldest of the sisters, always looked backwards and talked of the past which, in Viking tradition, influences not only a person's own present and future but also that of his or her descendants. The second Norn, Verdhandi, a young vibrant woman, looked straight ahead and talked of present deeds which also influenced the future. Skuld, the third Norn, who tore up the web as the other two created it, was closely veiled and her head was turned in the opposite direction from Urdhr. She held a scroll which had not been unrolled, of what would come to pass, given the intricate web of past and present interaction.

This was a forerunner of an idea now accepted in modern psychology that man influences his destiny by what he is and has been and so that destiny is constantly changing. Other cultures have the concept of the three sisters of fate and also the web. The web image is crucial to an interpretation of the future that makes clairvoyance possible without denying free will.

Throughout the web are nexus or change points where the threads cross and open out into a variety of paths. The Chinese *I Ching*, the Book of Changes, says that the key to understanding is to see and interpret these change points. Clairvoyants appear to see these change points that lie ahead where decisions can be made that will affect the future course of our lives. Good clairvoyance will help the enquirer to identify change points, which may not be at a set time. More importantly, he or she can identify the alternative routes that can be taken at these nexus points in order to gain control over the future and change it deliberately, rather than unconsciously fulfilling a prophecy made by a clairvoyant.

We can all, given practice, learn to identify these nexus points both for ourselves and for others to whom we may give readings. Such clairvoyance often works most effectively with a specific focus to trigger visions, such as runes (see p. 200) or some of the methods of scrying described below.

Scrying

Scrying (or looking into an object or substance with a reflective surface) to see clairvoyant or psychic images has been practised from the earliest times. The term comes from the English word descry which means 'to make out dimly'. In almost every culture, people have gazed into water by moonlight or looked into a piece of crystal or mirror and seen images either in the shiny surface or in their mind's eye. The practice, sometimes pronounced 'shree-ing', was developed by both the Ancient Egyptians and the Arabs. Until the middle of the nineteenth century, young boys would travel round Europe interpreting the crystal ball for their frequently fraudulent masters. In Ancient Greece, young boys were used for scrying by gazing into bowls of pure water lit by burning torches. They studied the changes in the water in the flickering light and invoked the gods or demons to provide their meaning.

The sixteenth-century French physician and astrologer Nostradamus used a bowl of water on a brass tripod to make detailed prophecies for ten centuries ahead. The predictions were made in obscure French verses but his admirers say he foresaw the assassination of Abraham Lincoln and John F. Kennedy, the rise of Hitler and the abdication of Edward VIII. Contrary to popular opinion, Nostradamus did not believe in a fixed future but thought it was possible to alter history by wise action.

Scrying with Water and Inks

Use a clear glass bowl or a wide, deep white bowl and either calligraphy inks or permanent ink cartridges which you can obtain in a whole range of colours and squeeze directly into the water, drop by drop. Alternatively, you can use a brush or dropper and add the inks, one or two drops at a time.

* Red, blue and black inks give the clearest readings and you can use more than one colour at a time.
* Let the inks swirl on the surface and obtain your first images of the present situation. This moving image stage is especially effective.
* Wait for the ink to sink and the water to begin to colour. If you have not used too much ink (and the only way is to

experiment), you will have a second deeper image in the bottom of the bowl for the underlying issue or influences.

- When the water is entirely coloured, hold the bowl between your hands and tip it gently. About halfway down, white rather than ink images will appear. These will suggest the way forward.

You now have three sets of images representing:

1. The present situation.
2. The underlying issues or influences.
3. The way forward and possible action.

Josh used plain blue ink with a dropper. He first created a snake on the surface that seemed to suggest to him that he was now trying to wriggle his way between various obstacles to obtain what he wanted, to start his own business. This image seemed to be circling a man on the surface which he took to be himself, afraid to leave a safe job that he hated, worried about jeopardising his family's security but feeling that he was being stifled and not fulfilling either his financial or mental potential.

The ink then settled at the bottom with a little still floating on top. The second image was of an anchor on a huge chain which quite spontaneously Josh saw as his own reluctance to face uncertainty. By now the water was blue but, as he swirled it, he saw half a cake and he instantly said, 'That's like half a loaf is better than none' and he admitted that he would like to start working part-time on a freelance basis and test the water. What the ink scrying had done was to bring to the surface Josh's preferred and wisest way forward, a particular nexus point or crossroads, so that he could determine not a once-and-for-all future but the next step. (See also Wax Divination in Water, p. 88–9.)

Magic Mirrors

Although crystal balls are the traditional tool of clairvoyants, an equally ancient method, mirror scrying, is far easier to use and very effective, although it is hardly ever practised by professional clairvoyants. Lakes used to be called Diana's mirrors because, when the full moon was overhead, diviners would scry in lakes, lit it was believed by the moon goddess's path across the skies and inspired with her wisdom.

Long before glass, polished metal was used for mirrors. Hathor, the Ancient Egyptian Goddess of Love, is said to have created the first magic mirror. One side was endowed with the power of Ra's eye to see everything, no matter how distant in miles or how far into the future. The other side showed the gazer in his or her true light and only a brave person could look at it without flinching.

Mirrors of highly polished metal were consulted in Ancient China to study what would come to pass. The Greeks also scryed in bronze mirrors to see into the future. Black shiny mirrors, often called witches' mirrors, were popular in medieval times but, because of their association with darker practices, they are now rarely possessed by ordinary scryers.

How to Make a Magic Mirror

A tray made of a silver alloy, or any flat wide surface of brass, copper or stainless steel, serves the same function as a traditional metal mirror. Experiment with a variety of shiny metals until you find one that feels right as a medium for you. You may wish to keep this exclusively for scrying, covered with a soft cloth when not in use, and polish it before each reading. I have even tried mirror scrying with a computer monitor or television screen when the power is switched off.

* Prop up your tray or shiny surface against a wall. Place six white candles in a semi-circle behind you so that their light is reflected on to the shiny surface. And switch off all the lights in the room so that everyday objects do not intrude into the frame.
* Sit slightly to the right so that your image does not appear in the mirror and also so that you are looking slightly out of focus.
* Ask a question and wait for the images to form either within the mirror or in your mind's eye. Both are equally valid and, with practice, you can throw the images from your mind's eye into the mirror in order to study them.
* Begin by visualising the image in your mind's eye on the

surface of your magic mirror. Then gradually see it receding deeper within the mirror and expanding so that it fills the whole area. You may see single images or whole scenes.

* Once you have an image, either look away or close your eyes again, then open and blink.
* Continue until you have a string of five or six images. You may see up to ten different images or pictures.
* When you feel that you are tired or losing concentration or can get nothing more, blow out the candles one by one, cover your mirror and write down the images in the order they occurred.
* If they do not make sense, join them with a spiral line and, as you do so, begin to weave a story with them. Do not force logical connections – just let the words flow. Alternatively, take out a paint box or some felt tips and on plain paper draw them into a backdrop. If you have a crystal ball or prefer to use a conventional mirror you can use the same technique.
* If nothing appears, close your eyes, open them and blink and then look into the shiny surface.

How to Read a Magic Mirror for Others

If you wish to read for someone else:

* Allow the enquirer to hold the mirror between his or her hands for a few moments and then sit to the right of the mirror with you directly behind, so that you both gaze into the mirror but the visions are the other person's.
* Ask the enquirer to concentrate on a particular question or matter of concern while gazing into the mirror.
* First ask what the enquirer can see. Often a complete beginner can see visions, especially if you explain that pictures in the mind's eye are just as valid.
* Describe what you see but ask how the enquirer would interpret the image. People frequently have quite definite ideas of what a symbol means to them and can often answer the question instantly. A reading is more helpful if it is a dialogue between two psyches, rather than a psychic guessing game. But it can be difficult for some enquirers, especially if they are paying for a reading, to understand that no one would expect

a doctor to guess symptoms and offer remedies without knowing about the sick person's problems and lifestyle.
* Again aim for between five and ten distinct images or scenes that you can combine.

Interpreting Images

There are traditional interpretations of images in different positions in a mirror or indeed a crystal ball. I tend not to use them but the rules established over centuries can offer guidelines while the technique is unfamiliar:

* An image moving towards the scryer suggests that the event will occur or the person appear very soon.
* An image moving away suggests that the event or person is either moving away from the scryer's world or that a past issue or relationship may still be exerting undue influence on the scryer.
* Images appearing on the left suggest actual physical occurrences.
* Images appearing in the centre or to the right tend to be symbolic.
* Pictures near the top of the ball are important and need prompt attention.
* Those in the corners or at the bottom are less prominent or urgent.
* The relative size of the images can indicate their importance.

What Do the Images Mean?

The images will, if you allow them to do so, suggest relevant answers to the question asked. We all have personal systems of symbols, built up from childhood and modified over the years. A symbol system is never fixed but most people's do have common factors, based on what the psychologist Jung called archetypes (meanings that have held true in many times and places), such as the wise man or woman, the messenger, the young hero/fool often identified with the self, the sun and moon.

7

Symbols for Scrying

This chapter lists 200 symbols that you may find useful for your scrying and divination work. The meanings given are only one interpretation. Many traditional lists concentrate heavily on a fixed fortune-telling meaning. Some of the meanings here may overlap with those listed in Chapter 15 on Dream Symbols, although symbols in dreams vary much more according to the context of the dream.

Originally I devised the list to use with tea leaf readings but I have found that the same symbols have appeared whether I have been using oils, candle wax or even sand. They do not foretell the future but signpost nexus points, suggesting hidden needs and desires and inbuilt solutions for future happiness or success. If the meanings do not apply to you, cross them out and insert your own or make your own personal symbol chart in your notebook.

1. **Abroad**: A foreign place suggests a desire for a more exciting way of life and often appears when people feel in a rut.
2. **Acorns**: From small beginnings ... Acorns tend to suggest hidden plans or dreams that could be realised.
3. **Acrobat**: A complete change of opinion or viewpoint may be needed. An acrobat hints at a desire to free yourself of restraints.
4. **Aircraft**: Exciting new prospects, perhaps involving travel, are bubbling away. Travelling even a short way may hold the key.
5. **Anchor**: There may be fears about material security. It is important to make sure that plans have firm foundations.
6. **Ant**: Hard work, involving co-operation with others, is vital now for success. It is possible to move mountains.
7. **Apple**: Fertility is needed, whether in terms of bearing chil-

dren or launching a new idea. Try a new approach and your efforts will bear fruit.

8. **Army**: If the army seems friendly you will receive unexpected help. If hostile you may be or may feel under threat and should seek help or reassurance from allies.

9. **Arrow**: Concentrate on a particular aim and do not be distracted.

10. **Ashes**: Try to build or rebuild using what has been lost or destroyed in the past.

11. **Axe**: Do not be deterred by obstacles as you have the means to cut through any opposition.

12. **Baby**: You are aware that a new stage will involve commitment. Alternatively, babies and young children may affect your life in the near future.

13. **Basket**: You are central to the welfare of others. Your efforts are not wasted as your caring role will bring you great satisfaction.

14. **Bat**: Hidden fears of the unknown will melt if faced in the light of day.

15. **Bear**: You should seek strength in others and allow them to support you.

16. **Bed**: You need to rest, as you have become tired by the demands of life. A large bed with two people indicates a close relationship, involving commitment.

17. **Bees**: You must communicate important facts to those close to you. There may be important messages on the way that will lead to changes.

18. **Bell**: A cause to rejoice, especially associated with weddings and relationships. Be confident that happiness will be lasting.

19. **Bird**: If the bird is flying towards the questioner good news is on the way. If it is flying away then try another course rather than persist. A flock of birds indicates the need to follow the sun, mentally or physically, rather than waiting for happiness to come to you.

20. **Bone**: Forget old injustices. Resolve any quarrels and accept what cannot be mended.

21. **Book**: Check information before acting. Rely on conventional wisdom.

22. **Bowl**: If full, you can afford to be generous, as your fortunes are on the ascendant. If empty, seek input from others, as you are giving too much.

23. **Branch**: A new friendship or an addition to the family will bring happiness. Take any chances to diversify and expand.

24. **Bridge**: There is a way to overcome present difficulties if you look hard enough. Meet people halfway.

25. **Broom**: Make a fresh start by clearing any backlog or clutter in your life.

26. **Butterfly**: Enjoy the moment without demanding permanence.

27. **Cage**: You are feeling restricted and need to free yourself from unreasonable demands.

28. **Camel**: Rely on your own resources and make sure you are prepared in every way.

29. **Canoe**: Be prepared to strike out alone and venture further than usual either physically or by adopting a new perspective.

30. **Castle**: You are in a strong position, as long as you do not lose faith in yourself. Defend your beliefs, as you are right.

31. **Cat**: You need to remain aloof and take life on your own terms. People will come over to your way of thinking if you do not compromise.

32. **Cauldron**: Inspiration and creative thinking are the keys to success.

33. **Chain**: Join forces with others to achieve what you need, but do not make binding commitments.

34. **Church**: You are seeking approval from conventional sources for a plan of action. Be sure this accords with your own principles.

35. **Cliff**: Move slowly towards any goal and do not take unnecessary risks until you are on firm ground.

36. **Clock**: Wait for the right moment rather than acting hastily.

37. **Clouds**: Confusion over an issue will clear, given time.

38. **Clover**: Take advantage of luck that surrounds you to take a chance.

39. **Comet**: You may be offered an unexpected bonus or an opportunity to streak ahead. Do not hesitate.

40. **Cow**: Be patient for a while. Domestic matters will resolve themselves if you do not over-react.

41. **Crab**: Protect yourself from unfair criticism or hurt. Retreating into your shell for a while may avoid hurtful conflicts not of your making.

42. **Cradle**: You may need to be kind to someone who is feeling vulnerable.

43. **Crocodile**: Beware of double-dealing in a friendly stranger or new acquaintance.

44. **Cross**: If it is upright, you have an opportunity to achieve an ambition if you make realistic plans. A horizontal cross indicates that you should avoid anyone who depresses you or puts you down. A Celtic cross indicates strong psychic potential that you should develop.

45. **Crow or Raven**: Listen to any warnings and act on them.

46. **Crown**: Do not be tempted to act less than nobly, since the short-term gain is not worth the long-term loss.

47. **Dagger or Knife**: Be aware of a false friend who criticises you behind your back.

48. **Dancer**: You may be spending too much time keeping others happy. Your own harmony and peace of mind are equally important.

49. **Deer**: You may need to hide your feelings and avoid direct confrontation.

50. **Dog**: You should rely on loyal friends and family rather than new acquaintances, however exciting they seem at the moment.

51. **Doll**: You may be acting a part rather than following your real wishes.

52. **Donkey**: You may have to persuade stubborn people rather than use coercion.

53. **Door**: A door will open for you in the near future that will lead to a better way of life if you have the courage to go through it.

54. **Dove**: You may need to act as a peacemaker between warring family or close friends.

55. **Dragon**: Be courageous. Confront any opposition head on.

56. **Drum**: Let people know your achievements and offer yourself for any promotion or gain.

57. **Duck**: Satisfaction at the moment is close to home.

58. **Eagle**: Take a long-term view for success in worldly matters and fulfilment of ambitions.

59. **Ear**: Ignore gossip about those close to you.

60. **Egg**: You will soon experience a project coming to fruition or a new birth.

61. **Elephant**: Do not be deterred by the size of a task. You know more than you think.

62. **Eskimo**: You may feel that you are not moving forward but it

is just a question of waiting for the ice to melt.

63. **Eye**: Rely on direct contact in any communication rather than leaving it to others.

64. **Face**: You may need to outface someone who seeks to belittle you.

65. **Fairy or Angel**: Seek happiness through psychic and spiritual matters.

66. **Fan**: Enjoy flirtations and flattery but do not take them seriously.

67. **Feather**: It is important to avoid vacillation about your plans or intentions.

68. **Figure**: A stranger will assume importance in your life and may provide an answer to a long-standing problem.

69. **Fish**: Use your intuition and natural empathy with others to understand what is really going on around you.

70. **Flag**: A gathering is indicated where you can muster support and make useful contacts.

71. **Flowers**: You will receive recognition and thanks for what you have done.

72. **Forest**: Do not get overwhelmed by details and trivia and miss the main issue.

73. **Frog**: You have the ability to move in different worlds so long as you are prepared to be adaptable.

74. **Gate**: A barrier to success or happiness is easily overcome.

75. **Genie**: Seek an unusual solution and widen the bounds of possibility.

76. **Ghost**: You are haunted by guilt or regrets. Let them go.

77. **Giant**: You need to make a huge effort or take a monumental step.

78. **Gift**: You may find that an offer or gift comes with provisos. As long as you are aware of them, it can still be to your advantage.

79. **Glove or Gauntlet**: You may need to challenge the assumptions or actions of others.

80. **Grapes**: You need to have more pleasure in your life and indulge your desires.

81. **Grass**: The temptation is to abandon the familiar, but the gains may be illusory.

82. **Guitar**: Listen to your inner voice and try to get in tune with yourself.

83. **Gun**: Resist others who try to get their way by force.

84. **Hag or Witch**: Do not be afraid to acknowledge your own negative feelings.
85. **Hammer**: You may need to push home any important issues.
86. **Hand**: Reach out to others who may be offering love or friendship, even if you have been betrayed in the past.
87. **Hare**: Move quickly to take advantage of any offers or changes in location.
88. **Harp**: You are entering a harmonious relationship or a period in one.
89. **Hat**: You will have a welcome visitor, perhaps from the past.
90. **Head**: Use logic rather than feelings to guide your decisions.
91. **Heart**: Follow your heart whether in love or family matters.
92. **Helmet**: Protect yourself from malicious attack or negative attitudes by your own positive attitude.
93. **Hen**: Domestic concerns and taking care of others predominate at present, but will soon be relieved.
94. **Horn (musical)**: You will hear good news or have cause for celebration.
    Horn (animal): Tackle any issue directly.
95. **Horse**: Hard work and perseverance are necessary to succeed.
96. **Horseshoe**: Good fortune favours any enterprise undertaken.
97. **Hourglass**: It is important to finish any tasks in hand and be aware of deadlines.
98. **House**: You will either be moving house or your concerns about material security will be resolved.
99. **Hunter**: You will need to look for the answers and should keep quiet about any intentions.
100. **Iceberg**: There are many hidden factors or feelings that are affecting a seemingly straightforward matter. Uncover them.
101. **Igloo**: You should temporarily retreat from inhospitable people or circumstances.
102. **Indian (Native American)**: Try to return to a slower, more natural way of life if pressures are building up.
103. **Inkwell**: Deal with any important correspondence rather than avoiding it.
104. **Imp**: Beware of trickery and petty spite from an immature person.
105. **Island**: You may be feeling temporarily isolated from others, so concentrate on your own happiness for a while.
106. **Jewels**: You have many hidden talents that you have not yet revealed.

107. **Jug**: Your unconscious wisdom will guide you if you allow it to be heard. Listen to your dreams.

108. **Juggler**: You need to balance different demands on your time. Decide on your priorities.

109. **Key**: The key to happiness is already in your life if you can use it.

110. **King**: A male authority figure is seeking to influence you. He may have useful advice but do not go against your own wishes.

111. **Kite**: If you allow yourself to be carried by circumstances for a while, you may find a freer way of life.

112. **Kitten**: You should have fun and relax for a while.

113. **Knot**: You need to extricate yourself from a tricky situation with tact and perhaps ingenuity.

114. **Ladder**: Promotion or work opportunities are on the horizon.

115. **Lake**: Look into your inner well of calmness and allow the disharmony of others to pass you by.

116. **Lamp**: There is light at the end of a particular tunnel.

117. **Leaves**: A cluster of leaves indicates praise or material rewards, while a single falling leaf says that it is time to let go of redundant feelings.

118. **Leopard**: You cannot be what you are not to please anyone. Preserve your identity.

119. **Letter**: You will receive a letter in the near future from someone with whom you have lost touch.

120. **Lightning**: A sudden flash of illumination or energy will help resolve a situation.

121. **Lighthouse**: You will need to guide others who cannot see the way forward.

122. **Lion**: Be courageous and you can achieve what you want.

123. **Locket**: Do not look back with regrets for you will find new happiness.

124. **Mask**: Beware hidden malice or anger that may suddenly burst out of someone seemingly affiable.

125. **Mermaid**: Trust your psychic insights to guide you into unknown fields.

126. **Messenger**: Do not act as go-between for other people's quarrels.

127. **Mirror**: If you feel that life is passing you by, step out of the shadow of whoever is blocking your own path.

128. **Money or Coins**: You will have an improvement in your financial situation through a new money-spinning adventure.

129. **Monkey**: There are many new skills to be learned, if you can be adaptable, that will offer success.
130. **Moon**: Listen to your dreams but beware of taking the easy option.
131. **Mountain**: An ambition that seems impossible can be attained if you take it step by step.
132. **Mouse**: Pay attention to small details and to the small print in any deals.
133. **Mouth**: Be careful what you say or you may be misunderstood or quoted out of context.
134. **Musical Notes**: You will find others very much in harmony with you and your ideas.
135. **Nail**: Direct, forceful action will succeed better than hints or sulks.
136. **Necklace**: A bond of friendship or love encircles you. If you see a broken necklace the friendship or love needs attention.
137. **Needle and Thread**: Improve your life or relationships by repairing any damage, rather than moving on.
138. **Nest**: You will be preoccupied with your home in a practical way.
139. **Net**: Look beyond your immediate environment to find friendship or happiness.
140. **Noose**: You may need to accept that you are restricted by circumstances.
141. **Numbers**: These often indicate a time scale, usually in months, for a projected change or improvement in circumstances.
142. **Oar**: You need to strike out into the unknown if you are to make changes. A floating paddle may indicate a fear of drifting or being carried along by others.
143. **Octopus**: Be versatile if a problem seems difficult.
144. **Ostrich**: Do not avoid tricky issues as they will not go away.
145. **Owl**: Seek wise counsel from an impartial source.
146. **Padlock**: Secure any deals or arrangements firmly to avoid misunderstandings or mistakes.
147. **Palm Tree**: You should take a well-deserved rest, perhaps a holiday.
148. **Parcel**: You may need to probe to discover whether an offer is to your advantage.
149. **Parrot**: Do not be afraid to be original and suggest new ideas, rather than following established approaches.

150. **Peacock**: First appearances can be deceptive. Trust your instincts, not outward show, in deciding whether to trust a stranger.

151. **Pipe**: Take time to think over and discuss a major decision.

152. **Purse**: You will need to watch your finances for a while, especially the financial demands of others upon you.

153. **Pyramid**: Seek wisdom from the past and learn from past mistakes.

154. **Question Mark**: Examine any doubts as they may be well-founded.

155. **Queue of People**: Make sure that others do not push your needs and wishes out of the way.

156. **Rainbow**: Happiness will soon follow a time of sorrow or greyness, if you believe in yourself.

157. **Rat**: Use strategy to outmanoeuvre a more powerful opponent.

158. **Rattle**: Children or someone who acts childishly may demand extra attention.

159. **Ring**: A deep emotional commitment will occur, perhaps a marriage or partnership.

160. **Rocks**: Care and tact are needed to negotiate a tricky situation.

161. **Roof**: You may be worrying about your material future unnecessarily.

162. **Rose**: Love, friendship and happiness will surround you in the near future.

163. **Sailor**: News or a visitor from afar will bring happiness.

164. **Scales**: Balance the pros and cons of a situation carefully.

165. **Scissors**: Cut through indecision and make a definite plan for the future.

166. **Sea**: If stormy, you may need to wait for calmer times. If the sea is smooth, then you can expand your horizons and begin new ventures.

167. **Ship**: Past efforts will bring results.

168. **Shipwreck**: Abandon a destructive situation if it cannot be salvaged.

169. **Snail**: Life is moving too slowly. You may need to shake other people's attitudes.

170. **Snake**: You may be tempted to stray or act in a sly way.

171. **Spade**: Dig deeper and you will discover the truth.

172. **Spider**: Avoid emotional blackmail and possessive people who try to entangle you in obligation.

173. **Star**: Try to make your dreams come true, if only in a small way.
174. **Sun**: Tomorrow is another day so leave behind yesterday's sorrows or anger.
175. **Sword**: Be prepared to fight for what you want or hold dear.
176. **Table**: Family togetherness or conferences can resolve misunderstandings.
177. **Telescope**: Look for the long-term advantage rather than expecting immediate gains from present efforts.
178. **Temple**: Your spiritual world matters just as much as material success. You should not be discouraged if others do not understand.
179. **Tent**: Temporary solutions should be accepted as they may lead to more permanent answers.
180. **Tiger**: Do not attempt to ignore your instincts, especially if they warn you of danger.
181. **Toadstool**: Beware of illusions and day-dreams.
182. **Tortoise**: Persevere, for your plans have firm foundations, even if they seem slow to materialise.
183. **Tower**: You may feel cut off from the crowd because of a strong principle or vision that others do not share.
184. **Train**: Take any opportunity to meet new people and visit new places.
185. **Treasure Chest**: You will discover a hidden treasure among your friends or a talent you have that will bring you immediate financial benefit if used.
186. **Tunnel**: A temporary depression or sadness will end if you do not lose hope.
187. **Twins**: You will meet someone who will help you to fulfil your dreams.
188. **Umbrella**: A person or place will offer refuge and consolation
189. **Valley**: A calm period of your life lies ahead.
190. **Violin**: Avoid being over-sensitive about criticism.
191. **Volcano**: A sudden, tempestuous outburst that has been building up for a while could be destructive if not faced.
192. **Wall**: You should relax your defences, as they are cutting you off from valuable support.
193. **Waterfall**: You may face a sudden and frightening challenge but should not fear it.
194. **Well**: Seek the wisdom that comes from deep reflection and drawing upon experience.

195. Whale: A huge undertaking or responsibility that lies before you promises great satisfaction in the end.

196. Wheel: Use any changes brought about by fate or circumstance to the best advantage.

197. Windmill: Harness available resources and seize a sudden opportunity.

198. Window: Look outwards instead of inwards for an answer that has been evading you.

199. Wolf: Strength lies in conformity rather than standing alone.

200. Yacht: Do not try to force issues as they may be resolved naturally.

Section Three

Divination

8

Automatic Writing

Automatic writing is sometimes regarded entirely as a tool of mediumship. However, like many forms of divination, such as casting runes or turning Tarot cards, it relies on unconscious muscular movements of the hand to convey, through writing, information that is not accessible to the conscious mind. As with other forms of divination, there is a debate over the source of the wisdom. Is it a communication from a highly evolved discarnate being or from a deceased spirit, whether that of a close relation or someone who needs to communicate information?

However many psychical researchers, myself included, believe that most of the information conveyed through automatic writing comes from the depths of the writer's subconscious mind or perhaps from ESP.

Because it is such a complex and important subject, I have included a number of different examples so that you can decide how you regard automatic writing and whether you wish to use it primarily for mediumship or, as I do, as a divinatory channel to the Collective Unconscious.

I was sent the following account by a sailor who served in the Second World War. I have changed the name of the ship and the location of the tragedy to avoid distressing any living relatives of those who were lost. William Brown, who lives in Lancashire, told me:

The experience relates to World War Two and training with the Royal Navy at a requisitioned holiday camp, in Scotland. Our instructor, a Chief Petty Officer Telegraphist, was an old sea dog, a kindly father figure and a Spiritualist medium.

Every instruction class was interlaced with talks and demonstrations on life after death. Taking any article, trinket or keepsake in his hand, Chief could give us insights into persons living or dead, houses, furnishings and information known only to the owner.

In one of his many interludes, our lovable instructor spoke to us of a submarine, newly built and lost with almost all hands on board while on trials off the coast of England. He went into great detail about the accident which he told us had not been published. Only details of the rescue operation from outside the submarine had been released at the time. This prompted questions from us all. Had he been involved in the rescue in some way? And, being given a negative reply, we wondered how he had come by this information. During our next instruction class, he revealed the answer.

Chief produced a couple of letters in different handwriting, one of which was written by a crew member of the ill-fated submarine, blaming himself for the tragedy. The letter spoke of test torpedo firing, torpedo tubes, inner and outer doors and special gauge cocks and visual gauge glasses that when opened would indicate that the outer door was fully closed, enabling the inner door to open. This, it stated, should never be undertaken without rodding through these open cocks and glass gauges, since a blockage could give an incorrect reading. This had not been done; it was taking an empty test glass at face value which had led to the disaster.

The gauges had in fact been blocked with seaweed, the writer maintained, and on releasing the inner door, had been burst open by a wall of water. The operator panicked, rushing through adjoining compartments, failing to secure these water-tight doors, before a petty officer answering the rating's cries had managed to secure one opening. The rest flooded, pulling the submarine down at this end by the sheer weight of water, denying an escape route and causing some gassing problems from wetted batteries.

He also mentioned that some personnel were not experienced submariners and that attempts at escape, with an experienced member nursing an inexperienced person, had resulted in a panic by the latter when a chamber was being deliberately flooded resulting in deaths.

The Chief Petty Officer was challenged on many counts. If

indeed the letters had come from crew members how had he come by them, since most had perished? The medium replied that the letters had been written from a dead submariner through him. Anyone could receive automatic writing, the Chief thought. Sit with a pen to paper, empty the mind and wait. It would take time, he told us – more than most are prepared to give – but eventually the body would be used and the written word would result.

Why then had he not passed on the letters, he was asked, to which he shrugged his shoulders and replied that no one would have believed him. 'You certainly do not. I could have brought troubles on myself. Better to leave it as it is.'

Many years later, when a civilian, I was walking home from work. It was a Saturday afternoon after five o'clock. I called as usual to collect a newspaper from the railway station, an *Empire News*, a Sunday newspaper that one could purchase late on a Saturday. There I found the official account of the submarine disaster. This information had come to light only when the ship was raised and refitted. Naturally there were similarities to the account in the letter, but one thing caught my eye. The official version was that the blockage was ship's paint not seaweed. The writer, if indeed it was a tormented soul, could be forgiven that mistake. He certainly would not have expected a brand new sub to have a blob of paint giving a false reading. Seaweed would be a natural assumption.

The letters had also given an account of the deaths of two people attempting escape. Also the statement that these deaths had prevented the use of that escape route for reasons which were also given, all of which were now proved true.

The letter was not only correct in the details but also in the motivation of the submariner who had died believing he had caused the tragedy. Time and time again, it has been discovered that the dead do not automatically gain full knowledge of earthly affairs, and ghosts can be prevented from resting by a sense of guilt or the belief that they caused a disaster. The most valuable automatic writing is based on emotion and real questions and needs.

Another case where spirit communication was also apparently involved in automatic writing was that transmitted through Pearl Curran, a housewife from St Louis in the US, in 1913. After initial contact through a ouija board, the spirit of Patience Worth began to dictate profuse quantities of literature through Pearl. Patience claimed to be an Englishwoman from a poor country family in Dorset. Born in 1649 and still unmarried, she was killed by Native American Indians not long after she emigrated to the US. She communicated through the ouija board, then increasingly through automatic writing, producing 2,500 poems, plays, short stories and epigrams, and six full-length novels set in different historical periods. She wrote a total of four million words in five years.

What was strange was that the stories were almost 90 per cent written in Old English, a far greater proportion according to academics than in any literature produced since the thirteenth century. Patience also wrote about periods after she had lived, giving facts which were authenticated. Is it possible then that Pearl had herself assumed the identity of Patience, as she unconsciously drew from what Jung called the Collective Unconscious and others have called the Great Memory (referring to a universal human memory)?

Certainly the nineteenth-century American philosopher and psychologist William James regarded automatic writing as a way of obtaining information that was buried deep in the subconscious and it became a valuable form of therapy.

Others considered it a telepathic process whereby information could be transferred from living minds. William E. Stead, the crusading journalist and spiritualist who died on the *Titanic*, at first considered automatic writing a means of communication by the deceased. When he first tried it he found the sentiments were exactly those expressed by a deceased friend who had been a journalist and did not reflect his own beliefs at all. However, Stead also found that he could write letters in the hands of various living friends, conveying any news they wished to tell him – facts he could only have obtained by telepathic means.

One remarkable example was a letter he wrote in the handwriting of a female friend who was travelling home on a Sunday evening from London after they had spent a weekend together. In the letter, which Stead wrote on the Monday morning, without any communication passing between them, the lady described how on her homeward journey she had been troubled on the train by the unwanted attentions of a gentleman passenger. The letter described how she had hit her attacker with an umbrella before he left the train at Guildford. The only discrepancy with the facts was that the umbrella had been hers, not the assailant's.

How Does Automatic Writing Occur?

Often it is an art that manifests itself spontaneously. A person, perhaps intending to write a letter, a list or even a story or poem, suddenly finds the pen moving over the paper writing words in an unfamiliar handwriting containing a message or anecdote. It may be that of a deceased relative, and if there are any samples of the deceased relation's hand they are often remarkably similar. It may be an unknown hand, perhaps an identifiable figure from the past or an unnamed source. Whether the source is a spirit or a memory from the well of the Collective Unconscious is perhaps a matter of interpretation, but the source of the knowledge often assumes a definite identity.

Should this occur, you should accept it as a natural mode of communication and allow the writing to manifest itself when it feels right and not try to force it. People who engage in automatic writing frequently experience a tingling sensation in the arms or hands immediately before a message is received.

Gordon and his wife Joanna engaged in spirit rescue work and communication with discarnate beings over several years, and recorded through Joanna's hand hundreds of conversations, many containing facts that had not been known but were subsequently verified. Gordon described the process:

> My wife remained fully conscious, but never knowing what her hand would write. The spirits communicated by directed writing through my wife's hand. I talked into thin air or sometimes thought my replies. My wife therefore sometimes did not even know my thought, to which the discarnate being would respond. Our spirit communicators normally came to us about nine o'clock at night and she would feel a slight tremor of the solar plexus which was the indication that she should get pen and paper ready.

How Does Automatic Writing Differ from Ordinary Writing?

Automatic writing tends to flow faster than conscious handwriting. Words may be joined together and perhaps be spelled unusually. The actual letters tend to be larger than the receiver's ordinary writing and be formed in a different way. Some automatic writers find that they are endowed with the most wonderful copperplate writing, but only during the process of the automatic transmission. Automatic writing can also be in mirror script or written left to right, even on occasions starting at the bottom right corner and ending at the top left. It may be in verse or contain complicated biblical quotations or even Latin. Once again, this may not indicate spirit communication but knowledge we have absorbed without realising it at an earlier period in our lives or that we have accessed from the unconscious wisdom of our forefathers.

Sometimes there are messages, seemingly from more highly evolved discarnate beings who may communicate about the state of the world and the need for conservation and peace. You should not worry about the nature or source of the communication. Accept what is useful or fascinating and discard what is not. You may even start a career as a novelist. Automatic writers do not seem to suffer from writer's block.

Beginning Automatic Writing

Even if you have never experienced a spontaneous flow of words, you can use automatic writing both for accessing unfamiliar information and for divination. Some people find automatic writing easier when they have first developed their natural abilities through scrying and divination; for others it is a good introductory method of allowing the unconscious mind to express itself.

To practise automatic writing:

* Find a good pen or pencil, a notepad and a quiet place at a table. Sit there and let your hand move as it will. You may like to ask your hand if it has any messages to transmit to you.
* Hold your pen loosely in whichever hand you normally write with, and let your mind roam completely freely, with images filtering through and floating away.
* If nothing happens after a few minutes, visualise a column of light made up of golden letters, forming and reforming words.
* Count down from twenty to one and let the light flow down your arm into your fingers and the pen. See the golden letters on the page.

* Wait until you feel your pen tremble and let it move. At first it may scribble and then make patterns and then words. Do not try to read or analyse the words or you will logically decide what should come next and lose the spontaneity.
* When you feel you are losing concentration stop.
* Try to practise at the same time each night – at first for no more than five minutes and eventually building up to ten or fifteen.
* At the end of each session, lay down your pen and see the column of light gradually fading and yourself in a dark, peaceful place.
* Keep the same pen and pad or book of paper for writing and do not use them for other purposes.
* Read what you have written. It may seem to relate to you or to another life or person, perhaps a past life, perhaps a persona that is deep in you. Keep it in your psychic notebook and you may find a story unfolding.
* Do something mundane or physical so that you do not go to bed immediately afterwards with the words buzzing round. It is important, with any formal psychic work, to have a clear demarcation between this and the rest of your life.
* Finally, remember not to get too involved in automatic writing. If it occupies your thoughts to the exclusion of other aspects of your life, cut down or even stop for a while. Because it is quite a direct psychic method, it can create a personality of the sender. It is especially important not to use automatic writing if you are feeling distressed or angry as you can dredge up memories or feelings that can be hard to handle.

My own mother's automatic writing ability began after a visit to a fortune-teller who identified a man with whom she was secretly in love. My mother began to receive messages in different writing from different spirits, the most persistent of whom said he was the late George VI. At first this was very exciting and my mother gradually spent more and more time receiving her messages. Her life was quite empty. She had a very unhappy marriage and few friends and my brother and I were at school all day. She came to rely on her spirit messages for advice, consolation and promises that the man she admired from afar would take her away.

Gradually the messages took over her everyday life, although few were of any significance. She then began to hear voices in her head that troubled her night and day and, although she continued her writing, the messages became mere scribble, unintelligible except to her. At last she became frightened and went to the local church to be exorcised by the parish priest. As she knelt at the altar, an old man ran up and down the aisle cursing. After that her ability and desire to practise automatic writing disappeared.

Using Automatic Writing for Divination

* Write down a question to which you need an answer, using an ordinary pen.
* Pick up your special pen and write down whatever comes into your head however unlikely or irrelevant it may seem. You may feel the special trembling but, if not, go ahead anyway. It may be a few words, a few lines or a page or more.
* When you feel the impetus fade, put down the pen.
* Do not read the answer but, with your everyday pen, write a second question that will come quite spontaneously. It may be unexpected but later you will find that it was pertinent.
* Pick up your automatic writing pen and let the second answer form.
* Continue with each question and answer without reading the answers, until you have five or six answers or feel that you have exhausted all the possibilities.
* Read all the answers through one after the other. They may take the form of a dialogue with yourself or they may be highly symbolic, in which case you can use the basic symbol system to begin to unravel them. The answers may even form a story, in which case consider how the characters and their actions relate to possible future choices of your own. Sometimes the symbols appear as pictures, or you may find yourself drawing a figure either in distinctive dress or someone you know. You may also develop a gift for drawing people you see around someone to whom you are giving a reading. These may be deceased relatives of the sitter or friends who have returned from beyond the grave to wish him or her well.

9

Candle and Wax Divination

Candles were a central part of the earliest magical rituals. Man learned to use fire around 600,000 years ago, and in early Palaeolithic times the inner caves that extended from cave dwellings were decorated with tapers made of animal fat, in honour of the Mother Goddess, statues of whom date from 22000 BC.

Beeswax tapers and eventually candles of undyed yellow were used throughout pre-Christian times, for bees were regarded as messengers of the gods and goddesses and beeswax candles thus formed a link between heaven and earth. In Neolithic times, the queen bee was symbolic of the Goddess herself. A vase depicting the Bee Goddess appeared on a frieze on a vase found in Thessaly, dated from around 6400 BC.

In the third century BC the priestesses of Demeter, the Corn Goddess, were called *melissae* (Latin for 'bees'). And in Christianity, beeswax candles have become associated with the Virgin Mary. Many people only use beeswax candles for magical and spiritual development and these can be bought, not only in yellow but also dyed with natural vegetable colourings.

Traditional Candle Beliefs

Because candles represented a way of measuring time, and because the brightness, direction and endurance of a candle flame were affected both by the inner composition of the candle and by external circumstances, candles were often seen as a reflection of the life of a man or woman. For this reason candles were linked closely with birth, death and love and it was believed that if a candle went out, death or disaster would follow. There was also a belief that, for every candle that went out in one place, another was lit and represented the spirit of one life passing into another.

A blue flame was said, in traditional lore, to indicate that a spirit or ghost was passing. And a bright spark suddenly flaring up in a candle wick suggested that a stranger or a letter bringing good news was coming for the person nearest to the candle. If a person wanted to know the date of the arrival he or she would knock the candlestick on the table and count, starting with the present date, until the spark fell out of the candle or faded.

To snuff out a candle accidentally indicated an unexpected wedding or birth. And it was forbidden to leave candles burning in empty rooms, except for the Christmas Candle which could be left burning in the window on Christmas Eve to light the Virgin Mary on her way. Large Christmas candles were given by grocers to their customers at Christmas for this purpose until the beginning of this century. This custom pre-dates Christianity and goes back to the Mid-Winter Solstice festivities around 21 December, when fires, torches and candles were kept burning to persuade the sun not to die but to shine again.

Candles were also used as love charms until late Victorian times. A girl would call her lover to her by putting two intertwined pins in a lighted candle and saying:

> 'Tis not these pins I wish to burn,
> But my love's heart I wish to turn.
> May he neither sleep nor rest,
> Till he has granted my request.

In country places at Halloween a candle was carried along a sheltered path from 11 o'clock until midnight, the witching hour, and taken around the houses, farms and barns in a village. If the candle went out, it was seen as a bad omen.

Candles were also traditionally used in curses. In the fifteenth century, several alleged witches were put on trial, accused of trying to murder people by naming a black candle after them, letting the wax fall, forming a doll from the wax, sticking pins in it and letting the candle burn away.

Using Candles for Divination

Different coloured candles can be used for different wishes. Burn a wish in the chosen candle. There are many different lists of candle colours. This one is a combination of several that have been found useful.

Candle Colours for Wishes and Needs

White is the colour of new beginnings, clear vision and ideas.
Red is the colour of passion, fertility and sudden change.
Orange is the colour for happiness, harmony and health.
Yellow is for communication, logic and learning.
Green is for love, romance and friendship.
Blue is for travel, justice and career.
Violet or indigo is for healing and psychic development.
Pink is for the mending of quarrels, patience and family matters, especially concerning babies and children.
Brown is for home, financial matters and for older relations.
Silver is for secret desires and intuition.
Gold is the colour of long-term ambitions and courage.
Black is for banishing guilt or regrets and for acceptance of people and situations as they are.

You can light an appropriate coloured candle as part of the magical rituals described in Section Five. You can also use them as a focus for candle wishes. To do this:

* Use a piece of paper the same colour as the candle or write on white paper in the appropriate colour pen. Make it into a taper about 22cm (9 inches) long. You can use one of the magical alphabets described in Section Six, ordinary writing or even pictures.
* Do not be afraid to pick a material wish. We all have earthly needs and meeting these is as vital a part of our existence as evolving into spiritual beings. If you need £500 for urgent repairs on your car, want to take your family on holiday or need a break yourself, ask for that.
* Be specific about your wishes. Any form of magic or divination works best with a definite time scale and a narrow focus. Be realistic too. You are more likely to get an unexpected rebate of £100 than £100,000.

* Light a candle and look into the flame, seeing what it is you most need or desire moving closer. Anticipate the pleasure, excitement or relief the fulfilment of your wish will bring, and visualise alternative scenarios of the source or the steps you will take to fulfil your desire.
* Hold the taper into the candle flame facing downwards. Have a saucer or plate beneath the candle to catch the ash so that you can use it for ash divination.
* It may be that your paper will not stay alight. This does not seem to depend on the type of paper, as members of my psychic class have used identical paper and pens, yet the tapers have burned in different ways.
* If your taper does go out, light it again. (I have sometimes had to make three or more.) If the taper burns quickly success will be instant. If it burns slowly, stops, smoulders and begins again you will also succeed; it will just take longer. As your taper burns look into the candle flame and see yourself happier, more successful but still the you that you are now.

Ash Divination

* When the ash has collected on the saucer, tip it on to plain white paper.
* Holding the paper firmly in both hands, gently shake the ashes until they form a picture. If you do not have enough, burn a second blank taper of the same colour in the flame.
* You may see a picture or several images, as you would in tea leaf reading: perhaps an animal, a bird, a person. You can refer to the 200 symbols listed in Chapter 7 if this is helpful. The first interpretation of the image that comes into your mind will be the right one.
* You may find that the symbol is one that appears in your dreams or will appear very shortly afterwards.

Wax Divination

This is one of the earliest forms of divination.

* Use your candle of need, and you can light candles of other colours to add to the picture.

* Drip the hot wax from your wish candle slowly over your ash image. You will find it becomes three-dimensional. Like a Chinese picture that is composed of a series of dots and splashes of colour, you may now see rivers, mountains, oceans.
* If you see nothing, add hot wax from other candles and half-close your eyes. You will probably see whole scenes so you may find the dream symbols listed in Chapter 15 helpful.

John at first saw in his ash picture a mountain which he took to represent a difficult task he had to face in order to overcome a financial problem left by a failed business. He could not see himself on the mountain and felt that he was getting nowhere. John then tipped hot wax on the picture from his white candle of need for a new beginning and decided to light a red candle to initiate change and a black one to put aside the bitterness he felt at being let down by his bank. The result was a picture of a dragon with huge wings emerging from the mountain – he saw this as himself facing the future courageously and flying away. He had been offered a fairly routine, relatively low-paid job in a holiday village whose logo was a dragon, through a relation who was working as a manager. John decided to cut his losses, abandon plans to get compensation from the bank and to start again.

Wax Divination in Water

Another method of wax divination follows the traditional way closely. Originally, wax or molten lead would be thrown into a bucket of cold water to make a picture or an initial. If you are skilled with a soldering iron (not an electric one needless to say), you could melt metal and drop it into water.

However, this technique works just as well with candle wax. It is especially potent when performed outdoors after dark.

* Use a heatproof pottery or metal bowl filled with water.
* Ring your bowl with candles of a strong single colour. Red, dark blue, purple or green show best.
* Tip a single candle on the surface of the water, thinking of a question or issue that concerns you. You need to interpret your first image very quickly, before the wax hardens. This first image shows you hidden aspects of the present situation

or any opposition that you are facing. Usually it is a single image.

* As the wax hardens, you will see a second static picture that you can study at length, perhaps an initial or a single shape. This will suggest a solution.

Paula used a deep purple candle which she dropped into water. She was considering moving in with a new partner, Stephen, after five years alone, following the breakdown of her marriage. Her first image was a cave, which she regarded as a refuge, a place to hide. Paula said that she was afraid that she was moving in with Stephen for the wrong reasons: because she did not want to spend the rest of her life alone and because she was thirty-eight and worried that she would never have a baby.

Were her fears justified? As the wax set, it formed a distinctive heart. Follow your heart, Paula said. What was that?

She dropped a second piece of molten wax, which you can do if the answer is not clear. That hardened almost at once, and formed what seemed to be a two-headed doll. Paula said that she and Stephen were close in many ways. Paula realised that even if she never had a child she would want to be with Stephen. She had had no doubts until her mother had started to question her motives. Paula said that she had been living with her mother since the divorce and knew that it would be difficult for her mother to accept Stephen, as she herself was a widow and tended to depend on Paula for company.

Divination does not offer guarantees of future bliss but can help us to uncover the best path and see the options clearly, unclouded by the considerations and anxieties of others. If a picture is not clear you can always add to it or start again.

Wax Divination Using Several Candles

A third method of wax divination involves using several small flat candles placed directly on a metal tray or dish so that the melting wax can flow freely.

* Make sure that the surface is flat.
* Use dark or bold, contrasting colours and watch as the colours merge to make pictures.

- Alternatively, if you are in a situation which involves several people, designate a candle for each one. Scratch the name of the person lightly in the wax if you wish.
- Watch how the colours interact and which candle's wax flows into that of other candles. The two furthest away may join. See how they interact, which is consumed first and which burns longest. You may find some surprising correlations with the people concerned and some unexpected liaisons may be revealed. You can learn a great deal about the hidden group dynamics by observing, for example, which colour is swamped by the other candles, which moves away and which allies (merges) with another.

Julian had recently returned to his wife and family after an affair for which he had left his wife had fizzled out. His wife Anna used a green candle for Julian. For herself she chose a blue one, for the mistress red and for the children bright yellow and brown. As the wax melted, the green candle wax flowed in turn towards all the candles and was almost surrounded by the red candle. The blue candle moved close but then diverted to the edge of the tray. However, significantly, the bright yellow and brown candles formed a finger-like flow that effectively blocked the access of the red candle to the green. The red candle went out first, the green one flickered but burned faintly, the blue candle went out next, then the green. And the yellow and brown candles were strongest, going out almost simultaneously some time after the others.

Anna saw the blue candle reflecting her own inability to reach out as Julian vacillated between his mistress and family. The predatory red candle was blocked by the two candles representing the children, who had reacted very angrily towards their father when he departed but had been very supportive of both parents since he had returned. It demonstrated to her the strength of the children's unquestioning love and the idea that they could rebuild a relationship that had foundered when she and Julian had drifted apart.

10

Crystal Divination

Crystal colour meanings are based on traditional usage and differ slightly from candle colours. However you may find that for you colour meanings are the same, regardless of whether they are the colours of crystals, candles or auric shades. You should adapt the lists accordingly or make new ones in your psychic notebook.

Colours form the basis for divination and, as long as you keep your meaning consistent, the system is remarkably effective, perhaps because crystals are formed from earth, air, fire and water, the elements of which life was composed according to Classical belief. Born in the ground, changed by volcanic fires, eroded by the air and their passage through many streams, rivers, even the sea, crystals take thousands of years to form. They are sometimes believed to contain the fifth element, made from the mixture, destruction and recreation of the others, the elusive philosopher's stone that was said to hold the key to wisdom and perhaps, as the ancients believed, to immortality.

Choosing Your Crystals

For divination you only need ten quite small crystals, one of each of the listed colours, not much bigger than a large coin, flat on both sides so that you can cast them. They can be round, square or an irregular shape. Go to any New Age shop or crystal shop. Increasingly, ordinary gift shops, especially near the coast, have a large selection of crystals. Look through each kind until you find the right crystal for you in each colour. Some you may find on a shore, a river bank, plain or hillside, especially quartz.

Hold the stone up to the light and you may well see rays of sunlight filtering through what seems the most opaque stone. You may want to keep your set of ten divinatory stones separately in a drawstring bag. I have suggested a list of crystals for each colour that are easily available but you may prefer to use stones from your own region. Choose one for each colour. However, you may enjoy, as I have done, building up a collection of small crystals of different shades, to use for chakra energies, healing and rituals for energy or tranquillity. The richer colours that are vibrant and opaque are good for energising and attracting love or success, while the softer, transparent colours promote calm and inner harmony and can also be used for banishing fear or redundant feelings.

White

White speaks of new ventures or beginnings (whether in love or business), clear vision, pure energy and original ideas. In divination, white says the concern is an energy issue when change is in the air and you need to take positive action. There may be a new beginning you need to make or an extra surge of energy at work or in a relationship.

Buy: clear quartz (cheap and obtainable almost anywhere); colourless zircon (the poor man's diamond); milky quartz; snow quartz; white mother of pearl (translucent); a white moonstone (soft iridiscent sheen); or find a white pebble on the shore or hillside.

Black

Black is for letting go of old sorrows, grief or guilt, for acceptance and for transformation. In divination, black represents the ending of a period in life, whether this is a natural change point or one forced on you by others. This may involve some pain but only then can you move on to the new world of opportunity that is waiting. Alternatively, it may indicate that you need to accept a person as he or she really is or a situation that may not be of your choosing.

Buy: hematite (brilliant silvery black); jet (actually fossilised wood that is millions of years old); obsidian or Apache's Tear (if you hold this to the light you can see through it, as it is a type of natural glass); black onyx (opaque); dark banded agates; blackish grey smoky quartz; or find a matt black pebble, such as flint, that may link you to earlier times.

Brown

Brown is for practical issues, money, home, order, animals and older people. In divination, brown is the colour of the earth. So, when you choose a brown crystal, it's telling you to go back to your grass roots, touch home base and trust the evidence of your eyes, ears and other senses, rather than relying on what others tell you or what you read and see. With money matters, check your figures.

Buy: brown tiger's eye; brown chrysoberyl; brown amber; brown or tawny single-coloured or banded agate; petrified wood stone (in various shades of brown that you can either buy polished or find on beaches where there were once prehistoric forests); smoky-brown quartz; or you can find brown stained limestones perhaps containing fossils, brown sandstone or a piece of brown flint.

Pink

Pink is for reconciliation, family (especially children and babies), patience, perseverance, caring for others and quiet sleep. In divination, pink represents the reconciliation of opposites or extremes and says that you are cast in the role of peacemaker but should not sacrifice your own peace of mind. Children bring joy and patience will eventually be rewarded.

Buy: pink coral; pink rhodonite (sometimes streaked with black); a bright to salmon pink rhodochrosite (often banded with paler pink); pink sugilite; pink sodalite; rose quartz; pink mother of pearl; watermelon tourmaline; pink kunzite (sometimes the woman's stone); or you can find some pink and white flecked granite or matt pink sandstone pebbles.

Red

Red is for fertility, courage, challenges, passion and anger which can be positive if channelled into positive change. In divination, red represents the need for courage and action. You should assert your rights and express any discontent in a positive way rather than suppressing it.

Buy: garnet; carnelian (a form of chalcedony, usually glowing, rich cherry red); red jasper; red agate or blood agate (resembling a carnelian, especially when highly polished); red calcite (can be brittle); red fluorite (similar to calcite but more glassy); red banded agate (opaque with more muted reddish-brown and pink colouring than the blood agate); or find a matt brick or dark red pebble (usually sandstone or shale).

Orange

Orange is for identity issues, for personal happiness, health, rivalries, balance and partnerships, whether at home or at work. In divination, orange is the colour of independence or equality in partnerships. It is often associated with the happiness and sense of uniqueness that gives us the confidence to assert who we are and what we believe. You should be optimistic about the future.

Buy: amber (not a true crystal but fossilised tree resin, usually about 50 million years old, which has a rich vibrant colour); rich orange carnelian; orange jasper; orange citrine; orange calcite (can be brittle); smoky-orange quartz; agate banded with muted orange; orange beryl; or you can find a matt orange stone, usually sandstone or a bit of quartzite that may have orange glints depending on which other minerals are present.

Yellow

Yellow is for communication, for undeveloped potential, logic, learning, examinations and interviews. In divination, yellow is the colour of the sun and communication. It cuts through doublespeak and jargon to the real issue and shatters illusions. You should use your head rather than your heart and be prepared to work hard to be sure of success.

Buy: yellow citrine; topaz; yellow zircon; yellow jasper; golden-yellow tiger's eye (has a beautiful lustre and rich striped markings); golden amber; golden beryl; yellow rutilated quartz (clouded inside with golden streaks for inner wisdom); or find a matt yellow pebble or piece of limestone, sandstone or shale.

Green

Green is for any matter of the heart, for sympathy, love, romance, friendship and intuition. In divination, green crystals are the stones of your heart and when you choose them it is your heart not your head speaking. So you should listen to your inner promptings and be guided by them, rather than the opinions of others. However, beware those who play on your sentiments.

Buy: brilliant emerald green opaque malachite (sometimes with black stripes or pale green streaks); bloodstone (flecked with red, a form of chalcedony); aventurine; green zircon (good substitute for the more expensive emerald); spinel; yellowy-green peridot (dazzling sister of the more muted serpentine); chrysoprase; jade (in many shades of green); amazonite; moss agate (really colourless but contains a profusion of branching growths of muted green minerals).

Blue

Blue is for matters of principle, altruism, justice, career and worldly wisdom. In divination, blue is the colour of high ideals, so your thoughts may be occupied with a matter of importance to you either at work or concerning official matters. You need to follow conventional steps, whether to make a career move or right a wrong, but you should not compromise or accept excuses from others for low standards of service or commitment.

Buy: hozite (a sky blue opaque stone that is a good substitute for the more expensive turquoise); turquoise; azurite (sometimes flecked with paler blue); lapis lazuli or lazurite (a deep blue flecked with gold); falcon's eye (a blue version of the tiger's eye); labradorite; blue lace agate; celestite; or a moonstone with a bluey sheen.

Purple

Purple is for healing and for psychic development, wisdom of the soul and spirit and for religious insight of any kind. In divination, violet, indigo or purple stones deal with our unconscious wisdom, intuitions and inspirations. There may be something that you really want to do or be that is unconnected with material gain or success in the world's eyes. Listen to your dreams.

Buy: sodalite (in many shades of purple, dark blue and deep indigo, with white being the most common); sugilite (more expensive but a beautiful bright purple); peacock ore (bornite); purple lapis lazuli; amethyst (which can vary from quite dark and mottled to almost colourless); purple fluorite; lilac kunzite.

Preparing Your Crystals for Divination

Wash your crystals under running water for a few minutes or, if you have a large crystal that you use, place your new crystals in water with that for a few hours.

Place your crystals on a glass or pottery dish in the open air or, if you live in an apartment, leave them near an open window or skylight to absorb the sun's first rays for the symbolic Fire element.

Leave the crystals in the open air or by an open window until dusk to absorb the Air element.

At dusk, place them in pure water with flowers for Earth and Water.

Finally leave them in the moonlight, real, or symbolic if it is a dull night, if possible on the first night of the New Moon or during the New Moon period so that your crystals can absorb the intuitive gentle lunar magic.

Casting Your Crystals

Casting crystals works in the same way as casting runes or choosing Tarot cards. The choice is made unconsciously, allowing your intuitive powers to select the most appropriate stone to answer the question you have formulated consciously or unconsciously. Sceptics say that the choice is random, or that all the crystals or cards could be applied to every aspect of your life. The second charge is true in a sense, because all forms of divination are based on real human needs and symbols that have held true for people in many times and places. However, I have helped many people carry out readings and have found that the stones not only mirror unexpressed feelings and needs but suggest solutions.

Sarah wrote from Oklahoma City: 'I have kept a record of stones I have chosen and what is going on in my life during this time and it was uncanny how the stones changed things for me. For years I allowed events to rule my life. Now I use my stones to prepare myself for life's challenges and hurts and it is a great "take charge feeling".'

On 19 April 1995, the day of the Oklahoma bombing, when several of her friends were killed, Sarah did an extended reading with many crystals that mirrored her own inner response to the tragedy and helped her to cope positively. Black stones were matched by the white of new beginnings, telling her that she could one day move forward and celebrate her friends' lives as well as mourning their deaths.

To use your crystals for divination:

* Draw a circle about 60 cm (2 feet) in diameter on a large white scarf and place it on the ground. Or you can draw a circle clockwise with chalk on paving stones or use a stick in firm sand.
* From your bag of stones take three crystals, one at a time, selected without looking. Standing or kneeling about 30 cm (1 foot) away from the circle, cast them in turn. You may think of a question as you cast your stone or let them form a coherent picture of what is around you.
* If a stone falls outside the circle, leave it and choose another one from the bag, again without looking.
* The first crystal represents your best course of action or inaction.
* The second crystal represents something unknown to you that could affect the outcome.
* The third crystal represents what lies over the horizon if you follow the suggested course.

Michael, who was in his early twenties, was uncertain whether to return to the US after working in the UK or go on to India with the money he had saved. His parents were urging him to go home and take up a job in a local firm. He cast an orange carnelian as his first crystal, a green jade as his second and a red jasper as his third.

Michael interpreted his best course of action as asserting his hard-won independence from his parents who had even crossed the world to try to persuade their son to be sensible.

The second crystal (this was not known to Michael) was green jade for the heart. Michael had met a young Chilean woman who was a student in the UK and was also planning on going to India. They had formed a strong friendship and Michael realised that Maria was one of the reasons he wanted to go to India. What lay over the horizon was red jasper for courage and asserting what Michael really wanted. It was likely that if Michael defied his parents there would be bad feeling. As an only child, he had always been desperate to please his folks. What is more, his trip to India and possibly a more permanent relationship with Maria would change him in ways that might make it hard for him to settle back into the bosom of his family in the small mid-west town from which he came. But not to go forward would mean denying an important part of himself as a separate person which he had already proved he was.

Crystal Options

You can also use your crystals to answer simple questions by throwing a single crystal. Either use your white cloth or draw a circle on paper so that you can sit at a table and throw. If the crystal goes outside the circle throw another. This method works if you ask a series of questions without consciously planning them first. Ask, throw, ask, throw again, and go on until you have perhaps answered a question you never knew was troubling you. This sounds like a fortune-telling method but in fact, if you rely on your intuition to guide you and interpret the answers, the results can be quite startling. Do not stop to interpret the answers in terms of your life and future until you have at least five questions and feel that you do not need to ask any more. Return the crystal to the bag after you have thrown it.

> **White**: Yes.
> **Black**: No.
> **Pink**: Be patient.
> **Brown**: Take practical steps.
> **Red**: Act now.
> **Orange**: Strike out alone.
> **Yellow**: Use your head.
> **Green**: Follow your heart.
> **Blue**: Follow convention.
> **Purple**: Use your intuition.

The Options Method

Rosa's first question was: 'How can I fill my time?'

Rosa worked part-time and, since her divorce, she had lived alone with teenage children who were preoccupied with their own lives. Her own life seemed empty, since she had devoted herself to her husband and family and had left all her friends behind when she moved after the family home was sold. In a new area the fresh start had brought loneliness.

Rosa threw a yellow citrine – 'Use your head.'

Her next question was: 'Should I get a more interesting job?'

This time Rosa threw an orange carnelian – 'Act now.'

Her third question was 'How can I get a better job?'

The yellow citrine, 'Use your head,' emerged again.

The fourth question was: 'How can I get out of the rut I am in?'

Her brown tiger's eye fell into the centre of the circle: 'Take practical steps.'

Her fifth question was 'Can I succeed?' and her clear white crystal quartz sparkled in the sunlight and answered: 'Yes.'

Trite? Rosa saw the first answer was telling her to use her brain. After the divorce she had lost all her confidence and taken a routine and boring job just to fill the hours, although she had run her home and her husband's firm for years. Her second crystal urged her to act at once, which was very significant since Rosa had completed an application form for a computer programming course at the local college, but had not sent the form and the deadline was fast approaching.

The third question was answered by another message telling her to use logic. Given that no handsome prince was on the horizon and Rosa hated the idea of a singles club, a college course offered a way out of her loneliness, boredom and the lack of money that prevented her doing many of the things she did enjoy.

The fourth question reflected Rosa's inertia and lack of confidence that left her arguing with herself, going round in circles and doing nothing. Practical steps would involve taking the form to the college and spending her free afternoons on a pre-course training scheme to improve her keyboard skills. The final promise of success and happiness lay in carrying out all the other steps.

The crystals were saying that her future lay in her own hands and only she could help herself. That sounds so self-evident but, for all of us who have been hurt or betrayed, such a step involves almost superhuman effort – or a magical push. Rosa sent her application, was accepted and is well into the course, on which she has made new friends. Her life has not been magically transformed but, as Sarah from Oklahoma said, Rosa has a great 'take charge' feeling, perhaps for the first time in her life.

Crystals for Personal Use

You will need three larger basic crystals that can be uncut and so need not be expensive. They should be about the size of an egg but they can be any shape.

A Healing Crystal

A piece of amethyst, either small shards of amethyst still in the rock or a single large uncut piece, provides a focus for all kinds of healing energies for yourself and your home. However, it's best to use two smaller smooth pointed pieces of rose quartz or crystal quartz for contact healing work with close friends or family (see Crystal Pendulum Healing, p. 259).

A Wish Crystal

An uncut chunk of crystal quartz or rutilated quartz forms your wish crystal (see Chapter 25 on Spirit Guides) which contains an angel or spirit of the crystal and acts as a focus for wisdom from your own subconscious. These are crystals you can ask to fulfil your needs and from which you can request advice.

A Self Crystal

Your self crystal can restore your sense of balance, self-esteem and energy when you hold it. This can be a piece of citrine – either shards in a rock or an uncut piece with many golden lights if you tend to be a person who is constantly giving to others – or a rose quartz if you prefer solitude and harmony.

Finally you need a small talismanic piece of crystal to carry with you always to connect you with the energies of the Earth, Air, Fire and Water elements contained in the crystal and acquired in its formation.

This you can also talk to and hold, when you are in a crisis situation or facing a challenge, as a reminder of your worth, strength and integrity.

These are only suggested stones and you should choose ones that feel right for you for each function. Take time to choose them. You may buy one on a particularly happy outing or, as I often do, receive them as presents in the most unlikely circumstances.

Rest your crystals after a crisis or a period of intense use. Wash them in pure running water, pass a candle flame and incense over them and finally wrap them in soft dark silk for a few days.

11

Herb Divination

This is an ancient form of divination that was practised very widely in many countries because herbs were so easily available to ordinary people in hedgerows and in their gardens. While herbal medicine has been the subject of widespread research, the magical practices have received less attention.

However, researchers such as Lucy, a field botanist from Norwich, are increasingly interested in the folklore not about only health, but also about the divinatory and magical uses of herbs and flowers, as a way of understanding the ancient links between mind, body and spirit that the modern world is only now rediscovering. Lucy writes:

> We are increasingly aware of the wholeness of things. My own research into flowers has echoed your discoveries, although we approach from different angles. Ancient herbalism is increasingly found to have basis in scientific fact. The parallels between ancient and modern use are now being discovered. For example, as you study plants you find that each has its own inbuilt remedy for any side effects. The meadowsweet flower is used in the manufacture of aspirin. Its leaves contain an antidote for stomach irritation, a side effect of aspirin.

Divination with Growing Herbs

Until recent times young women would decide between two or three possible suitors by planting the same number of small pots of fast-growing herbs, one for each. The one that grew tallest would be the chosen swain. The relationship between plants and people is one that has not been fully explored, but plant growth has been shown to be affected by emotion. Plants that are talked to and encouraged flourish more than those that are ignored or spoken to harshly over a regular period. What is more, plants react even in the absence of the person to whom they are emotionally connected.

For example Pierre Savon, a New Jersey researcher, found an intense electronic reaction from his plants at the time he was making love almost 160 km (100 miles) away. Could it be possible then that herbs planted to make a decision are affected by unconscious feelings in the planter, so that the plant that grows faster is reflecting the person's deep unconscious choice?

Certainly this method of deciding between different options has worked for many people over the centuries, as long as the question or issue is something important to the person asking.

To use this technique:

* Decide on several options, whether between people – go/stay/stay but make plans to go, act/wait, speak/be silent.
* If you are in a hurry you can scatter an equal number of mustard and cress seeds on cotton wool or blotting paper in saucers and keep them well-watered. Label each saucer with the name or option and see which grows first.
* However, if the decision is not one that has to be made in a few days, you can buy small pots of herbs. As long as you use the same species for each option, at the same size, thickness and state of development, you can choose a herb that is traditionally associated with the issue, whether it is love, career, family or health:

Sorrel and vetivert are associated with love.
Bay and rosemary are for career decisions and the law.
Feverfew and garden mint can be used for family matters.
Fennel and parsley are for travel and communication.
Basil and dill can answer money questions.
Sage and thyme can decide options involving learning and examinations.
Coriander and mugwort are for health decisions.
St John's wort, chaste-tree and rue are for fertility.

Growing your own herbs means that you can watch not only which herb seeds grow first, but how the different plants progress and which is the longest-lasting. This may be important if you are seeking a permanent commitment and not just excitement in love or a career move that will be better in the long term than one that is initially better paid or more interesting.

You can, if the matter is one that concerns a long-term future, plant the herbs from seeds or tiny cuttings. Place a tiny rose quartz or crystal in each pot and, as you do so, visualise in turn the designated person or option coming to fulfilment.

Herbs should be planted during the waxing phase of the moon, especially three or four days before the full moon. This has been found by gardeners throughout the world to promote healthier and more rapid growth than those planted during the wane.

Keep a chart of growth, week by week: the first to grow; how the first to sprout initially may be overtaken by another; or the tallest may suddenly wither.

Alexandra wanted to know whether she should move with her husband Tom to the sea, as he had always dreamed of doing when he retired, or stay in their city centre flat where they had many interests and continue her freelance art work for several companies where she covered for sickness and holidays. Tom was ten years older than Alexandra and she did not feel ready to retire. The decision did not have to be taken for several months and so she planted rosemary seeds, one pot for retiring to the sea, one for continuing with their present lifestyle, and a third for an alternative (that suddenly occurred to her when she was planting the first two) that they should buy a mobile home with Tom's insurance policies which were due to mature. They could then commute between the town and the sea as work demanded.

The herbs representing retiring to the sea came through first but then failed to thrive. The second option, that they should remain in the town, grew slowly. However, the third pot, to commute, after a slow start grew steadily and became thick and strong. Surprisingly, Tom was also in favour of the third option, as he had doubts about leaving his old life behind completely. So they decided to buy the mobile home before Tom's retirement and gradually spend more time there.

Divination with Chopped Herbs

Fresh finely chopped or dried herbs can also be used as a medium for creating symbols or whole pictures to answer questions. Scattering herbs is another traditional method of divination and has the advantage of creating a three-dimensional moving picture that can be easily rearranged by shaking, much like a kaleidoscope image. It is like taking a dream image, and being able to hold it and study possible interpretations.

The four true divinatory herbs are parsley, sage, rosemary and thyme. You can mix these divinatory herbs to create a herb picture. However, any fresh or dried herbs of the kind sold in jars can be used, as long as the individual leaves are solid and separate, rather than powdery. Dried rosemary, parsley and chives are especially effective for herb pictures since each grain is distinct.

To use this technique:

* Find some firm white or cream paper with a rough surface, about 30 cm (1 foot) square.
* Think of a question, an issue or a person who is occupying your thoughts, or let your mind roam freely so that your unconscious automatically focuses on the area of concern, which may be very different from that expressed in a conscious question.
* Shake a handful of herbs on to the paper and, holding the paper at either end, gently tip and shake it until it forms an image or a whole scene. If an interpretation does not spring to mind, close your eyes for a few seconds and then open them and look at the herbs through half-closed eyes.
* When you have identified your first image, gather the herbs together in the centre of the paper and toss the paper or swirl the herbs around to see what new patterns emerge. Note the image at each stage but do not try to interpret it in depth, although you may wish to sketch each picture in your psychic notebook.
* Repeat until you have five images or scenes.
* Finally, study each of the images in turn. If the areas suggested below do not seem to fit, read the images one after the other and weave them into a scenario.

Image 1 will tell you the real issue or question, which may be different from the one you consciously considered.

Image 2 will tell you the obstacles you need to overcome to achieve success or happiness. These may be internal fears or external opposition. Again, this may be unexpected.

Image 3 tells you of helpful influences, whether your own talents or resources or other people.

Image 4 indicates the best way forward.

Image 5 is the likely outcome or change.

How to Interpret the Images

The correct interpretation is the one that comes into your head without prompting. You can look at the list of 200 divinatory symbols in Chapter 7 but you should rely primarily on your own inbuilt symbol system, developed through your childhood and linked through your unconscious mind to the universal archetypal meanings that have held true for people in all times and places.

Antonia used parsley and sage mixed and her first picture was a dragon breathing fire, which she saw as her husband who was in a perpetual rage about life and whose frequent tantrums were making her feel constantly exhausted and depressed, as she sought to placate him and shield him from any crises which arose. That was her overriding concern, although she had actually asked a question about her health, which was linked to her stressful situation.

The second image was a picture of children's faces hiding in the shrubbery. This represented the opposition to her happiness. I suggested these were her own children whom she was trying to shield from the situation, but she disagreed. Antonia said that, from childhood, she had always hidden from confrontation and so she was going along with her husband's unreasonable attitudes.

The third image was a boat, indicating helpful influences. This was not a long sea cruise from her troubles but, to Antonia, represented the ferry from Southampton to the Isle of Wight where her godmother lived. Her godmother had asked her to bring the children to stay many times. And, as often happened, inner and outer worlds merged for she had received an invitation that morning to use her godmother's house for a month while her godmother went to see her daughter in South Africa.

The fourth image was a pair of scissors. Antonia wondered what course of action this indicated and answered her own question – cutting free from her difficult domestic situation if only for a month.

The final image promised no magical answer but was a pillow – a chance to rest at her godmother's while she made a decision about her relationship and also to give her husband time to reflect on his future if he did not control his temper.

An Alternative Method

If you find the herb images too unstable you can try lightly brushing the paper in a large rectangle or circle with a paper glue before scattering and shaking the herbs to get a more permanent image. This limits you to a single picture. You can, however, add herbs to different areas of the paper or make five separate images and read them in the order you made them. Keep them in your psychic notebook.

If your herb picture does not make sense immediately, go and sit at the other side of the table and change your perspective. Once you have identified one element, the rest usually follows.

Herbal Infusion Magic

Herbal teas and infusions have a two-fold purpose. First, they have magical and health-giving properties, according to the old principle that you absorb magical energies when you eat or drink a magical substance. However, although you can quite safely drink any of your herbal infusions, the main purpose is to use the leaves in hot water in a technique halfway between ink scrying (see p. 59) and tea leaf reading. However, you should not wait until the water is deeply coloured, but make the reading while you can still see the herbs clearly at the bottom of the cup. Culinary herbs are quite safe to drink, although if you are pregnant you should check with a herbalist or pharmacist if you do not regularly use the herb. For example, rue, sage, tansy and pennyroyal are best avoided in pregnancy.

Scrying with Herbal Infusions

* Use a mug or a large plain light-coloured cup and either 1 level teaspoonful of coarse dried herbs or 2 level teapoons of freshly chopped leaves or flowers crushed between your fingers. Powders colour the water instantly so they are no use.
* Fresh finely chopped herbs in most varieties do not make the water murky.
* When using dried herbs, use bright or pale green herbs. Parsley and chives are especially good for herbal infusion scrying, as is peppermint. You can add more than one kind of herb. Dried parsley, chervil, cloves and tarragon mixed make a good combination to read and the infusion tastes quite pleasant.
* Pour on boiling water.
* At first the herbs will be swirling on top of the water. Read your first image as the herbs float. As with most scrying, this first image will identify where you are and the main issues.
* Most of the herbs will gradually sink to the bottom, forming a single image. Read this second image which will tell you the future if you continue on your present path.
* Note how many herbs remain floating on top. This does not depend on the type of herbs and varies from reading to reading. The number will tell you how long you will have to wait for the results of any change you make. You can regard single leaves as weeks and clumps on top as months.
* Swirl the cup around between your hands. You will find that the herbs at the bottom are separating out and that the third image now appears in the white lines between them. This will suggest an alternative approach or change you can make that will bring happiness or success.
* Note each image as it occurs and either interpret it as it emerges or sketch the image and analyse it later.
* Finally, drain off the leaves and read a likely outcome in the separate images left around the edges of the dry cup.

Helen loved gardening and wanted to join the local horticultural society. However, many of the members were very set in their ways and tended to discourage newcomers, especially those who had not lived in the area for long. She made an infusion with parsley and saw first on the surface of the cup a high circular wall.

She interpreted this as her inability to find a sponsor to nominate her as a member.

When the herbs sank to the bottom she saw an empty garden with wilting flowers. She admitted that she had been very discouraged and had not been bothering with her own garden so much. There were five separate leaves which suggested that any change would come in about five weeks. Helen then swirled the cup around and, as the mass of herbs separated in the white areas at the bottom of the cup, she saw clear images of a computer, a net and tall flowers. It made no sense to me but Helen connected it with accessing the Internet on her computer and decided to try to contact other keen gardeners in her area.

The fourth image was a group of spades which Helen saw as fellow gardeners. In fact she did not make any local contacts but via a new contact about 80 km (50 miles) away discovered a county organisation that ran meetings for keen gardeners at a local college which had a good horticultural department. Helen went along and within a few weeks met a whole range of people who shared her interests. She then decided to take a course at the college.

Whether you want to increase your spiritual awareness or need to solve a problem that is affecting your sense of well-being, herb divination is equally effective. Once the earthly matters are settled, we have the peace of mind and energy to explore our inner world.

Section Four

Harnessing Natural Energies

12

Earth Energies

Earth energies are the natural powers of the earth that we can feel beneath our feet on open land or in the smallest garden and through the fingertips when we hold a crystal or stone or touch a tree or flower. They can manifest as earth lights that hover over plains or rocks and seem to respond to the thoughts of people or as strange animals such as the legendary demon Black Dogs of East Anglia. These energies can be used to give psychic visions at natural sites of great antiquity and, by using a stone or crystal on a chain, to provide information from deep within our unconscious to guide our actions.

Leroy Bull, from Doylestown, Pennsylvania, quotes from *The American Dowser*, vol. 35, no. 3 (Summer 1995):

Energy ley lines are natural flows of cosmic energy that are of the electrical sign plus (+). By definition they come down to the earth at places we call power centres which have domes. Domes are places where water rises vertically through the earth's strata. All of the water flows away from the centre of a dome formation. Where a water dome and energy ley line come together we have a power centre. Water is of the electrical sign minus (–). Therefore, at a power centre we have the presence of (+)-(–) or yin-yang or male-female. We might liken these places to acupuncture points of the earth.

Before the Renaissance, these sites were sought after and used as places for ceremonial sites. Stone circles, pyramids, churches and public meeting places were built on these sacred sites. The presence of balanced energy at these locations left the participants with feelings of comfort, energy and well-being. Everything in the universe has its own energy and vibrates to its own frequency. This biosphere that we live in is a primordial soup of frequencies. We are born into and feel it at all times. It is the stuff of universal consciousness. Dowsers are people who are consciously connected to this universal flow of energy. They feel it, code it and identify things by their brokerage of this energy.

The Magic of Stones

Whatever the source of earth energies, few would deny that, at sites of great antiquity, standing stones and stone circles, there are forces that can be felt by almost anyone who touches a stone. On a misty morning or evening, our feet will follow an instinctive path along lines of psychic energy, often called leys, that cross or merge at these places.

To discover the magic of stone and earth energies, go to one of the ancient stone circles that may date from 3500 BC, such as Newgrange in County Meath in Ireland, perhaps the most spectacular prehistoric cemetery in the world and close to the sacred hill of Tara, seat of the ancient Irish high kings. Other centres of natural power include the stone ships circle in Vastmanland in Sweden, the stone circle at Almendras in Portugal which may have been created as a temple to the stars, Stonehenge on Salisbury Plain, or the stone Medicine Wheels of North America such as the Big Horn Medicine Wheel near Sheridan in Wyoming.

My own favourite stone circles are at Avebury in Wiltshire, both because they lie on converging powerful lines of psychic energy and because, unlike many ancient monuments in the UK, they are still accessible to the public.

Avebury Stones

The Avebury stone circles, which lie about 130 km (80 miles) west of London, have been described as a British metropolis of 4,600 years ago. They are part of a huge prehistoric complex which includes Silbury Hill (Europe's tallest prehistoric monument, sacred to the Earth Goddess, and one of the world's largest man-made mounds) and the West Kennet Long Barrow.

The great outer stone circle was created about 2600 BC and originally comprised 100 huge stones, though many have been taken away or destroyed. Avebury was used continuously for worship for more than 2,300 years before falling into disuse under the Saxons.

Like many of the ancient stone circles, Avebury may have been a giant astronomical calculator and the top of some of the dipped stones were perhaps used as sights for star-gazing. But the truth is that we know little of the lives of the first peoples who built the stones except that they worshipped the Earth Mother who was seen in these early times as permanently pregnant. For this reason, the stones have always been associated with fertility.

Indeed there are clearly differentiated pointed male and diamond-shaped female stones, some with natural wishing or love seats. The solstices and equinoxes would have been celebrated with great fire festivals and circle dances to rouse the earth energies. Sacrifices of animals or even people may have been made to ensure that the earth remained fertile. By Celtic times, May Eve and Halloween marked the beginning of summer and winter and so were celebrated with great fertility festivals to encourage the land and tribes to be fruitful.

Until the early twentieth century, on the Celtic summer festival of Beltane or May Eve, village girls would sit on the Devil's chair at midnight, on one of the huge stones, and wish for love and happiness. As with so many love rituals, the lover would appear in vision or actuality and the fertility powers of the stones would be reinforced.

The energies inherent in the stones have manifested in many ways. Small luminous figures have been reported dancing around the circles, especially on the old festivals; strange lights have floated above Avebury and the area has been a centre of crop circle activity for several decades.

Linking into the Energies

Whether you visit Avebury or another of the many great monuments, you can tune into the spiralling energies immediately surrounding the stone circle. Although there will be stones missing, if you allow your feet to guide you or use a pendulum (made from crystal or a stone strung on a cord) you will find that your course is similar to a maypole dance. Ley energies (psychic grid energies) tend to run in straight lines along the former avenues of stones and these can be powerful too. Use a map to trace the lines between ancient monuments. A place such as Carnac in Brittany has many avenues still standing and the pull of the earth is immensely strong.

To do this:

* Study a plan or picture of the circle as it was originally, when it was first used for worship and ceremony.
* As you walk, feel the power of the earth entering your feet and rising through your body in an upward-spiralling path, before centring around the base of your spine. You may see visions either externally or in your mind's eye, especially close to dusk, of those who danced here before you. You may also glimpse the guardians of the place as shadowy forms.
* Note any special dreams you have on the night after you have visited the site. If possible, try to stay in the area – not in a modern hotel but a more homely one. If you can visit the stones at sunrise you will gain more psychic impressions than from a whole library of psychic books.

If you have a stone circle within easy travelling distance, try to walk the circle at sunset on the Eve of the Summer Solstice or Longest Day and at noon. If you can be in sight of stones at sunrise, it can be a magical experience on the eve of the Shortest Day. Other circles apart from Stonehenge are aligned to the Solstice sunrise (for example, the Big Horn Medicine Wheel) or to other equinox points or even the May Morning sunrise, as is Avebury. Check the alignments of your nearest site in a guide book. It is thought that, throughout the world, groups of stone circles and monuments may be aligned in a single giant astronomical clock. Certainly it is believed that if you touch stones at Avebury then your vibration will be felt in other linked circles around the world.

However, you can go to any stone circle or hilltop barrow to feel the union of sky and earth energies on the Longest Day. There are many ancient monuments around the world that are not fenced in any way and are rarely visited by tourists. Alternatively, go into the garden at dawn on the Summer Solstice and place a marker stone at the spot where you see the sun rising. In the southern hemisphere this will be in mid-December rather than June. Light a golden candle, and you will join with the millions of people all over the world who have tried, by sympathetic magic, to make the sun keep its power. At such moments you are part of Jung's two-million-year-old man and your own psychic awareness is amplified by connections with the stones.

Charging Personal Crystals

* Carry two or three large crystals in each hand, or smaller ones in a drawstring bag, clockwise around the first stone, beginning at compass North, or an approximation of the northerly direction from a map. Go anti-clockwise round the second and continue right around the circle, remembering to circle the approximate location of any missing stones, as their energies will still be implanted in the soil.
* Sense the powerful misty-grey stone energies reinforcing your own inner psychic powers. Unlike crystals, stones do not emit golden or white light but a silvery grey colour, almost like mercury.
* Complete the circle and leave from the same place to complete the spiral.

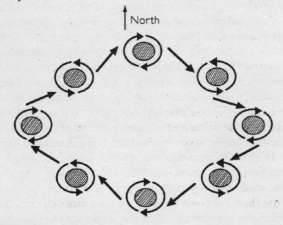

Walking the stone circle

* Leave an unobtrusive offering close to the northernmost stone, either a single flower or a tiny crystal in one of the hollows, so that it may be found and taken home by another visitor.
* Near the entrance to the site, or in an adjoining field, bury one of your newly charged crystals in the soft soil in order to help renew the land. Whenever you give or leave a crystal, a replacement will inevitably appear in your life.
* Once you have buried your crystal, take a pointed stone about 15 cm (6 inches) long, not from the actual monument but from just within the boundary of the sacred site or an adjoining field, which will be imbued with the same energies. You can use this as your dowsing stone.
* If you can renew your crystals in this way every few months, you will find that they retain this special connection with the earth and will be especially potent, whether for healing or giving you energy. You can also charge a larger crystal that you use for scrying by carrying it around the stones in a spiral and placing it on every third stone for a few moments to imbue it with extra power.

Special Stones

When Mary, the healer we met in Chapter One, was in Ireland she was sitting on the beach and saw a stone wedged between two rocks not far out in the sea with the waves washing over it. Mary knew that it was a very magical stone and wanted it for her healing work. At low tide she went out to the rock but the stone was firmly embedded and would not move. Mary said to the stone: 'I really want to take you back to England for my healing work. If you will come with me, I promise that one day I will build a healing sanctuary here and bring you home.'

She touched the stone and it came away at once. It is now one of her most powerful stones. Years later, Mary is negotiating to buy a cottage in the area for a healing sanctuary.

You can find special stones, as Mary did, not only near old stone circles but washed up by the tide on river banks or on a hillside. You can use these for dowsing, perhaps even more effectively than a crystal pendulum or metal or wooden rods, because opaque stones are repositories of earth energy that are not depleted by reflection.

Let the stone choose you, whether from an ancient stone circle or from further afield. It should be about 15 cm (6 inches) long and quite narrow. Walk along the field or shore in ever-increasing circles until you feel compelled to stop and you will find it.

Personal Dowsing with Stones

Dowsing is the skill of searching for minerals, oil or water beneath the earth, using, it is believed, a mixture of geomagnetic and psychic forces. However, the fact that some people can locate minerals or water from a map would suggest that psychic ability is predominant. People have also successfully dowsed for lost people, pets and objects, ghosts and ley lines.

The word comes either from the Middle English *duschen* ('to strike') which is an early Germanic reference to rods striking the ground, or from the old Cornish *dewsys* ('goddess') and *rhodl* ('tree branch'). You can use the energies of the earth as a psychic amplifier for your own personal psychic powers through dowsing. Dowsing for decisions is very potent using a stone strung on cord or chain.

Making a Stone Pendulum

Some stones already have a hole and these are a traditional focus for seeing past, present and future. Alternatively, you can drill or chisel a hole in your special stone. Make your chain or cord about 22 cm (9 inches) long so that you can hold it comfortably between the thumb and first finger of your writing hand.

To charge the stone, circle it with amethyst, rose quartz and clear quartz crystal, perhaps those you charged at the stone circle, and place it in running water until the water is full of bubbles. You can use a clear glass or Pyrex bowl held under a running tap. Add salt to the water and leave it in the sunlight from dawn to dusk on a clear day to absorb fire and air power.

Making Dowsing Circles

Draw circles with white chalk or wax crayon on grey paper or draw your circle outdoors in the earth with a large pointed stone.

Alternatively, you can dowse in three circles marked out with tiny stones (see diagram) that you can keep permanently either in a corner of your garden on smooth earth or on a small slab of stone supported by bricks in a conservatory or greenhouse. The largest circle should be about 30 cm (1 foot) in diameter, with two smaller circles inside it.

The first circle is the circle of the self and involves the essential you. If your pendulum pulls you here, then the answer lies within yourself, in your own actions or in striking out alone.

The middle circle is the circle of interaction. If your pendulum pulls you here, you need to compromise, to seek the help of others or to commit yourself to a shared objective for the time being.

The outer circle is the circle of fate. Here lie the constraints temporarily imposed on you by life or other people. For now, you need to go with the flow and not waste energy fighting the inevitable.

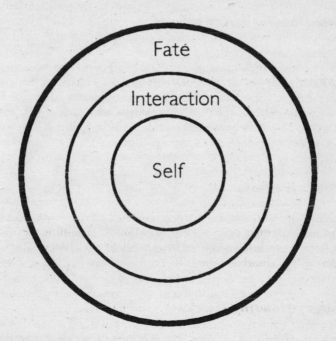

The dowsing circles

To use your dowsing circles:

* Think of a specific issue or question and hold your stone between your hands for a few minutes, endowing it with your hopes, fears, feelings and conflicts on the issue.
* Hold your stone on its cords and let it turn gently over each circle, beginning in the centre and moving outwards.
* When you have passed your stone over each area of the three circles, return outwards from the centre. As you do so, you will feel a strong pull downwards towards one of the circles.
* Hold your stone to your eye with the poorest earthly vision, using the knot on the cord as a sight marker. Half-closing your eye, look through the hole and let an image or picture form itself on the other side. This will clarify your stone message and, more importantly, give you insight into possible future outcomes if you follow the suggested strategy.

Stone Dowsing Using a Grid

If you seek more specific answers, or want to choose between a number of options, you can draw a grid of squares in rows of three or a series of circles close to one another, in which you can put different options and allow your stone pendulum to guide you to the right choice. Pass the pendulum slowly over each option and you will feel a pull downwards towards the best option, which will not usually be the one you consciously expected.

Asking Questions

Alternatively, you can ask your pendulum a series of separate questions and the stone will answer yes or no. Start with a question and, after each answer, ask another without conscious thought. Again, you may be surprised, as the questions you ask and the answers you receive may not be the ones you were thinking of. To find the 'yes' response, think of a happy scene and your pendulum will respond to your positivity.

For your 'no' response, briefly relive in your mind a rejection or unhappy moment and your pendulum will make a negative response. Tests rarely work with pendulums unless emotion is involved. Each person has a unique response. Although a yes is often indicated by a clockwise circling or ellipse I have met people whose positive affirmation is an anti-clockwise motion. If your pendulum does not respond, rephrase the question. You can record your questions and answers or arrange them as a flow chart.

If you prefer, you can use a conventional crystal pendulum to conduct earth energies. Clear quartz is probably the best, followed by rose quartz or amethyst.

Recharging Your Stone

To recharge your stone, when it seems to be losing its power, bury it with a rose quartz, an amethyst and a clear crystal quartz in a clear glass jar in the garden for a full lunar month, beginning on the first day of the dark of the moon (the period between the old and new moon when it is no longer visible). For this month, use other methods of divination or a different stone as a pendulum. When the month is over, wash your glass jar in pure water and leave it in the sunlight until the day when the crescent moon is in the sky.

Justine from Reading described her work with a stone pendulum:

> I have been dowsing for about three years and was introduced to it by a hypnotist who gave me a small stone on a chain which I always use. I try to blank my mind so I do not consciously influence the pendulum and its answer. I also test it with dummy questions, which it seems to know I am doing, which I find encouraging. Just recently I have found that, in accordance with your methods, there is real power in the pendulum. If I write down very precise statements in their own circles and put about nine questions to a page, I can feel the pendulum physically pulling towards the circle it wants and away from other circles like a magnetic force. The difficulty is trusting the answers.

Focusing Your Energies

In an earlier book, I suggested creating a stone cairn or pile in your garden, adding a stone for each step of a new venture taken as an affirmation of intention. Christine wrote to me to say how helpful she found this:

> The pile of stones which I started in a patch of the garden where honeysuckle grows up the fence, a favourite spot of mine, was wet and shiny this morning after overnight rain. Around the stone pile is a clump of columbine and pansies to keep the growing pile company. I have always loved stones and drop one into an old large square bottle if I like the colour, shape or texture. It stands in the bathroom window.
>
> I have taken to going out to my stone pile when I am miserable and taking my crystals with me. Sometimes I tip them in my lap and hold them, look at them and feel that special energy seeping into me. Then I walk round the garden which is only a small one, tiptoe past Jenny Wren's nesting box, see the baby birds peeping out, then catch the delicate fragrance of petunias in the wooden tub by the back door. As I go back, I think perhaps things are not so bad after all. I have looked at my growing stone pile and it reminds me that it must be different from now on. As my stone pile grows and changes shape, so must I adapt to my changing world.

Culloden Ghosts

At places of great human sorrow, the earth can be stained with blood so deeply that the imprints or actual spirits of those who died remain and are activated, especially on the anniversaries of great battles. The ghosts seem to use the energies of the earth to appear. Perhaps the most striking example is that of Culloden Field in Scotland where thousands of hauntings have been reported over the years. Few can walk across the moor without tuning into the emotions stamped into the land – pain, fear, anxiety, hope, triumph and despair. I am indebted to Mark and Hannah Fraser, who publish the journal *Haunted Scotland*, for the following material.

On 23 July 1745 Prince Charles Edward Stuart landed on the island of Eriskay. On 19 August he landed at Glenfinnan, Loch Shiel, where the standard was raised. By 17 September, Edinburgh had been captured and, with an army of about 5,000 Jacobites,

Charlie now marched into England. After many victories the Jacobites found themselves less than 190 km (120 miles) from London. In the capital were many supporters, including the Prime Minister who was preparing to hand over the crown.

Then they turned back to Scotland. A lot of blame is heaped upon Charles Stuart. But if they had marched upon London, as he wished, there is no doubt that events would have turned out differently. After several more battles, the Hanoverians and the Jacobites met at Culloden on Drummossie Moor on 16 April 1746. The battle was short. The Jacobites were slaughtered but not disgraced, and a purge of Highlanders ensued. Women, children, the old and infirm were murdered, raped, tortured or shipped to America. Scotland was lost forever but then it had never really been united. It is commonly assumed that the Hanoverian army was entirely made up of Englishmen, but many Highland and Lowland regiments took part in the massacres and hated the Jacobites even more than their English comrades. This, to all intents and purposes, was a civil war.

It is said that descendants of those who fought at Culloden are sometimes treated to a grisly re-enactment of the battle if they visit the site on its anniversary. Many have said they can feel the energy and the sadness of the clansmen who are now said to visit or haunt the ground of their last heroic stand.

Mark Fraser received the following story from a couple who live not far from Inverness. As John and Mary walked over the ground where the battle took place they both heard a lone piper playing a sad lament. Look as they might they could not discover the source of the music. The pipes faded away, to make way for the sound of many marching feet and a monotonous drum beat. Then the sound of desperate fighting filled the air. There were screams and shouts, the clash of swords and the resounding crack of musket fire all around them. Already shocked, John and Mary now saw a terrible scene unfolding before them. Highland men ran, screaming, towards the ranks of redcoats. They dropped like flies, as the English muskets fired. Mary and John stood in shocked silence as several clansmen died while carrying away an English standard. As they fell, a horse trampled their bodies, a hoof splitting open the head of a young clansman who looked no more than fifteen years of age. The blood seemed to pour away far across the moor, as large as a river, as it joined the blood of other Highlanders.

At that instant a tall man in Highland battledress bellowed out the name 'Jamie', which drowned the sounds of the battle and hung in the air long afterwards. The scene stopped suddenly 'as though someone had pressed the freeze frame on a video recorder' and there in front of the now motionless battle was the Highlander who turned to look at John and Mary with his grief-stricken face. The man stood well over 180 cm (6 feet) tall. In his hands he held a great two-handed sword. His left shoulder seeped blood from a large wound. On his head he wore a bonnet with a feather. Broad black belts crossed over his shoulders; tartan trews stopped at the knees; the rest of his legs were covered with some kind of socks. His leather sandals were fastened by thongs which were wrapped around the lower parts of his legs several times. A long plaid was draped over his shoulder. He had red hair and a beard and above his left eye ran a cruel battle-scar reaching down to under his chin. His forearms were also covered in many scars.

Then the tall Jacobite turned to face away from the couple. As he did so, the scene behind him changed to that of many dead clansmen lying on the ground. The tartans of their clothes swirled in the wind, only to fall again in pools of dark red blood. Now the tall Jacobite searched the faces of the dead, gently turning them over as he did so. Who was he looking for? John and Mary will never know, for the scene completely vanished and they were left looking at the bleak landscape.

They knew that John had at least one ancestor – Euan – who had fought and died in the battle.

13

Auras

It is believed that people, animals and plants radiate a form of electromagnetic energy. This is the aura, which acts as a transmitting and receiving station for emotions and thoughts and can reveal information about the physical, mental and spiritual well-being of the individual. Kirlian photography, named after the Russian professor Semyon Kirlian who discovered the technique in 1939, is a method of high-frequency electronic photography that reveals beautifully patterned sparks and flares of energy emanating around the outline of living creatures. Plant auras fade when the plant is cut or deprived of water. And if a dead leaf is removed you can still see the ghost image of the missing part.

In experiments carried out at the Neuropsychiatric Institute at UCLA in California, Kirlian techniques were used to record energy flares emanating from the fingertips of healers.

Gilbert Attard, a French psychic researcher with a special interest in physics and magnetic energies, has an intriguing theory concerning auras:

Each of us can emit an 'aura' which is one of the fundamentals of the visible spectrum. Several people together will emit the sum of the frequency which is a white light, the sum of the three fundamental colours, blue, red and yellow. The point of impact of the white light will be the convergence point of all the human eyes. What is interesting in this natural physical phenomenon is that it can explain some of the phenomena called supernatural, for example the apparitions of the Virgin Mary or the white that is often mentioned. In effect, several individuals focus their attention on a particular point in space to create a virtual image. If my theory is correct, it raises a question: what provokes this phenomenon? Is it the combination of different energies coming from the ground (magnetic fields, static charges, etc)?

Are certain places, such as Lourdes and San Damiano, more propitious than others?

There may be a new possibility, which perfectly combines the two preceding ideas. Is there an intelligence outside our own which knows this physical principle and can use it to communicate with us by using mental power to project holographic images? In such a case, are we dealing with extra-terrestrial beings?

Gilbert's theory recognises the complex interaction between the physical and psychic aspects of the aura and is one that deserves to be thoroughly investigated, in order to fit disparate elements of the universe into a coherent whole.

The Spirit Body

Certainly the aura has several levels that are not clearly defined or agreed upon. There are many conflicting theories. Many people believe in the existence of a spirit body within us, upon which the physical body is imposed. When we die or travel astrally this spirit body, linked to the physical body by a silver cord, separates, and when the silver cord is severed, then we are said to die. Some see the etheric or spirit body as a silvery essence and others see it as a direct double, a doppelganger. This may be the form people see as living ghosts.

Rosemary told me what happened when her daughter nearly died from whooping cough when she was ten months old.

As Jane lay dying in the oxygen tent, in hospital, the Sister told me that all I could do was will her to live. I can see every detail of her years later, her Viyella dress covered in white smocking. There was a drip in her head. Then I saw a silvery white line going from her out of the tent. It was like a piece of wool, not a bright line and not silver, not white but between silver and white. I'd heard about the silver cord we all have but this was nothing like I imagined. From then on a fantastic peace came over me and from that moment too she started to get better.

Children routinely see pink and blue auras around people, especially their grandmothers, a sign of the love that pervades all levels. Auras can extend from a few inches to a vast distance. The spiritual aura of the Lord Gautama Buddha was said to extend 320 km (200 miles).

While the physical body lives on food, air and water, the etheric body is said to absorb *prana* or cosmic energy from the sun, as well as earth energies from the ground and from crystals, standing stones, flowers and trees. Indeed it is often said that, if you feel drained of energy, you should go out into the sunlight and hug a tree.

Predominant Colours

Many people see auras without acknowledging the fact on a conscious level. This is reflected in popular sayings such as 'she is feeling blue' or 'he is in a black mood'. When you first begin to read auras you will see one or perhaps two dominant colours. It is only as you develop that you will be able to distinguish between the different layers. However, this first overall auric colour is central to formal aura readings and also to understanding the current concern or mood of the person on a level deeper than that of non-verbal signals. It will always form the first stage in any aura reading or assessment and in the everyday world it is the level that will be most helpful to you in 'people reading'.

Red

Red is a very creative, life-enhancing auric colour and can vary from brilliant scarlet to deep ruby. An overall red suggests energy, activity and courage. When the impression is of a harsh or murky red tone, there can be great anger, perhaps suppressed, that needs to be resolved or harnessed.

Orange

Orange can appear as the predominant auric colour when a person is independent, confident and optimistic. A very pale orange aura can reflect uncertainty and low self-esteem.

Yellow

Yellow is the auric colour of communication. When the aura is golden yellow, the person is open, articulate and very creative while possessing a keen intellect and love of learning. However, when the yellow is dull, there may be many secrets and sometimes less than honest intentions.

Green

Green is the auric colour of the heart and the emotions and is especially dominant when relationships are the main issue. In matters of love, a clear green aura is a good sign of fidelity and in friendship it indicates trustworthiness. Pale green can suggest emotional dependency. A dull, muddy green can conceal conflicting emotions or an emotional leech. Yellowy-green can be a sign of possessiveness and unwarranted jealousy.

Blue

Blue is an aura concerned with principles, justice and ideals. Bright blue is altruistic and the person will put their principles before personal gain. It is also, like purple, the colour of healing. Navy blue has an unworldly quality and a dull blue can suggest that concern for convention is leading to rigidity.

Purple

Purple is the auric colour that deals with the spiritual and psychic side of human nature and is predominant in an intuitive person. Deep purple is the colour of spiritual awareness and becomes more prominent as psychic awareness evolves ritual areas. When the auric purple is muddy or blurred it implies that its owner is spending too long on day-dreams and illusions.

Pink

Pink in an aura is a sign of a natural peacemaker. If the pink is bright and clear, then you know that, whether you are in a work, social or emotional situation, the other person will be receptive to your suggestions, fears and feelings. A pale but clear pink reveals inner harmony but, if the pink is misty, you may be dealing with someone who sees other people's point of view so much that he or she is unlikely to reach any decisions without firm direction.

White

White is the synthesis of all the other colours and is most often seen emanating from the crown of the head. Unlike the pale colours of an aura that is drained of energy, this white is vibrant and glowing. It is the colour of spirituality, of the innovator and creator, and, though not often seen, draws pure light from the cosmos and in return sends forth inner lights in all other colours, so that the whole aura will sparkle.

You may see one or two predominant colours, from which you can learn a great deal about a person's present state. Often this initial auric image is seen most clearly around the head. For some people this level of auric awareness is adequate for everyday interactions and divinatory readings. However, it is also possible to differentiate between the different three levels of the aura and see an auric glow around the whole body. This can give information about bodily health, emotions, mind and spirit.

The Three Basic Levels of the Aura

The Aura of the Etheric Body

The etheric aura, from the spirit or astral body, is usually seen a few inches from the physical body and follows its outline. The inermost aura reflects the state of health or dis-ease of the physical body. The colours of this aura are like a merging rainbow and parallel on both sides of your body (see aura diagram, p. 129), beginning in normal healthy circumstances as red beneath your feet and merging as they rise up the body through yellow and orange.

If you get areas of blue these are natural healing energies at work on any areas that may need it. These energies can come from the earth, the cosmos and from absent or contact healing work and may be seen as darts of energy coming inwards. If these auric colours are clear, all is well, but if they are generally dark, your natural physical energies may be blocked or your physical well-being clouded by stress. If this aura disappears over large areas then the general energy level of the physical body is depleted, whereas if the aura bulges or has black patches or breaks in a particular place, there are blockages of energy in the area concerned or in nearby organs. You can try one of the healing rituals described in Chapters 27 and 28 to heal any breaches in your own aura and the auras of others.

The etheric body is the seat of the chakras (see p. 20), which enable the universal life force and the earth energies to enter and heal the physical body.

The Aura of the Emotions

This aura forms an oval beyond the etheric aura, rather than following the outline of the body, and is generally perceived as green. The emotional aura surrounds the whole body and head in an unbroken ellipse. We are creatures of feeling and it is increasingly recognised by medical science that our emotions not only help to trigger bodily illness but can also help to activate our immune system to fight disease. A clear green aura indicates that a person is in tune with his or her own feelings and is receptive to the emotions of others. A dull green suggests that the person may be overwhelmed by the emotional demands of others. Yellow-green may imply that jealousy or resentment are clouding the natural emotional flow and there may again be dark patches around the heart or in other areas. These often indicate the bodily area where a person is feeling physical pain or knots of tension in muscles where emotional pain has penetrated the etheric layer. Breaks here or dark patches can also indicate hurt and unresolved guilt.

When a person is in love, this is the level at which the auras of the loved ones merge around the heart. Equally, if two people feel strong dislike, their auric fields may clash and damage the emotional body. An intuitive, sensitive person will have a very fluid layer between the emotional body and the outer auric level and this should protect them from negative influences, especially in psychic work.

The Aura of the Mind and Spirit

This is usually regarded as the outer layer of the aura. Like the emotional aura, it forms an oval rather than following the outline of the body. In some people this aura is rigidly bound; in others it instantly melts and gives access to the emotions and to influences from other people's minds and the cosmos. When this layer is fluid a person may be very telepathic and clairvoyant.

This is the area of the mind and is coloured blue, merging into purple as it rises higher in the body. In very spiritual people white, silver or gold can be detected above the head, as in medieval paintings of saints. In contrast, a murky grey, brown or black above the head suggests that logic is clouded by depression and a feeling of being overwhelmed by life's cares.

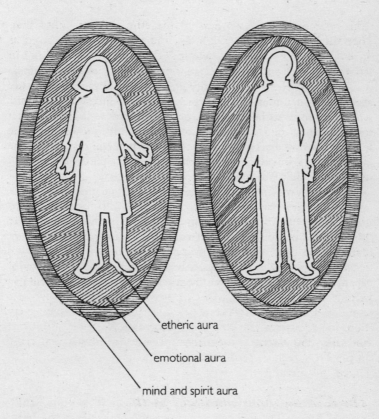

etheric aura

emotional aura

mind and spirit aura

The auras

Clear auric colours indicate that thought processes are in harmony with the rest of the body and the outside world. As with the other layers, there may be areas of darkness or breaks where flecks of colour from the other layers have penetrated. For example, it may be dull red if thoughts are being clouded by physical discomfort or anger. If green clouds this outer aura, emotions may be colouring thought processes unduly.

Healers' outer auras are often pure purple or brilliant blue, merging with white or golden rays from the cosmos, as are those of evolved psychics who are concerned with using their gifts to help others.

How to Read Auras

Reading auras is an important step in psychic development, since it can not only help you identify areas that need healing but can also help you understand the predominant concerns of anyone whom you meet socially or in a work situation as well as in psychic work. Reading an aura can reduce conflict and promote positive interaction with friends, bosses or lovers by enabling you to see beneath the non-verbal signals which many people are becoming increasingly skilful at masking.

At first you may need to practise reading auras under controlled conditions but in time you will see them even in broad daylight or under harsh lighting, especially the first predominant auric impression. Finally, you can learn to draw an auragram in order to offer a sitter a great deal of information about his or her own deeper well-being and feelings. Auras can be seen in the mind's eye, although some people see them physically. Neither method is better.

Sensing the Aura by Touch

To use this method:

* Ask a friend to lie down or sit in a chair. Pass your hands 5–7.5 cm (2–3 inches) away from the body, from the head down to the feet, until you feel resistance. This is the etheric

aura. Now move out a little further and try to trace the oval shape of the emotional aura. Finally, move your hands and feel the resistance of the outer mental aura. You may find it easier to use a crystal pendulum to trace the outlines and you can note any places where the pendulum reacts negatively as a sign of stress, knotted muscles or pain.

* Close your eyes and see in your mind's eye one or two predominant colours. Alternatively, close your eyes, open them and see if you can make out one or two major colours as a haze around the head where they are clearest. You may at first see a silvery haze. This level of auric awareness will serve many purposes and indeed many aura readers will base the pictures they paint or the colour of your aura on this overall impression.

* Once you are happy with this process, you may wish to examine the separate layers. If so, after the initial reading run your hands again over each auric layer in turn, noting any breaks or bulges in the natural shape and any places where the aura disappears. After you have sensed each layer, briefly scribble down the predominant colours or better still record them on an auragram (see p. 133). Do not talk over your aura readings until you have finished all the aspects but, as you talk to your subject, be aware of any auric impressions that emerge naturally.

Seeing the Aura

Seeing the aura, either physically or in your mind's eye without tracing it, is not difficult. To use this method:

* Look at the person against a darkish background, with a northern light (either natural or candles), while he or she is totally relaxed in a comfortable but well-supported chair that does not obscure the outline. Alternatively, the person can lie on a bed or couch, again wearing fairly close-fitting clothes, and facing upwards.

* Sit quietly and throw your eyes slightly out of focus by concentrating 15–22 cm (6–9 inches) beyond the subject so that he or she is only vaguely discernible but the general outline can be seen.

* Begin with your overall impression of the predominant

colours and record these. The head is the source of these
stronger overall impressions.

* When these are clear, close your eyes or blink to clear this
picture and concentrate on the separate levels. You may find
it easiest to begin reading at focal points – around the feet, or
the area level with the base of the spine for the etheric body,
around the heart for the emotional layer, and around the head
for the mind/spirit aura – and then trace the aura around the
rest of the body.

Studying Your Own Predominant Aura

It can be quite difficult to see your own separate auric layers until
you are very practised. However, almost everyone can see the
predominant aura and learn to strengthen it for everyday encoun-
ters. Look in the mirror, either in soft sunlight or with a candle or
soft lighting behind you. Close your eyes and let the picture of the
rainbow emerge around your head (the easiest place to see it). Now
open your eyes and see what colours are left. That is your predominant aura at present.

Try this at regular intervals: after a quarrel; after making love;
after a success at work or home; and when you are sad, tired and
sleepy. Note down the colours. Try this for two or three weeks to
get a representative pattern.

If you keep an aura diary in your psychic notebook, you may
find that certain situations evoke the same auric pattern, perhaps
before visiting a difficult relation or even going along to an activity
you feel you ought to enjoy but don't any more.

If you always present the same auric colour or colours, regardless of the situation or person, then you may need to become more
adaptable. Equally, if you have no predominant auric pattern, you
may be influenced too much by people and situations.

Strengthening Your Aura

The easiest method of strengthening your aura is to use crystals.
However you can use any dense block of colour, although those

from natural living sources – like the sun, flowers and trees – will work fastest and can boost low energy levels. Gold, silver, orange, yellow and white are potent restorers of auric vibrance. Blue or purple can help before healing or psychic work and pink or lilac can create harmony and tranquillity over knotted auric sections. If you tend to make heavy emotional demands use a rich vibrant green to give you emotional strength.

Hold the crystal, or focus on the flower, and in your mind's eye see the colour rising up and flowing around your outline, permeating every pore, until your whole body vibrates with the brilliant colour. Now let the colour rise so it forms a halo round your head. If you look in the mirror you may see the auric glow of the input colour around your head or a faint white radiance.

Making an Auragram

Recording an aura is best done on an auragram. All you need is a large sheet of dark cream paper, so that you can draw white, and a set of paints, markers or crayons in a range of colours so you can differentiate between shades. Draw four circles, each inside the other. The outermost circle is for the predominant aura, the first impression, and will be one or two major colours. Colour this first.

Then move to the innermost auric circle to record the etheric body. Colour it as you see it, which may not be the colours you expect at all. For example, I have seen a completely green inner aura when a person was so flooded with emotion that it penetrated every fibre of her being. I have also witnessed no colours whatsoever when someone is totally exhausted. Use a dark colour for any breaks or clouding.

Then colour in the second innermost circle of the emotional aura, noting particularly any darkness and the shade of green. If you see a hole in this layer around the level of the heart, ask if the person has formed a deep attachment or is reaching out emotionally to someone else.

Finally, colour in the third layer, which may be penetrated by both inner and outer influences that can be seen as shafts or rays. Cosmic rays were often pictured as coming from the halos of saints.

Some people prefer to draw a person and the auras around him or her as they talk. Even an untrained artist can produce a meaningful picture.

Talk to the person for whom you are reading and ask about any areas of darkness that do not indicate serious illness but perhaps an aching joint or a neck held stiff with tension.

Use the aura reading as an opportunity for the sitter to talk about their hopes and fears. This, in itself, can be immensely healing.

In Chapters 27 and 28 there are several techniques that can be used for healing breaks in all levels of the aura. However, pranic breathing, using the technique described in Chapter 1, or simply inhaling the light (slowly counting one and two and breathing out the darkness) are also very effective. Find a rhythm that is right for you. For energy, breathe in rich golden light for matters of the spirit; a rich clear red to unclog any physical blocks; rich green to heal the heart; and purple or pink to restore general harmony. As you breathe in the coloured light, exhale any murkiness or darkness and continue until you see in your mind's eye that your exhaled breath is clear, light and fluffy.

14

Dreams

For thousands of years, in all cultures, dreams were held to be the doorway to another world, offering insights into the present and future. Science has explained them away as products of our imagination or digestion but the Dreamtime, when all the world was created, still plays an important part in the lives of the Aborigines of Australia. Pauline, who recently moved to Queensland, Australia, has natural mediumistic abilities. As part of her work as a healer and aromatherapist, she offers her services to the Aboriginal community. She describes her experiences:

> Since arriving I have had two visits by the Dreamtime, the ever-present first world of the Aboriginal spirits. Also my daughter Jenny heard the didgeridoo at about 3am when we were visiting my husband David's cousin in Caloundra which is right on the beach behind some trees. That night I had a visit and my son Tod felt someone trying to get his sheet off him.
>
> My first ever encounter with the Aboriginal Dreaming was when we visited in July 1990 and it was the second night in Brisbane at my husband's cousin's home. I had gone to bed on our separate camp-type beds and David had been reading. The light was turned off and I was in the middle of my healing prayers when I felt something touch me from the far side. When I opened my eyes, animals made of dots which were swimming around the room, started coming so close and touching me right next to my face. I was terrified at first and asked for protection and that they move back a bit. I realised quickly, however, that this was a wonderful experience and that they were just inquisitive about me. All the dots seemed

to be able to change into other animal species.

In September 1996, I had a similar experience in Sarina Beach near Mackay, about four hours' drive from Rockhampton, in a motel. Out of the curtains appeared a huge Aboriginal man and behind him women and children. On the other wall, which was plain dark brick, were all the animals again, only this time much smaller – the size of cats, as opposed to large dogs as on my first encounter.

These areas were once the home areas of the Aboriginal tribes who live off the land and sea during various seasons so, although they are nomads in essence, they tend to frequent certain areas at various times of the year.

I now work with Aboriginal Health, doing aromatherapy sessions free for them, and they were amazed I knew about the Dreaming, as many have only heard of it themselves and not experienced it.

When the Dreaming comes, I always thank them for accepting us into their land and ask for protection for my family and myself and that we be given the opportunity to work together, their people and mine.

In Aboriginal Lore, the Dreamtime is not separate from the material world but co-exists with it, and can be accessed in sleep and meditation as a source of inspiration and wisdom direct from the first hero creator gods who are the ancestors of modern man. It is the archetype of dreams themselves. It is a formless state, from which various Sky Beings emerged to shape the land and bring culture, law, ritual and religion to the Aborigines. All Aborigines and not just their *mekigars* (magic men) contact the Other-World.

In the modern Western world we have lost touch with the world of dreams as a rich source of psychic wisdom beyond our own personal unconscious mind. If we learn to listen to our dreams they can give us access to the universal pool of past, present and perhaps future experience through Jung's Collective Unconscious.

Creative Dreaming

The Greek philosopher Aristotle said, in his *Prophesying by Dreams*, in 350 BC:

The most skilful interpreter of dreams is he who has the faculty of observing resemblances. Anyone may interpret dreams which are vivid and plain. But, speaking of resemblances, I mean that dream presentations are analogous to the forms reflected in water, as indeed we have already stated. In the latter case, if the motion in the water be great, the reflection has no resemblance to its original, nor do the forms resemble the real objects. Skilful, indeed, would he be in interpreting such reflections who could rapidly discern, and at a glance comprehend, the scattered and distorted fragments of such forms, so as to perceive that one of them represents a man, or a horse.

Dream interpretation is therefore a skill like scrying and divination, through which you can access this deeper source of wisdom. The key is to dream creatively – that is, have dreams which are full of symbols, have several levels of meaning and are rooted in the wider experience of mankind rather than those which are, in Aristotle's words, 'vivid and plain' and relate only to immediate problems and concerns.

Preparing for Meaningful Dreams

Ring your bed with small scented candles. Alternate purple for psychic awareness and pink for peaceful sleep (for example, rose, lavender, patchouli or jasmine). Or you can use unscented candles and burn one of these psychic and sleep-inducing essential oils for a short period in your bedroom before you go to sleep. Make sure these are extinguished before you fall asleep. If you feel you might drop off under these restful conditions it might be wise to set an alarm clock to wake you up.

Lie quietly enclosed by the gentle light and focus on a single image in your mind's eye – a huge pink glass tank containing tiny translucent fish that float gently before your eyes. Let each fish become a rainbow bubble that as it leaves the water expands into a rainbow and floats away.

Blow out the candles alternately round the circle, beginning with the one furthest away, the first to send light to your friends and family, the second for peace to your enemies and those who have hurt you by word or deed. It is important to empty your mind and heart of negativity so that your dreams are positive.

Carry on until you have one candle left burning.

Gaze now into the light of the last candle and let it draw nearer and nearer until you are bathed in the warm, golden glow and pass through into a glorious rainbow. Let the colours filter round and through you and, as you close your eyes, let the light radiate within you. Now let the colours fade and merge into soft cotton wool clouds of white or pink that cocoon you as you drift gently wherever your psyche takes you. In this half-dream state you can create your own entrance to the world of sleep.

Blow out your final candle and, in the darkness, recreate in your mind's eye the golden glow and cotton wool clouds until you sleep.

Recording and Interpreting Your Dreams

Keep your psychic notebook or a special dream notebook next to your bed so that you can record your dreams the moment you wake, even in the middle of the night. Note down absolutely every detail you can recall, however disjointed or surreal.

You may find that the same symbols occur quite frequently and that you even see an unusual symbol very shortly afterwards in real life. Jung called this synchronicity (or meaningful coincidence) and it indicates that the symbol is relevant to your present situation.

While you may find that conventional dream symbolism can offer clues to dream meanings they only provide a template and should always be interpreted according to the context and feelings they evoke within a specific dream. I once dreamed quite vividly of a woman carrying a white peacock and the very next afternoon I saw a woman carrying a white peacock under her arm when I was nowhere near a bird park. In my dream, the bird had been associated with the strong feeling that I was letting an unexpected opportunity slip away.

I took the white peacock's second appearance, this time in real life, as a message from my psyche to indicate that I should take a recently offered chance that would involve a risk in my work life. I took it, as my subconscious or psychic insight was prompting me, and it worked out well. In conventional dream analysis a peacock means either vanity or wealth, or conversely loss of wealth, and white the colour of spirituality and distancing yourself from reality, but together they offered an entirely different meaning.

Predictive Dreams

I have experienced many dreams in which one of my children has faced danger or even death and this is due to the natural anxieties that we play out in our sleep. True precognitive or predictive dreams, whether sent from our own unconscious radar that can detect danger before it occurs or some discarnate force, are far more urgent, real and frequent, though they do not always offer a point where the danger or potential tragedy can be averted. A place or incident can be clearly indicated, recognition of which in the outside world (as with my white peacock) can alter the ending of the dream in the real world (see also Lucid Dreams, below).

For example, David, a vicar, described his predictive dream, in which a car came out of a field and smashed into the family car. David told his wife but, as he was not expecting to go out in the car, he was not worried. However, David was then unexpectedly called out some distance away, to an area with which he was not familiar, and he and his wife set off in the car. After some miles, David reached the spot which he recognised from his dream. The conjunction of the dream and reality had the effect of making David slow down, just as a car did come hurtling out of a field. David was thus able to swerve and avoid a bad accident.

However, precognitive dreams can also be about quite ordinary events and push us in a direction that may be one we had subconsciously desired. Pamela dreamed about owning a black Manx cat, although she did not have a cat at the time. Later in the week a friend at work mentioned that another friend's husband was going abroad and they needed a home for their cat. Pamela decided to see the cat, partly prompted by her dream, and the cat was indeed black. He was not Manx but, like Manx cats, did not have a tail since he had lost it in an accident. Pam became the proud owner of her 'witch's cat'.

Lucid Dreams

Lucid dreams refer to the state of psychic dreaming in which the dreamer is aware that she or he is dreaming but nevertheless does not wake up, in much the same way as Aborigines enter the Dreamtime. We have all experienced these dreams, which are sometimes called 'waking sleep'. It is in this state that dead relatives may appear and give information not known to the dreamer or in which the dreamer may travel to strange lands and other dimensions.

These dreams are described as 'more vivid than dreams'. The dreamer is often surrounded by a golden light that may remain with him or her and the dreamer may take control of or change the dream while still within it. In this state those close to us may share a dream or pick up each other's distress, and information gained through these channels should not be ignored. One woman whose daughter was in the army dreamed of her daughter's distress, although her daughter wrote happy letters home and denied that she had any worries. At last she admitted to her mother that she was experiencing severe financial problems and her mother was able to resolve them. Stephen LaBerge, founder of the Lucidity Institute in California, believes that lucid dreaming, in which symbols and characters can be examined and interacted with, is a powerful spiritual tool in taking charge of your destiny.

If you can learn to take control of your dreams, whether talking to a deceased relative or a friend, visiting other realms or receiving information that may be of use in the waking world, then gradually more and more of your dreams will become lucid and your nightmares will grow less fearsome.

Sam worked at a light industrial firm on the South Coast of England and used to talk to Harry who did not seem to have many friends outside work and lived alone. A few weeks before Harry was due to retire, he did not turn up for work, which was unusual as he never took time off. News came later in the day that he had died suddenly in the night.

Not long after the funeral, Sam had a dream in which Harry was walking up the road dressed in the flat cap and overcoat he wore for work. He looked really well and young, smiled and said: 'Hello, Sam, I just came to see how you were. I didn't get a chance to say goodbye.'

Sam woke up and was convinced Harry had come to him in the

dream and that he had contacted another dimension. Harry did not bring any vital advice or warnings but the experience was reassuring since he looked so well.

Robert Louis Stevenson did not see the deceased in his dreams but what he called the Little People, fairy folk who gave him access to material for his books that his own conscious mind could not reach. Perhaps, also, the material was beyond his personal unconscious and came from a deeper well of human experience. Night after night, he dreamed episodes of stories that were told to him, he said, by the Little People. These formed the substance of many of his famous books. He also dreamed the story of *Dr Jekyll and Mr Hyde*, in which the figure of Hyde was pursued and took powder which made him change in the presence of his pursuers.

As well as stories, inventions have been discovered in dreams. For example, the American Elias Howe invented the sewing machine in the US but was unable to find a way of attaching the thread to the needle. Conscious efforts failed to provide the answer. One night, however, Elias dreamed he was being taken to his execution and noticed that his guards had spears with holes near the top. Within his dream he made the connection, quite irrelevantly in view of his impending execution, that would solve the problem of the needle on the sewing machine. He woke himself before the execution and the next morning the sewing machine was perfected.

Where the psychic or psychological, innate creative or divine or cosmic inspiration through the dream state begin and end cannot be measured. What is crucial is to access this well of unconscious wisdom in which answers to all kinds of problems can be found. And whether we do it is less important than how we do it.

Changing Dreams

Spontaneous dreaming is a vital part of our dream processes and to try to direct every dream is counter-productive and may leave you feeling tired or irritable in the morning. So you should aim for three lucid or controlled dreams a week at the most and some weeks only one. Certainly try to change your dreams only if you are feeling positive, as fears and negativity are best left to unravel even at the expense of the odd nightmare. Indeed you may sometimes need to see a dream through, and face whatever the crisis is, as part of your creative dream work, in order to overcome your fears and leave you ready for the next day.

* Begin with day-dreams, letting a scene unfold. Consciously change a detail, the colour of the flowers, the nature of an encounter, beginning with the physical and gradually changing negative people and responses into positive ones.
* As you wake from a nap or sleep, before you are fully awake, move back into the dream, as you did when influencing the content of your dreams, and rerun the dream so that first the physical details and then your reactions become more positive.
* Create a dream beginning as you drift into sleep and, when you wake, shape the dream to fit with the dream beginning.
* Influencing the outcome of a dream and keeping control in the middle of a dream can sometimes be achieved by using pre-arranged signals from natural sources. Whenever you feel afraid, worried or angry in real life, hold a particular crystal (perhaps a clear crystal quartz), a flower in season, a silver ring, a protective medallion such as a St Christopher, a small white china dove symbolising peace, or a row of beads such as amber that have a link with the unconscious world and consciously quieten yourself.
* Use the same symbol in your day-dreams and keep it by your bed at night.
* Hold it as you drift back into your dreams and in time it will become a talisman, triggering your power to create change and to protect yourself from harm in your dreams.
* Sleep with it close to your pillow and you may find you wake in the morning holding it and that it has featured almost as a magical token in your dreams, enabling you to overcome danger or fear and open doors.
* Once you have associated the crystal with your dreams, tell yourself before sleeping that you will use the crystal to change the dream, especially if it becomes frightening, or to enable you to talk to people or travel in your dreams. As with the white peacock, the inner and outer states are fused through the symbol.
* Alternatively, you may use a particular word such as *Shalom* (Hebrew for Peace), Blessed Mother/Father, Isis or even the

Hindu and Buddhist OM as a chant – whatever seems to evoke in you a feeling of positive power. Use the word as a mantra in real-life situations, in your day-dreams, and when you wake. If you say it last thing at night before you drift off to sleep it will gradually come to be a trigger whereby you recognise your own power within your dreams.

* If you want to dream of a lover, follow the age-old custom of placing a love token or his/her picture beneath your pillow; for travel a tiny silver charm of a plane or boat; for money a coin. And you may find that, not only do you dream of your lover or travelling to exotic places, but creative solutions also come to you in sleep that can help you realise your plans in the outer world. Like the Aborigines, you can, by creating your own Dreamtime, bring past and present, the archetypes and their earthly reflections, closer together and so be able to influence your own destiny.

Making a Dream Catcher

Both the Native North American Indians and those in Central and South America make and use dream catchers to prevent bad dreams and encourage wise ones. These are increasingly on sale in tourist locations in the US and in New Age shops in the UK.

However, it is far better to make your own and use it as a focus for your increasing psychic powers.

* The easiest way is to use an old badminton or tennis racquet and remove the handle. Cut a small hole in the centre and overstitch round it, as dream catchers often have a hole in the centre through which the good dreams filter.
* Alternatively, you could make the circle with soft bamboo or wire. You need a circle of thin metal. Copper, the metal of Venus and love goddesses in other traditions, offers gentle protection.
* You also need a net. You can either improvise a net from one used for holding fruit or a child's fishing net or, better still, weave your own, using a strong wool or natural cord in soft blues, pinks, purples and greens.
* Each time you cross the frame, make a protective knot.
* Ready-made dream catchers have feathers, tiny crystals and

shells around the frame, according to the area from which they come. Originally each child would have his or her own dream catcher made with personal symbols – feathers or a claw from his or her special totem animal; crystals that were given to the child; shells he or she had picked up and perhaps woven into stories that children were told about the talking animals, birds, and fish who gave wisdom and sometimes their name to the tribe.

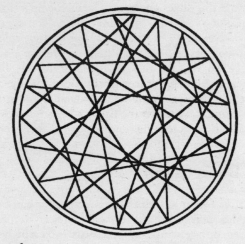

A dream catcher

* Collect small objects to decorate the outside of your dream catcher and tiny crystals to sew on, glue or pin to the cords. You can use dried or silk flowers, and special twigs perhaps from protective trees such as the rowan, hazel or hawthorn.
* Place some tiny clear quartz crystals or mother of pearl in the central hole, if you have one, or near the centre so that they can catch the light.
* You need have only one or two decorative items to begin with. You can add to your dream catcher or remove objects according to the seasons, with dried spring flowers or the first nuts of autumn for fertility. Hang your dream catcher in your bedroom window or above your bed.

You will find not only that your dream catcher gives you good dreams but that your dream recall improves dramatically.

15

Dream Symbols

The following symbols appear frequently in dreams. The meanings suggested here are drawn from both psychology and traditional dream divination. You can use the list as a basis for your own list, substituting your own meanings and adding to the list any others that appear regularly in your dreams. You may find these dream symbols reflected in your scrying, divination or past life work as well as the scrying symbols listed in Chapter 7. Jung talked about big dreams that used universal symbols and occurred at change or crisis points and little dreams concerning everyday matters in which the symbolism was more personal.

Dream symbolism acts not only as a release for any deep-seated anxieties, fears and wishes but also as an indicator of what is moving into your life just beyond the present horizon. Many dreams are precognitive, in the sense that they may reveal possible courses of action that we 'know' on a psychic level will bring us happiness or fulfilment.

Equally, some warnings of disaster are not an indication of the immutable hand of fate, but may alert you, for example, to a fault in your car that you had not registered on a conscious level. The Duke of Portland, who organised the coronation of Edward VII, dreamed that the King's coach stuck in a particular archway on the way to Westminster Abbey. As a result, he measured the arch which he found was 60 cm (2 feet) too low.

Premonitory dream warnings can also alert you to unhappiness in a child or partner, or potential treachery in a friend which has been picked up by your unconscious radar.

1. **Abandonment**: If you find yourself abandoned, something or

someone in your present situation is making you feel insecure. If you are abandoning others, you may have an unacknowledged resentment concerning present relationships.

2. **Absent Friend**: This can be an indication of telepathic communication. You may hear from your absent friend soon or you should contact them, as a link has been made. The friend may also have dreamed of you on the same night or shared the same dream symbols.

3. **Accident**: If you are involved in one, this is a warning to be careful of your health and avoid carelessness in the area shown in the dream, e.g. if it is a road accident, check your tyre pressures, etc. If others are involved, you may be very anxious about their welfare or be feeling guilty for neglecting them (a feeling which may or may not be valid).

4. **Actor**: If you are in a play, you may want to have a more prominent and more recognised role in life. If you forget your words, you may be worried about others spotting your inadequacies.

5. **Assassin**: If you are being stalked, you should seek to discover the identity of the enemy in your real life. This may be someone seeking to assassinate your good name. If you are killing someone, it is a sign that you need to be ruthless to survive the present situation or demands.

6. **Ball**: If you are playing ball, you are secure in your present situation and relationships. If you are not playing, you may feel excluded from the happiness of others.

7. **Band or Orchestra**: You are trying hard to fit in with others. However you may be happier following your own path.

8. **Blood**: If you are bleeding, you may feel that your energy is being drained from you. If you are afraid of the blood, especially if someone close to you is bleeding, you may be afraid that something important in your life is slipping away.

9. **Burglary**: If your home is being burgled, you may feel that outsiders are intruding upon your private life or that an outsider is posing a threat to an important relationship.

10. **Cards**: Playing cards for money can indicate the desire to take a risk but anxiety that it will fail. If you are winning, then the risk is worth taking.

11. **Cave**: If you are happy in the cave, then you may be in need of nurturing and mothering. If you are trapped in the cave, then you are being stifled by the protectiveness of someone close.

12. **Chase**: If you are being chased, the pursuer – whether an animal or person – usually represents a hidden problem from which you are unconsciously trying to run away. Confronting the pursuer indicates that a positive approach will drive away any opposition. Analyse and identify the pursuer.

13. **Children**: If you are the child, you may want to shed some of your current burdens and be free again. Returning to childhood can also indicate the desire to recapture some aspect of earlier life that was fulfilling and could be helpful now. It could also suggest a reluctance to accept impending change. If you dream of a child and want to have one, you may be preparing the way to become a parent. It may even be the night you conceive. Some people believe that they are contacted by the essence or spirit of a future child. If you lose a child, whether your own or an unknown child, you may be worrying that you have taken on responsibilities you cannot handle.

14. **Clothes**: Buying new clothes implies a desire to change your image. Wearing inappropriate clothes, or none at all, in public can mean that you are afraid of the disapproval of those around you. If, however, you are pleased to have no clothes on, then you have a desire to be unconventional.

15. **Crossroads**: A turning point in your life involving choice. If the signs are clear, you should make a fast decision. If, however, the sign is broken or no signpost is present, you should wait until you are more certain and look for guidance. The actual places marked may be of deep significance.

16. **Crowd**: A sense of being lost and swept along by other people's opinions and lifestyle. Holiday or fair crowds suggest the need to have fun without getting too deeply involved.

17. **Crying or Grief**: This may reflect a disappointment or sorrow you have not acknowledged but need to express. If you are comforted, then the dream can be healing and may suggest you need to talk through your fears. If a friend or family member is crying, you may need to ask tactfully if they are unhappy and then offer support, as the dream may be a telepathic signal of hidden distress.

18. **Darkness**: If you are walking or driving in total darkness, perhaps because your lights have failed, it suggests that you need to find sources of help and positive input into your life as you may feel totally unsupported. If you are walking from

darkness into light, it may be part of an out-of-body experience, or there could be real hope of resolving a difficult situation.

19. **Death or Funeral**: This indicates the desire to lay a situation to rest or make a new start. Dreaming of your own death or that of a loved one may suggest an unresolved hidden fear about your health that should be taken seriously, if only to allay your fears, or an ailing relationship that may need extra input to thrive.

20. **Devil or Demon**: You are tempted to act in a way that your upbringing says is wrong. Acknowledge your negative feelings and your own hidden needs.

21. **Earthquake**: An indication of insecurity in a relationship or work situation, based on warning signs you may have missed on a conscious level. Collapsing buildings may indicate a financial problem you need to face.

22. **Eating and Food**: You may feel deprived of physical affection or sex and, if you are paying for the food, you may be paying too highly for love or friendship. A dream banquet may occur if you have been dieting but can also suggest you need to indulge a particular need or desire.

23. **Examination**: If medical, you may be worried about your health. If a school examination, you may be afraid that your ideas will not stand up to scrutiny or that you know far less than other people. Do not be too harsh on yourself but check your facts.

24. **Falling**: Falls with rough landings indicate a fear of failure and that you are feeling out of control in your life.

25. **Father**: Whether your father is alive or not, the appearance of a father or father figure indicates a conflict or matter concerning authority or convention. Dead fathers and grandfathers often return with advice and warnings while deceased mothers and grandmas usually offer comfort and reassurance.

26. **Fire**: Lighting a fire means that you need to get started on a job, as others will not do it for you. A raging fire suggests a deep fear of having your home, or whatever is on fire, destroyed by the interference or ill-intent of others.

27. **Flood**: If you are trapped, this can suggest that you are feeling swamped by life and afraid of others emotionally blackmailing you. If the flood is blocking your route, others may be frustrating your efforts. If you do not fear water, water dreams

can be very positive (such as tranquil lakes), but if the water is dammed you may be keeping your emotions too tightly in check.

28. **Flying**: Often associated with sex, dreams of flying are also a sign of an astral or out-of-body dream and can be very empowering. Flying dreams, especially with gentle landings, represent the opening up of opportunities.

29. **Fountain**: If flowing, it signifies a source of inspiration and creative power, either from within you or from others you meet. If the fountain has dried up, you should seek a new source of help and friendship and those with new ideas.

30. **Garden**: If the garden is beautiful and wild, your natural fertility of ideas should not be held back by convention or the fear of standing alone. A formal garden suggests fulfilment within a structured environment or situation that will bring harmony. A barren garden suggests a gradual loss of natural growth and power, and the need to escape from the negative influences that constrain your growth and happiness in whatever area of life.

31. **Ghost**: If you know and like the ghost, he or she may have a message for you or may reassure you that everything will be fine. If not, or if the ghost is frightening, then you may be afraid of some old problem coming back to haunt you or some relationship that you have not completely buried.

32. **Glass**: If you are enclosed in glass, you may feel that no one is listening to you. If the glass is broken, especially if you break it in the dream, frustration is welling up in you and should be faced before you give vent to your anger in the wrong place.

33. **God or Goddess**: This indicates striving for perfection and spiritual fulfilment. Your desire to communicate and to be understood on the deepest level is not being met in your present situation or relationships. You may need to develop psychically and spiritually in a more formal way and to see wise people, especially in the spiritual arts.

34. **Harvest**: If the harvest is good then your efforts will bear fruit before long. If the harvest is trampled, you need to find a new approach or simply try again when the time is right.

35. **Holiday**: If pleasurable, it is an indication of a desire for relaxation, travel and holiday that should be translated even into a day off or a short trip in real life. Dreaming of the end of a holiday, and not wanting to return, indicates a reluctance

to face up to the reality of your present situation.

36. **Hospital**: If you are a patient, it may be that you feel temporarily unable to cope with the demands of your life and have a need to be cared for. If you are visiting a patient or you are a doctor or nurse, you may be anxious to help someone close but may not wish to interfere. The dream could also be a telepathic call from the person who needs help.

37. **Ice and Snow**: If you are trapped in the ice and snow, you may feel that a particular situation is insoluble. The answer is to wait for circumstances to improve. If you fall through ice, you are perhaps afraid that, if you speak out or make a move, you may lose what you have. If, however, you are skating and enjoying it, you are in control of your emotions and fears and will succeed in any delicate negotiations.

38. **Incubus (Male) or Succubus (Female)**: Dreams in which you are crushed or sexually attacked by a demon of the opposite sex usually occur from later adolescence right through to the thirties and are more common in women. Such a dream may indicate a sense of powerlessness and an awareness of the darker side of life rather than a spiritual attack.

39. **Inn or Hotel**: If you are comfortable, you need a temporary respite from your responsibilities, even a short holiday, or to relax and seek the company of others. If the hotel is crowded and inhospitable, you may feel temporarily out of place or unwelcome at home or at work and perhaps you need to re-establish your niche in a more positive way.

40. **Insanity**: If you are trying to convince others of your sanity, you may feel that you are being unjustly treated and that no one will acknowledge your point of view.

41. **Insects**: Insects crawling around your home or even on you indicate that you are being invaded by small worries and irritations that disturb you more than you admit. Beetles suggest a fear that hidden omissions on your part may be uncovered. Bees flying around hives or in orchards imply fertility and creativity resulting from hard work. The way to fulfilment is through your own endeavours. Bees were traditionally messengers of the gods, and in Christian as well as pagan rites beeswax candles have been seen as a symbol of purity and the spirit. Wasps tell you to beware of spite and gossip.

42. **Invention**: You may well find an answer to a problem or a new way of doing something in a dream. You are in a very

creative period of your life so try out any original ideas, especially those specifically revealed in dreams.

43. **Jar**: A jar with the lid so tightly screwed on that it will not open is sometimes a warning not to reveal secrets except to those you are sure you can trust. An open jar with its contents spilled suggests that someone close has betrayed a confidence or is gossiping about you.

44. **Journey**: A never-ending journey or one involving a series of delays indicates too much stress in your life and an urgent need to slow down. A journey on holiday or to a new place can indicate excitement at inner changes which can prompt physical moves and travel.

45. **Judge**: If you are being judged, there is a fear of being called to account over an undiscovered wrongdoing. If you are the judge, you feel an injustice keenly and need to seek redress, not necessarily by recourse to law.

46. **Kitchen**: If the kitchen is a warm, orderly place, you will find happiness in the home and any home moves will be good ones. If the kitchen is messy, you need to tidy any clutter, financial and emotional, as well as clearing any jobs you have been putting off.

47. **Knight**: A knight in shining armour means you are looking for a magical solution or the ideal person to transform your life. However, if you ride off with the knight, you perhaps have someone in your immediate circle who, though less glamorous than your dream figure, will offer you warmth and reassurance if you let down your defences.

48. **Lizard**: This is a very ancient symbol of protection and wisdom, suggesting that the dream is tapping into a deep well of knowledge and wisdom and should be analysed carefully.

49. **Love/Lover**: If you are not in love at present, this indicates that you are receptive to love and will soon meet someone who could become a new love given encouragement. If you dream of your present love or he or she is dreaming of you, there is a shared meeting on the astral plain. Dreaming that your lover is faithless may indicate that your relationship needs care and a little vigilance, while dreaming of a past love suggests that your present relationship is lacking in romance or passion.

50. **Magic**: If you are doing the magic or are being shown magic, then your intuition and psychic powers are awakening and

you should trust your instincts. If you are the victim of bad magic or witchcraft, then there may be deceit close to you, of which you are aware on a deep level.

51. **Moth**: Fluttering around a light suggests that the course you are taking is heading for disaster and you should fight against the destructive relationship or obsession that is dominating your life.

52. **Mother**: Dreaming of your mother, whether she is alive or dead, indicates an instinctive need for reassurance and wise counsel. Dreams of dead mothers returning are numerous, as are those of grandmothers, and can often be very healing, especially when there has been a bad relationship in life.

53. **Recurring Dream**: Any recurring dream indicates that you should listen or act on it, especially if it is a warning. The inner voice will often use recurring dreams if it is not being heard.

54. **Recurring Place**: If your recurring dream is of a particular place, try to locate it, as you may learn something there or meet someone who can help you.

55. **Royalty**: Kings and queens, according to Freud, stand for the dreamer's parents or parent figures, while princes and princesses represent the dreamer. If you see yourself as royalty, you may feel out of touch with the people around you. If you are mixing with royalty and talking to them on intimate terms, you may have an urgent, deep need for promotion or public recognition.

56. **School**: Being back at school suggests that you need to solve problems by following a conventional path. If you are having a bad time in the dream classroom, you may lack confidence in your abilities and have perhaps been listening to unjustified criticism from others.

57. **Success**: Dreams of jumping over a high wall, winning a prize, completing a task and being rewarded indicate that you have the power to succeed if you believe in yourself.

58. **Teeth**: Dreams of teeth falling out can be caused by fear of having a quarrel or falling out with someone close, or worries about aging and physical deterioration, perhaps when someone close is being critical. Breaking teeth indicates worries about a deteriorating relationship or a health fear that should be alleviated by professional advice.

59. **Telephone**: Dialling the wrong number on a phone, forget-

ting a vital number or being unable to make yourself heard, usually in an emergency, indicate frustration at not being able to communicate with someone close and fears of failing when put to the test.

60. **War**: If you are in the middle of a battlefield, you may be standing between warring factions in your everyday life and should step back. If you are living in a war zone, you are afraid of your own inability to control your life.

61. **Wedding**: If it is yours, whether you are married or not, you are anxious for a closer relationship with someone and assurance that the relationship will last. If you are a guest, you may feel that you are being disregarded at work, or in a relationship, in favour of someone else.

62. **Zoo**: Zoos indicate hidden aggression or repressed anger that should be expressed in a controlled way.

Use your dreams to guide you. Do not be afraid of symbols of death, as these are signs, not of impending death, but of the need to leave behind old sorrows and move on to a new stage in your life.

16

Out-of-Body
Experiences

Belinda, an actress and writer living in London, had an out-of-body experience as a child but it was not until she was much older that she understood its significance: 'I was very ill with asthma when I was a child,' she told me:

> One day I was sitting in bed, unable to breathe, and heard my gran coming up the stairs with my dinner. Suddenly I realised that I was up on the ceiling and could breathe quite well. I could see my body on the bed leaning forward in the fighting-for-breath position. However, much as I loved the sensation of being able to breathe freely, I knew I had to get back into my body before my grandmother came in and suddenly I was there fighting.

It is estimated that more than a third of people in the Western world have had at least one out-of-body experience. In some cultures, however, the experience is a normal aspect of sleep. The Eskimos of Hudson Bay believe that the soul leaves the body during sleep to live in a special dream world. If you wake someone who is sleeping, the soul will be lost forever. In tribes as far afield as Greenland and New Guinea, the soul is said to travel astrally during sleep and the experiences are remembered on waking. In parts of Africa, dreams are as important as waking since dream activities actually occur during nocturnal astral travel. In the *Dictionary of Mind, Body and Spirit* (Aquarian Press, 1990) Eileen Campbell and J. H. Brennan distinguish between etheric projection, 'stepping out of the body to function like a ghost', and true astral projection, which is 'closer to visionary experience and is believed to be experienced nightly by everyone during dreams'.

The majority of out-of-body experiences involve 'etheric body travel' but there are many overlaps between the two states. Zulus interpret dream images as messages and visions, sent by the ancestors. Some dreams of deceased relatives involve out-of-body experiences. Michael, who lives in the West Midlands, experienced several out-of-body experiences as a child and into adult life, although many people lose the childhood ability to float in and out of the body at will. Michael also contacted his late father during one of his experiences:

> I was lying on my bed fully conscious. Some force gripped me and I was propelled downstairs and slammed head first into the dining room floor. I cried out several times, aware that the ceiling above my head was transparent and I could see myself lying in bed. I was very frightened and continued to cry out. Suddenly I was rushed upstairs, by a force I can only describe as slow-motion, back into my bed.

Michael's first adult oobie (out-of-body experience) was quite frightening but a later astral experience was more tranquil and helped him to come to terms with the death of his father:

> Four days after my father died I found myself floating above Wordsley Church, about 1½ miles from where I live. I floated down and ended up in the church. I had not been in it since I was a small boy. I was particularly aware of the church organ on the left side of the aisle. As I looked down the aisle a panel slid open behind the organ and my dad stepped out, wearing the clothes he usually wore for his job as lorry driver and mechanic. Dad told me he was fine and I wasn't to worry. He had died from cancer and the last days hadn't been easy.
>
> Then Dad went inside the panel again and it slid shut. It was the church where my mother and father got married in 1937. Perhaps my father's spirit returned to the place where he had experienced one of the happiest days of his life and that was why he met me there. I recall floating home over the rooftops of the houses where I lived as a boy.

Out-of-body experiences can also involve travelling to planes that are perhaps some time in the future or in another universe. An oobie can be regarded as one way of being contacted by aliens and such experiences can be quite surreal.

Paul was thirty-six when he had oobies on two consecutive nights. They seemed to take him to a world that was very different from his own but was superimposed on the everyday world. Perhaps when two dimensions move close this is a way of describing being on two planes at once.

I woke and ascended in a spiral from my body. A reptilian creature crawled across my bed and over my chest. I threw it to the ground and a man stood up. From the neck down he was scarcely detectable in the blackness. But his head was handsome, hair snow-white, his eyes dark brown, his head set in an aura of light. He moved me from the bedroom to the sitting room and I became aware that I was not walking but floating. I was dressed in a white robe. From the blackness of his body came an arm and white hand. He took me to the window and I looked out and the landscape had changed to a beautiful golden view. The man promised me it would be mine and then I was out there trying to get back into the house and calling for my wife.

The next night, I again ascended spirally and then, from the void of darkness, I found myself on the surface of a planet. I was aware that there was no atmosphere, rather like the moon but without craters. I could see a stooped figure walking along. His appearance changed and he was covered in bandages like a mummy and then I became the figure. I heard the roar of beasts and they were dogs with lions' heads – I climbed up something like a tree and then I was lying in bed awake. In fear I went to embrace my wife and my arms went straight through her.

Are Oobies Possible?

If the mind/soul is a separate entity from the brain then it can exist independently. This would be the essential person that survives after death. Evidence from the study of near-death experiences throughout the world, in which certain phenomena such as seeing lights, tunnels, angels and even deceased relatives (when the physical body dies for a few minutes either in an operation or during a serious illness or accident) consistently feature, would suggest that people can exist independently of the physical body.

Shamans, magicians who enter states of altered consciousness, are said to fly to other realms to heal or gain wisdom or, in the case of Inuit shamans, dive deep into the ocean to contact Sedna the Sea Mother, ruler of the fish and seals. Shamanic practices are recorded in Palaeolithic cave paintings, for example the dancing shamans pictured in the Trois Frères Caves in Ariège, France, dating back to about 14000 BC. These ancient rites have appeared in many cultures and are still used by Siberian, Eskimo and Native American shamans. One of their chief symbols is that of the bird or bird mask, and a bridge or ladder between dimensions is often depicted. This mirrors the Ancient Egyptian belief in the three souls. The Ba was the bird soul; the Ka was the spirit double of the actual body; and the Ib the heart that was weighed after death against a feather from the headdress of Ma'at, the Goddess of Truth and Justice, to see if it was free from sin.

Ways of Experiencing Other Dimensions

Many out-of-body experiences are quite spontaneous. But there are various methods that people can use to try to free their etheric body. Sometimes the methods will not work at the time, but an experience may occur a few days afterwards or you may have particularly vivid dreams involving flying or visiting other planes.

Astral travel in the widest sense is very creative and can expand psychic horizons of awareness. You should be aware, however, that such experiences can be frightening, because they are so powerful, and you should therefore only attempt astral travel when you are calm, in a positive state of mind and with no preconceived goals. The only danger is when a person resorts to drugs to obtain what is not a true oobie but a chemically induced state of euphoria, or when people become so excited by an out-of-body experience that they use this technique too frequently.

Fortunately, oobies have a self-limiting effect. People who have had a spontaneous oobie and did not enjoy it rarely have another. Equally, if a person induces more out-of-body states than the psyche is able to cope with, the method does not work.

Tattwa Cards

This is an Eastern method, made popular by the members of the Golden Dawn magical tradition, that has been used to create out-of-body sensations and visions of other dimensions. It is a technique used successfully in progression (moving forwards in time). Although the symbols were each said to give access to a certain area of the astral plane, in practice you may find that each acts as a doorway to a different level of consciousness and what you see depends on your own unique needs and stage of psychic development, and the way your psyche interprets abstract concepts pictorially.

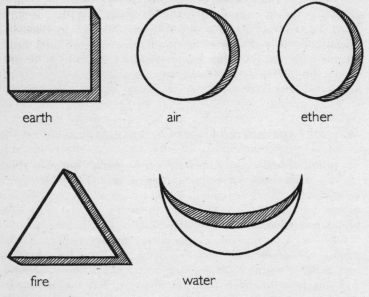

earth   air   ether

fire   water

Tattwa cards

The astral plane is not a specific place but a symbol used to understand the concept of different dimensions and levels of experience beyond the everyday. Some people talk of a temple where there is an actual book containing the Akashic records (which are supposed to hold all knowledge and experience and show you what you need to know). These records are a symbol that you may or may not find helpful in your astral explorations.

To make your own set of Tattwa cards:

* Draw the symbols on pieces of thin white card about 6 cm (2$\frac{1}{2}$ inches) square, painted red for fire, yellow for air, blue for water, green for earth and silver for ether. You can buy some lovely fluorescent paints, as the more brilliant the symbol, the better it works.
* At a time when you are relaxed, shuffle the cards face down and choose one at random. Sit in a comfortable but well-supported chair or lie on a bed, hold the card about 15 cm (6 inches) from your eyes and stare at it intently for about a minute, allowing the image to slip in and out of focus.
* Close your eyes and visualise the symbol becoming larger until it forms a curtain that enfolds you as you pass through it. Be aware all the time that you can pass back through the curtain whenever you wish. Visualise your body resting quite peacefully on the other side of the curtain, waiting for you to slip easily back into it. You can even visualise a silver thread joining you safely to your body all the time that you are travelling.
* When you wish to return, go back through the curtain or allow the colours to fade and let the everyday world slowly impose itself again until you are quietly sitting in your chair or lying down. You may even feel a gentle bump as your etheric form re-enters your body.

The Ceiling or Window Technique

* Sit or lie comfortably and fix your gaze on either the top corner of a large window or the corner of the ceiling furthest away from you. Count to 100 in your mind and gradually project yourself to that spot so that you can visualise your body down below. Move now towards the roof or through the window, seeing the hard surface melt to allow you through quite smoothly. See yourself flying over a specific route you know well, noting the familiar details. Return by the same route and back into your body.
* When you are happy with the technique, choose someone you know well and visit him or her during the daytime. Use the same method but follow the route you would take to his or

her house and enter the house by the front door, seeing it melt as you enter and then close behind you. Astral journeys should follow the same etiquette as any other visit and not be intrusive or invade private conversations or areas of the house. If the house is empty, look for a new ornament or change of position in furniture – anything unusual. If the person is present, touch or kiss him or her very gently on the cheek.

* Retrace your path and re-enter your body. Find an excuse to visit the person and see whether the different item is there – he or she may mention thinking about you at the time you were astrally projecting. This is very common, but it is probably not a good idea to mention the visit unless you are sure that the other person will not feel frightened or invaded.

* If you have a friend who is interested in the psychic or are part of a psychic group, pre-arrange an time when you will visit and be visited and place an item in a very prominent but unusual place. Compare notes. Laboratory experiments in out-of-body experiments are less successful than home-made ones where experimental conditions are less rigorous, but a bond of emotion exists between the visitor and visited.

Sounds

Sound is one of the strongest triggers of naturally occurring out-of-body experiences. Lesley, who had several out-of-body experiences as a child and a teenager, recalled triggers such as the wheels of a pram passing by, classical music and a doorbell ringing. There are two distinct aural triggers – a sudden noise and being enveloped by music.

Sudden Sounds

Ask a friend to help you experiment with sudden but persistent sounds, when you are relaxed, e.g. a doorbell ringing for about a minute, a telephone, a clock chiming twelve, a workman's hammer. Use the initial sound to project your etheric body – in Lesley's case, her pram wheels precipitated her to the top of a tree.

Discordant or harsh sounds, such as those that burst from a road drill, do not seem to trigger oobies. The sound is only necessary as a trigger for your psyche to take over, although the experience is usually quite a short one.

Music

Musical boxes, especially those continuously playing a tune such as Brahms's *Lullaby*, are excellent triggers for a longer oobie.

Experiment with different excerpts from classical music, for example Bach's 'Jesu, Joy of Man's Desiring', the 'Jupiter' from Holst's *Planets*, Grieg's 'Morning' from *Peer Gynt*, Tchaikovsky's 'Dance of the Sugar Plum Fairy' from *The Nutcracker Suite* and selections from Handel's *Water Music*. The beginnings of Beethoven's *Fifth Symphony* (the sound of fate knocking at the door) or Tchaikovsky's *1812 Overture* are also good stimuli.

You can gradually increase the length of the pieces. Dvorak's *New World Symphony* is very sustaining, as are any of Tchaikovsky's ballets or Delibes' *Coppelia*.

In and Out of Time

However, in spite of conscious development of astral powers, the most fulfilling astral visions may occur in those spontaneous moments (what T. S. Eliot called 'in and out of time') when we are physically occupied in a mundane task.

Vivian wrote:

I am eighty-two years old and recently had been thinking a lot about the after-life and not looking forward greatly to the Victorian heaven – pearly gates and lots of harps playing and the rest. I was ironing in my living room and suddenly I was not there. I seemed to be on a mountain top, like one I visited once in Austria, looking out over every lovely place I have ever seen and surrounded by and recognising all the people I have ever loved, not in bodily form but the essence of the person. I was not conscious myself of having a body.

It's true that there are no words to describe the emotions I felt or the beauty of what I saw. It exceeds earth's greatest joy, of giving birth, all family joys, making them pale and insignificant.

I do not know how long I was absent from the body. It seemed as if I continued with the ironing but I came back in the act of putting a garment on to the clothes horse. And when I was back a voice as clear as a human voice in the room said, 'That is heaven.'

Section Five

Ritual Magic

17

What Is Magic?

Magic, says my friend Lilian (white witch, healer, past-life regressionist and clairvoyant), means carrying out a symbolic action on the psychic plane to give power to external action or intention in the material world.

Magic is akin to the increasing power of a plane leaving the tarmac. It is the impetus of needing or wanting, finding a focus for that need, concentrating energy from within and from natural sources by visualisation or a ritual until finally the power reaches a climax and is released into the cosmos. There are many different kinds of magic but they all follow the same principles:

Sympathetic magic involves performing a ritual that imitates what you would like to happen in the outer world (for example, pointing to a toy plane and a tiny Australian flag in the direction of Australia while visualising yourself there, if you would like to visit the country for a holiday).

Contagious magic is very similar (for example, young people who traditionally made love in the fields on May Eve in a two-way transfer of fertility between land and people).

Attracting magic embraces both sympathetic and contagious magic, using a focus (for example, a silver heart to attract love). The ritual might involve surrounding the heart with a circle of candles and symbolically drawing the love into the flame.

Banishing and protective magic drive away negative feelings and fears by casting away or burying the focus of the negativity (hence the old expression 'burying the hatchet', meaning mending a quarrel).

Ritual magic means following definite steps in order to attain a magical goal. This sort of magic can include formal rituals involving magical tools that symbolise elemental powers and specific words and actions to be carried out at certain times of the year or for certain magical needs. These are not necessarily ancient and, indeed, many covens began following rules only after the repeal of the Witchcraft Act in 1951. These rules can be learned through joining a pagan coven and the Pagan Federation is listed under Useful Addresses at the back of this book.

However, many people prefer a more relaxed approach, adapting any words or actions to each need. The success of magic lies, not in following the rules of others to the letter, but in understanding the reasons behind certain prescribed steps (for example, that yang/yin or male/female energies, which are present in us all, are essential in differing proportions according to a particular aim). For instance, a desire for courage might need a surge of yang power. In formal Wicca (witchcraft) this would be akin to the power of the High Priest or Horned God and symbolised by the sword or athame, a black-edged ritual knife. Equally an executive can use a paper knife or even a computer-drawn image to represent this yang power. What is important is to follow the stages in the right order, but these can be carried out using the implements in a kitchen or even entirely visualised while travelling on a busy commuter train.

As your psychic awareness increases, so the need for physical symbols decreases, although for many people they mark any rituals as separate from the everyday world and therefore special. There are times for sitting with candles and crystals and drawing magical circles and other times when your water element is represented by a paper cup of water and your air element represented by an environmentally friendly aerosol spray.

Performing Magic

First you need to create an area where your magical energies will be focused, whether by drawing an actual circle, creating one as a computer image or visualising your magical space surrounded by powerful light. You are not summoning up occult powers or spirits but channelling your own inner powers, and those that occur naturally in the sky and the earth, to give your desire the initial powerful impetus that will turn it into reality. Keep your wish fairly specific. For example, if you want courage, specify the particular need that has made it important. Equally, as I mentioned in the section on visualisation, if you want a house or car, see the particular kind you would wish for. The more detailed a visualisation, the more focused the energies can be. The four stages of any magic are: focus; action; raising the power; and releasing the power.

Focus

This means finding, drawing or even visualising a symbol to represent what it is you want or need: a silver heart for love; a tiny doll for a baby; a key for a new house; a computer image of a plane if you want to travel; or the actual words written on a piece of paper. This stage is vital, as the focus you choose is endowed with all your desires, hopes and fears concerning the wish or need and will be the vehicle for the increasing magical energies.

Action

This is the stage where you use actions, whether physical or mental, to endow the symbol with magical energies, by touching them with your ritual objects or passing the symbol through the areas of the circle belonging to different elemental powers. Alternatively, you could write a wish on a stone or on a piece of paper which is then burnt. Light a circle of candles around the symbol, or ring it with crystals, begin a chant or dance, tie a knot or visualise the steps you are taking towards success or happiness, seeing in your mind's eye your new house or car or the place you wish to visit. This is the first step towards transforming the desire encapsulated in the symbol into action that will eventually reach the outer world.

Raising the Power

This is achieved through the ritual or visualisation according to the focus and tools you are using and is the building up of the magical energies, for example by chanting a word or phrase faster and faster. You would begin dancing in a circle with increasing speed, pulling your knotted cord tighter and tighter or adding more knots. You might concentrate in your mind's eye on the wish you have written or made being carried to fruition by magical energy (perhaps wind swirling faster and embracing more within it as it gains momentum, a golden cone of light rising higher or a fast-flowing river getting wider and more powerful as it surges to the sea). At the point when the climax is reached comes the release of power.

Release of Power

This may be a final shout, a leap, or word such as 'It is free, the Power is mine' – whatever seems natural. Or, if you have tied a knot, you may suddenly release it or see the whirlwind rising into the sky or suddenly becoming a silver cord and forming a star or a glittering rainbow. This is the moment when you consign your wish to the flame, extinguish the candle and send light and energy into the cosmos; throw the stone with your wish, or what you want to be rid of, into a river or the sea; release a balloon into the air; even run fast down a hill. There are many ways of releasing the energies and, both on the physical and psychological plane, it is a joyous and positive conclusion that leaves you ready to use the impetus.

Making Magic Come True

Some practitioners put away their chalice and candles and then wonder why, having followed every word and order of the most complex ritual, success, happiness or love remain unattainable. Real magic, in the sense of the union of inner and outer naturally occurring energies, has lifted the symbolic plane to soar through the skies but, like any real mode of transport, it needs fuel and direction to reach its destination. You now have to write that letter, learn the hundred pages necessary to pass that exam, sort out those accounts, ask for a rise, say 'I love you', 'I am sorry' or 'Goodbye'.

The Four Elements

In any formal magic, the four elements are seen as providing natural energies for transforming wishes into actuality. Earth, Air, Fire and Water are not chemical elements, but are symbols of the four forces that traditionally make up life on the physical, mental and spiritual plane. Together they combine to form the fifth element, Ether or Akasha, which represents pure spirit or perfection. Medieval alchemists worked at creating this elusive substance, often called the philosopher's stone, which was said to turn base metal into gold and, according to Eastern tradition, could cure all ills and offer immortality.

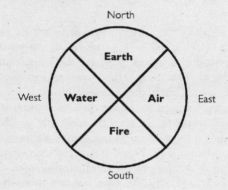

The circle of the elements

Earth

Earth is the element of order, in both nature and institutions, such as the law, politics, finance, health and education. It represents the female/yin/nurturing Goddess aspect, Mother Earth. Its elemental creatures are gnomes, with their stores of hidden treasure, wisdom and above all common sense. You may see them only fleetingly in your garden amid the autumn leaves.

The guardian angel of the Earth quadrant is the Archangel Auriel, who is associated with Venus or love and sometimes called Hamiel. The ritual artefacts associated with Earth are the bell and the pentacle (see Chapter 22 on Talismans and Amulets). Its colours are green or brown, its quarter is North and its direction Night.

Air

Air represents life itself: logic, the mind, communication, learning and healing, and the male/yang/God in the form of sky deities. Its elemental creatures are sylphs, gentle spirits of the air, who can be seen fleetingly as butterflies, and offer ideas, ideals and transient happiness. Its guardian is the Archangel Raphael, who is associated with Mercury, the messenger and healer.

In the Golden Dawn, one of the main magical traditions, the ritual tools associated with Air are the sword and the athame (the ritual black-handled knife). The colour of this element is yellow, its quarter is East and its direction is Dawn.

Fire

Fire represents light, the sun, lightning, fertility and also destruction of what is no longer needed. Like Air, it represents the male/yang/God in the form of the sun deities. Its elemental creature is the salamander, the mythical lizard (though the name is now given to a species of amphibious newts) who lives within fire.

Its guardian is St Michael, Archangel of the Sun, who is linked with all the solar deities, especially Apollo. Its tools are the wand and the pure quartz crystal. Its colour is red, its quarter is South, and its direction is the Noonday Sun.

Water

Water represents love, relationships, sympathy, intuition and the cycle of birth, death and rebirth. Like Earth, it represents the female/yin/Goddess in the form of the moon-goddesses. Its elemental creatures are undines, spirits of the water. The original Undine was created without a soul, but gained one by marrying a mortal and bearing him a child. However she also lost her freedom from pain and her immortality. The Archangel of Water is Gabriel, often associated with the moon. The ritual implements are the chalice or a silver cup and the cauldron or a silver dish. Its colour is blue, its quarter is West and its direction is Dusk or Sunset.

The Magic Circle

Intrinsic to all magic is the idea of the magic circle, a space marked out for conducting rituals, concentrating power and providing a protective boundary against negative influences.

Earth, Air, Fire and Water, representing law, life, light and love, are central to all ritual magic and in the Northern Hemisphere are sited at the four compass points in any magic circle: Earth in the North; Air in the East; Fire in the South; and Water in the West. In the Southern Hemisphere, some practitioners follow the Northern tradition. However, you may wish to follow your own seasonal patterns. Since the Sun travels from East to North to West, you can reverse the Earth and Fire Quadrants, place the altar in the South of the circle and cast the circle anti-clockwise or widdershins (which is sun-wise in the Southern Hemisphere). If you follow this method, you will also need to move the seasons forward six months.

Casting the Circle

You may decide to make casting the circle the first part of any ritual. However, some people like to prepare this, and any artefacts that will be needed, in advance so that they can concentrate purely on the ritual.

* Traditionally, witches swept out their circle before use to remove any bad feelings or vibrations. Brushing your hair in the centre of the circle is a way of removing negativity from yourself. You can sweep out the area you intend to use or, if carpeted, sweep it in clockwise circles.
* A compass is remarkably easy to use and you can keep a magic circle marked out with stones in a corner of your garden or painted on the floor of a room covered with a large rug. Attics are especially good, since you are high up.
* Alternatively, once you know your directions you can draw a chalk circle in your backyard or patio when you need it or visualise your circle and draw an invisible outline, beginning in the North and continuing in an unbroken circle.
* When you draw a circle for the first time, use paint, a clear quartz crystal, an athame or chalk. And, as you draw or

visualise your line, see a golden protective light enclosing the area of magical working.

* When you open an existing circle, trace clockwise round the markings of the circle with your quartz crystal or see a golden thread circling the area.
* Begin by drawing your circle from the North (in the Northern Hemisphere), clockwise, deosil or sun-wise, and make a single unbroken line.
* Make your circle large enough to walk inside and have a table or platform in the North – a piece of unpolished wood such as hazel, ash, rowan or oak (one of the magical trees), or uncut stone supported on bricks, will do.
* If you are working with friends then make your circle large enough for all of you to sit or stand inside it.
* When you uncast a circle, begin again from the North, but trace with your crystal or finger anti-clockwise, or widdershins, so that you end where you began. If it is a chalk circle you can rub it out.
* You may decide to divide the circle into four quadrants but this is not essential.

If you can personalise the objects you use, rather than buying expensive ceremonial artefacts that are disconnected from the real you, then your magic can more easily spill over into the real world.

Materials

Materials you will need for ritual magic include a set of small silver symbols, such as those found on a charm bracelet (for example, a thimble for domestic affairs, a padlock for security at home, a boat for travel). However, you can also use soft wax or even clay to fashion any symbol that feels right – a flower for love, a coin for money, a tiny teddy bear for friendship or children. These will act as a focus for your own inner power and the elemental energies.

Elemental Substances

Salt can be used as the Earth symbol (see Chapter 19 on Salt

Magic), as it is the purest element and vital for human life. Use sea salt and keep it in a small unglazed pottery jar or a tiny pottery dish.

Incense can be used for Air, with different perfumes used for different rituals: allspice for money rituals; bay for rituals concerning health; cinnamon for increasing psychic awareness; Dragon's Blood for sexual attraction and fertility; frankincense for success and new beginnings; myrrh for endings and banishing sorrow; rose for love; pine for courage; rosemary for memory and learning; sandalwood for protection.

Candles can be used for the Fire element, with different colours according to the need.

Water, either pure spring water from a sacred spring, such as Buxton water, or tap water, should be left for a twenty-four hour cycle in a crystal or clear glass container in the sun and moonlight.

Elemental Tools

Earth

The bell is a symbol of the Earth. It should be made from either crystal or brass and can quite easily be obtained from an antique shop. If you buy one that has already been used, your dedication ceremony (described on p. 175) will override any negative vibrations from previous owners. You can sound the bell in each of the four elemental quadrants as you pass your chosen symbol around the circle. Of, if you have created a large circle, you can walk around it carrying the symbol. The bell can also be rung nine times at the beginning and end of each ritual, standing in the South of the circle facing North. Nine is the number of completion and perfection.

The pentacle

The pentacle is also a symbol of the Earth and is familiar to users of many Tarot packs. It can symbolise material possession, especially money and practical endeavour, and you can place crystals or the focus of the ritual on the pentacle to endow it with Earth energies. It is very easy to make your own pentacle from a piece of clay, wood, wax or metal. On it mark a pentagram, a five-pointed star enclosed in a circle with the single point extending upwards. On p. 230 the two different ways of drawing a pentagram are illustrated – one of which is for attracting magic, the other for banishing.

Air

The athame or air dagger is a ritual black-handled knife, usually with a double-edged blade, traditionally engraved with magical or astrological signs. You can obtain one from a specialist magical shop (see Useful Addresses), many of which will sell by mail order. However you can also buy a camping knife with a black wooden handle, on which you can engrave your personal astrological sign with a pyrographic set which you can obtain from an art shop. You could engrave your name in a magical alphabet (see Chapters 20 and 21). But any dark-handled kitchen knife will do. The athame is traditionally used for drawing circles in the earth, directing magical Air energies into a symbol and sending negative energies skywards where they can be transformed into sunbeams or rainbows.

The sword is rarely used in ritual magic at home. The ritual black-handled knife serves the same purpose or a white-handled knife can be used as a substitute for the sword. This can also be used for cutting herbs, cutting the Halloween turnip or pumpkin, and marking candles with runes or astrological signs. Pearl-handled knives are considered especially magical.

Fire

The wand or fire stick is not usually an elaborately carved wand with a crystal on the end, of the kind wielded by fairy godmothers. Rather, it is a thin piece of wood about 52 cm (21 inches) long, rubbed smooth and preferably cut from a living tree (some conservationists find this unacceptable unless the tree is being pruned). After a strong wind, or in a forest where trees are being constantly felled, it is often possible to find a suitable branch from which the wand can be cut.

* Ash is a magical wood, associated with healing and positive energies.
* Elder wands are symbols of fairy magic and so are good for any visualisation work.
* Hazel comes from the tree of wisdom and justice and is linked with the magic of the sun.
* Willow is the tree of intuition and is said to be endowed with the blessing of the moon.

You can also use a long, clear quartz crystal, pointed at one end and rounded at the other, as a wand.

Water

The chalice or ritual cup represents the Water element and can be filled with pure or scented water. The chalice or cup used for rituals is traditionally made of silver, but you can also use crystal glass, stainless steel or pewter. The cup need not be large. If you are using essential oils in your chalice, use a small earthenware or dark glass cup rather than metal.

The cauldron or ritual dish is also a symbol of Water, although it is occasionally regarded as an Earth symbol. It can take many forms, but if a dish is used it is frequently made of silver. The cauldron can vary from a deep earthenware dish to a small iron pot with a handle that symbolises the womb of the Mother Goddess. It is used for brewing potions, burning incense or as a container for flowers or herbs. You do not need to buy a special cauldron from a magic shop unless you wish to, as there are many suitable pots available from kitchenware or gift shops. You can also use your cauldron for scrying, especially on the old festivals, such as Halloween and May Eve, by using pure water and dropping dark inks or oils on the surface. If you are able to scry with direct moonlight or a candle behind you, you may see many images that will suggest ideas or answers to questions that are concerning you (see Scrying, p. 59).

The Book of Shadows

The Book of Shadows, beloved of witches in traditional covens, has no sinister connotations. It is just another name for your existing extensive psychic notebook, although I always call mine a Book of Light.

In traditional lore, the Book of Shadows was handed on from mother to son or daughter and you may find that your children are very interested, as my own are, in flowers, herbs and trees. My ten-year-old daughter Miranda makes beautiful essential oil mixes quite instinctively.

You may decide to use a special leather-bound book and pen and ink for any ritual magic, and include pressed flowers and herbs from special occasions. Or you may be more pragmatic and use a special ring binder with dividers in which you can rearrange and rewrite information as you discover better methods.

Preparing for Rituals

To dedicate your ritual tools, sprinkle each one with a few grains from your dish of salt. Hold the salt in your right hand and the tool in your left. Next, circle clockwise over the new tool with incense, frankincense or rosemary for the sun; and jasmine or sandalwood for the moon. Finally, sprinkle it with pure water, scented with roses.

Before you carry out a ritual:

* Do not eat a heavy meal or drink alcohol. You no longer need to fast for twenty-four hours, as the resulting physical weakness not only interferes with everyday functioning but the state of otherworldliness it induces does not make psychic awareness any greater than a general moving away from the world.
* Have a fragrant bath with eight to ten drops of lavender, rose, neroli, ylang ylang or another floral oil. Dress in something loose and comfortable.
* Prepare your magical place with candles and crystals of purple, pink and green for psychic awareness and intuition. You can choose candle colours, according to the need on which you are focusing (see Candle Colours, p. 86). You can also light candles of green for Earth, yellow for Air, red for Fire, and blue for Water.
* Burn some oil in an unglazed pottery or metal heater, using

one of the essences for psychic awareness: jasmine for the moon; frankincense for the sun; rose for love; lavender for harmony; bergamot or lemon for heightened psychic perception; and patchouli or neroli for psychic dreams.

When to Carry Out Rituals

Magic is often associated with darkness and the moon. One of the reasons was the need for privacy, especially before the repeal of the Witchcraft Act. However, the moon, because of its link with feminine intuition and mystery, in the form of the early Moon Mother and the pagan lunar goddesses, has always been regarded as a symbol of magic.

For magical purposes the lunar cycle is divided into three – waxing, full and waning – and each is considered appropriate for a particular kind of magic:

The new moon period, most powerful when the crescent first appears in the sky, is for rituals involving new beginnings, love, money-making and young people.

The full moon period, most powerful as the full moon first appears, is potent for magic involving power, fertility, energy, success, mature people and mothers.

The waning moon period, most powerful on the first day of the waning moon, is good for banishing, protective or healing magic, in the sense of removing illness, and for old people.

Some people do not practise rituals on the last three days of the moon cycle, the dark of the moon, but this can be a very valuable time for banishing regrets, guilts and secret sorrows.

You can use a newspaper to check the phases of the moon (usually given along with the weather report) or follow your instinctive feel for the right time. You may wish to work with friends and decide whether you are attracting the yang/God or yin/Goddess energy from the sky and the natural energies of the earth. You can absorb both equally for balance and harmony: first one and then the other, and fuse them within you.

Covens traditionally meet on the full moon or on Fridays, the day of the Norse Mother Goddess Frigg, but modern ritual magic can be carried out whenever there is a need. You can also use the old festivals that featured in Celtic worship but actually date from much earlier and recognise man's link with the seasons. Each festival began at sunset and lasted for three days. The date of the equinoxes and solstices can differ by a day either side so check your diary. As Christianity swept across Europe, the Church decreed that traditional festivals should be given a Christian meaning. Hence the festival of the Mid-Winter Solstice became Christmas. In the same way, ancient sites of worship were often used for the building of churches to eradicate the pagan ways.

Samhain

The Celtic winter began with Samhain on 31 October, the Christian All Souls' Eve, which is still celebrated as Halloween. During the three-day festival, the cattle were brought down from the hills and kept in barns or slaughtered for the winter stores. Families also returned from the hills, and departed family members were supposed to return for nourishment. It was a time when the boundaries blurred between past, present and future. The three-day festival is good for rituals concerning older people, endings and psychic development. It has been Christianised as All Souls' and All Saints' Days at the beginning of November.

Mid-Winter Solstice

The Mid-Winter Solstice or Shortest Day falls on 21 December or thereabouts, when evergreen boughs were used as decorations to persuade the trees to blossom again. Yule logs were burned so that the sun would not die on the Shortest Day, but would bring back light and life. You may wish to light a red candle or gather evergreens. You can use this festival for rituals about money and business or practical concerns. It has been Christianised as Christmas.

Oimelc or Brigantia

The eve of 31 January begins another ancient lunar festival, Oimelc or Brigantia, when the first lambs were born and fresh ewes' milk was available to the community after the worst of the winter. It was a time sacred to the maiden aspect of the Goddess and has survived today in the Outer Hebrides as the festival of Brigit (who merged with the Christian St Bride). The womenfolk would make a bedecked bride bed of straw by the fireside and men would come to wish on it. You can use this festival for rituals about love and children. The Christianised feast at the beginning of February is Candlemas and St Valentine's Day is also associated with this period.

The Spring Equinox

The eve of 20 March or thereabouts heralds the Spring Equinox of equal day and night and is sacred to the Anglo-Saxon Goddess Ostara or Eostre, whose sacred hare we remember in our Easter bunny. Eggs were placed on her altar to celebrate new life. The yolk represented the solar deity and the white the White Goddess who carried new life within her. In the Christian tradition, 25 March is the Annunciation of the Virgin Mary and Easter falls on the first Sunday after the first full moon after the Vernal Equinox. Use this festival for rituals involving new beginnings.

Beltane

The Celtic Summer began on Beltane, the eve of 30 April, when the cattle were let out of barns after the winter and purified of disease by driving them between two fires. This is the origin of our May Day revels when youths leaped across the fires. Tree worship was recalled in the maypole dances when the ribbons traced out the patterns of the energies of the earth. May Day is still celebrated and an early true Whitsun, as opposed to the new Spring Bank Holiday in the UK, falls in May as does Mothering Sunday in the US (the third Sunday in May). Use this festival for rituals concerning fertility of all kinds.

The Summer Solstice or Longest Day

The Summer Solstice, on 21 June or a date very close, marks the celebration of the sun at its height when great wheels of fire were rolled down the hills and oak bonfires lit on hilltops to persuade the sun to continue to shine. The sunrise on the longest day is seen as a very sacred time by Druids and many of the old standing stone circles are aligned to the summer sunrise. St John's Eve and Day, on 23 and 24 June, mark the Christian Midsummer. Love rituals were practised on Midsummer's Eve, connected with St John's wort, the golden herb of midsummer that was said to bring fertility. This festival is potent for rituals involving success, power and good health.

Lughnasadh or Lammas

The beginning of High Summer fell on 31 July. This was the feast of the Goddess of the Land when the first hay was harvested and, as an added bonus in ancient times, you could try out a new partner for a year and a day. The Corn God was symbolically slain with the last sheaf of corn cut and corn dollies made from this sheaf are symbols of growth and a good harvest. The Christian festival on 1 August was Lammas or Loafmass when the loaf made from the first corn was traditionally offered on the altar. Use this festival for rituals of justice and all kinds of partnerships.

The Autumn Equinox

Around 21 September was the second festival of equal day and night. It was the feast of the second harvest and of fruit and vegetables, the time of traditional harvest suppers and preparation for winter. Many Christian churches hold harvest services around this time. Use this festival for rituals concerning the home and tasks that need completion.

Your First Rituals

There are no absolute rules and, so long as you follow the principles of magic and remain consistent in your rituals, the magic that springs from deep inside you is always far better than words written by others, no matter how poetic. Magic rarely works if you are desperately trying to remember some complex ritual gleaned from a third party, no matter how reputable or esteemed the source.

The best witches and wizards always improvise and adapt and, like any skill from driving to typing, once you can take your eyes off the manual and forget the mechanics, then you are able to tune into the real situation.

You can and should create your own rituals. The following ritual is based on one practised by Wiccans but can be used as a basis for increasing intuition and psychic awareness by one person or a group of friends. It concentrates on linking your own inner energies and those of the elements with that of the moon. It is not a dark ritual but a positive affirmation of our connection with the cycles of nature.

Drawing Down the Moon

There are many versions of this Goddess-focused ritual. It is practised to give you, whether man or woman, wisdom, heightened intuition and psychic power, and the ability to love and be loved. Some people see the moon symbolised as a specific ancient lunar goddess form. The most famous one, still central to modern Wicca, is Diana, Roman Goddess of the Moon, the Hunt and Fertility. Though, like her Greek counterpart, Artemis, she was worshipped originally as the maiden aspect of the moon, in time she also came to represent the full moon.

Sometimes the Triple Lunar Goddess of modern Wicca is represented by the classical deities: Diana (the Greek Artemis), Selene and Hecate (being maiden, mother and wise woman or crone).

Isis, the Egyptian goddess, was both Moon Goddess and Mother of the Sun. However you may prefer to tune into the light of the silver moon as a source of power.

To perform this ritual:

* Wait until it is dark and the moon is bright in the sky. If it is sufficiently warm, cast your circle with your willow wand, black-handled knife or crystal, in the open air, in a quiet place where you will not be disturbed.
* If you are visualising the circle, see a golden cord emanating from the sky and gradually, as you draw the line in the air with your crystal, making a golden cord that entirely encloses you. You may wish to invite a trusted friend or two, male or

female. It does not matter which, since both men and women can draw the feminine intuitive power of the moon.

* Consecrate the North, East, South and West compass points of the circle: the Earth and North by sprinkling salt or potpourri; the Air and East with an incense stick or oil burner, using a moon fragrance such as myrrh, jasmine or sandalwood; the Fire and South with a candle of silver, the colour of the moon. Finally, water steeped in rose or lavender should be sprinkled in the West for the Water element.

* Have at least one of the appropriate ritual tools in each quadrant: a pentacle or bell for Earth; a knife for Air; a wand, if possible made of willow, for the moon in the South; and a chalice, cup or deep dish filled with pure water in the West. You can improvise, if you do not have anything suitable, with a piece or object made of iron for the Earth; stainless steel for the East; brass for the South; and copper for the West.

* Hold each in turn as you pass clockwise round the circle, seeing the Earth power of old standing stones and tall trees; snow-capped mountains mingling with rushing wind, scudding clouds and the rumble of thunder. Add to them the brilliance of the lightning flash, the fierceness of the forest fire and cascading waterfalls, mighty waves breaking on the shore, whirlpools and rapids.

* When you have completed the circle, adding words as and if you wish, light a circle of nine silver candles with tiny moonstones in the centre.

* Look through the candlelight at the moon and see the moon grow larger and larger, closer and closer, until you are part of it and one with it. Become the moon and absorb her psychic power, her mysterious wisdom and her intuition.

* Then slowly see the silver light withdrawing and the moon moving further away until it is in its former position in the sky.

* Blow out the candles one by one, beginning with the candle in the most extreme North-Westerly position and ending with the candle in the North. See the silver light shimmering around those you love or who need it most. Do not forget your own needs.

* Finally, uncast your circle, beginning in the extreme North-West. Erase the marks, if they are made in chalk or earth, or see the shimmering golden protective cord coiling back into itself and finally disappearing into the cosmos.

18

Attracting Good Fortune

Find a focus for whatever it is you want to attract. In earlier times, men and women would take a lock of hair, a fingernail clipping or even the earth on which a would-be lover had trodden and use this as a focus for attracting love. Teenagers who have a poster of a singer or film star on the wall and kiss it are practising a form of sympathetic magic in the incredibly remote hope that the love object might suddenly materialise on the doorstep.

However, were they to use a photograph of a fellow student, or the guy or gal in the office, the positive vibes might well reach the desired target so that at the next meeting, both would be giving 'I'm here' signs from a deep unconscious and psychic level.

To perform a good fortune ritual:

* Be realistic in your target and specific as to the person, the amount of money and the source of the happiness you desire. If meeting the right person would make you happy, try to visualise the kind of person, usually someone with similar interests and aims that would survive the initial surge of 'falling in love'.
* Choose your focus. If you need a new home, use a picture of one from an estate agent that is similar or perhaps even of a house you would like, that is just beyond your current means. Don't overstretch your imagination. A luxury Hollywood mansion may be completely unrealistic within your current budget. Equally, rather than focusing on a million pounds, which is not absolutely vital to your happiness, settle on £3,000 to fix the roof. For weight loss or gain, find a photograph of someone who is not model girl skinny or with biceps like Mr

Universe but a toned-up version of the person you are now.

* Spend a few minutes holding your symbol and endowing it with images of yourself in the new situation (for example, arranging in your mind your present furniture and favourite items in your new house). Anticipate the excitement, happiness or contentment you will feel, as emotions are the most powerful transmitters of energies.

* Having prepared your circle, pass your symbol clockwise through the different elemental quadrants, touching it with ritual tools or salt for Earth, incense for Air, a candle flame for Fire and scented water or oils for Water, seeing the different elemental energies entering your focus.

* When you have passed round the circle once, begin a repetitive action to raise the power, so that it rises and increases in a cone of light as you. For example, you could stand in the centre of the circle, chanting faster and faster the name of the person, what it is you want, or a repetitive phrase such as 'Let [him/it] come to me', or 'Be mine', and finally shout out loud or in your mind, 'The wish is true' or 'The power is free'.

* You could move round the circle faster and faster in a simple stepping motion, holding the symbol or holding a helium balloon taut and letting it tug on the string until you eventually have to let go. You will soon find your own 'right way'.

Lucky Bottles

Bottles have always been used for both sympathetic and protective magic. I have a beautiful glass bottle covered with gold stars and filled with a golden oil. Such bottles were traditionally used to attract fertility, love or money.

Fertility Bottles

Whether for babies or bringing a project to fruition, a fertility bottle acts as a powerful focus for sympathetic magic. These bottles used to be filled with red wine and rosemary. After a wedding ceremony (in times when nuts as well as rice were thrown as fertility symbols), the bride would choose a number of hazel nuts and a number of walnuts (representing respectively the number of boy and girl children she wanted). The nuts would be placed in a bottle or flagon (sometimes one used for the wedding mead). This was sealed and placed under the threshold or in a wall the morning after the first night spent at home. This form of sympathetic magic was said to ensure that the bride would have the chosen number of children.

Do not bury your bottle but keep it in a high, safe place where it will not be disturbed. Use a sunflower oil or even a golden bath oil and in it place one nut for each step of a new project or the number of months you hope it will take for a dream to come true.

Money Bottles

Choose a wide-necked clear glass bottle and keep it in a place that is warmed by regular sunlight. Begin your money collection, if possible, with a coin you have found, as there is an old magical tenet that something found is worth ten times that which is given or bought.

Fill it with coins of any denomination or currency and when it is full to the brim seal it in order to attract money to you. Money jars or pots, containing copper coins, are sometimes found in farmhouse kitchens in the Mid-West of the US. The kitchen or your work space at home are best for money bottles.

Use:

* golden coloured coins to attract the power of the sun
* silver coins for the power of the moon
* copper-coloured coins for the power of Venus
* tin coins (can often be obtained from museum shops) for the power of Jupiter

On the eve of the summer solstice, place your bottle in the garden at sunset to catch the first rays of the sun at dawn the next day.

Love Bottles

Choose a bottle made from a gentle green or pink glass. In it, put:

* tiny green crystals such as jade or green glass nuggets
* nine small red or pink roses that are not yet opened
* a thick colourless oil (such as baby oil) to which nine drops of rose, geranium or lavender essential oil have been added

Do not fill the bottle but allow the roses to float gently and the crystals to settle at the bottom. Place the bottle in your bedroom out of bright sunlight but where the moonlight can filter through it. With each crescent moon take your bottle into the garden and visualise love coming to you or remaining with you and shake your bottle so that the crystals can float around. Fill it with a golden oil, such as wheatgerm or virgin olive oil, and add to it.

You can create also bottles for health, using pure spring water from a sacred well and adding clear quartz crystals. You should keep this, if possible, near an air vent or a window.

Banishing Magic

Banishing magic can be used to remove an old sorrow or regret, or to gain the strength to leave a destructive situation, or to neutralise the negative words and feelings of others. It may be tempting, especially if someone we love is being hurt, consciously to use awakening powers in a negative way; when we have been wronged there may be an urge simply to lash out on a paranormal plane as a gut reaction to earthly malice. But negative magic, no matter how worthy the cause or unworthy the target, often rebounds quite badly on the sender.

Janice, who lives in Surrey and is in her thirties, had become very clairvoyant and was using sympathetic magic regularly to focus her aims. However, she became so incensed by a problem at work that she tried to use banishing magic in a negative way. She explained:

> I desperately wanted an administrative job. It was well within my capabilities and I had deputised successfully many times for the previous employee. However, my boss was being difficult and insisted on appointing an outsider. He offered the job to Sarah who was less well qualified than I was and who on her first morning did not have a clue how to tackle the work. I became so angry as the day wore on that I visualised Sarah's desk surrounded by pentagrams and set fire to them.

Sarah did not return the next day and resigned without giving a reason. My triumph was tempered by a fear that my negative actions would rebound on me and I waited for something bad to happen. About a week later we were burgled, and burgled for a second time not long after. Strangely enough, no one ever settled in that job again.

The most effective defence against negative feelings and influences in any form of spiritual development is a positive attitude, a determination that you will only ever focus on necessary and worthwhile goals, and a strict avoidance of any form of divination or deliberate contact with the paranormal if you are feeling negative. If you have an argument, feel angry with someone (however justifiably) or just feel generally negative, it is advisable to sort out matters on the earthly plane and divert any bad feelings into physical work or activity. Banishing rituals should *only* ever be carried out with the positive aim of removing dark feelings, rather than attacking a person or institution.

In the earlier section on Protective Rituals (see p. 27), I suggested ways of enclosing yourself in a psychic energy field to keep out harmful influences. You cannot and should not interfere with other people's thought processes but you can deter gossips and those who are actively hostile from turning their attentions to you.

Fighting Ill-Wishers

Every time someone who is habitually unpleasant approaches you, visualise him or her wrapped in a soft pink mist or a lovely warm pink blanket. In your mind's eye, turn the person very gently in another direction.

In the outer world, keep a small mirror or reflective surface, such as a pair of glasses, and shine it away from you, towards a door or towards another area of the office or building. You will find that the person concerned will veer away. The more confident you get, the further away you can begin diverting the person.

Alison, a young writer in her first job, was the target of two older women in the newspaper office where she worked who delighted in coming over to her desk, pointing out her mistakes and deliberately flustering her. Things got so bad that she would become flustered as soon as she saw them approaching, which only encouraged them. She decided to try visualising them wrapped together in a soft pink blanket which she lifted and placed in the far corner of the open-plan office next to the coffee machine. She took to keeping on her desk, ostensibly as a paperweight, a clear crystal quartz with a sharp point which she pointed away from her desk. To her amazement, she found that the office harpies would approach, stop, look puzzled and turn completely around and go over to the coffee machine. Their intake of coffee increased directly in proportion to Alison's new-found confidence.

Protective Magic

In Chapter 2, I mentioned crystals traditionally endowed with protective powers. These included black agate, amethyst, blood-stone, carnelian, garnet, black and red jasper, lapis lazuli, tiger's eye, topaz and turquoise. You can also use a cloudy crystal quartz to absorb negative energies.

Protection at Home

In many ancient societies each home had its protective spirits that were given offerings at the family hearth in return for their watchfulness. In Rome, Vesta was the state Goddess of Fire and also of the domestic hearth. Just as the Vestal Virgins guarded her sacred fire, so the domestic fire was the province of the unmarried daughters.

You can light a single pillar candle of red or gold in a deep pottery holder to symbolise the hearth, if you have no fireplace in which to ignite a small protective flame. Although the vestal flame was perpetually burning, you can use a large quartz crystal to represent this and light your vestal candle (which should never have been used before) or fire at times when you feel in need of protection, or at the same time each week for a few hours. Place the crystal and candle in an iron holder or basket in your living room where a hearth would stand.

Another Roman protective deity was Terminus, God of the Boundary Stone, property and peace among neighbours. In other places, griffins and lions were placed on either side of the gates of a large house as guardians. In Ancient China, stone lions outside official buildings were believed to repel all hostile forces.

Protective Artefacts

You can endow any object with protective powers and make it a guardian of your home or work space. However small your apartment or house, you could have a pair of carved creatures guarding either side of the entrance or just inside the front door. You could even have matching wooden or onyx animal book ends on your desk in the office to serve as guardians.

Place under each animal a small protective crystal that you have passed through an oil burner for the four elements. The burner itself represents Earth; the fragrance Air; the heating candle Fire; and the oil Water. Alternatively, you could sprinkle the crystal with salt, pass it through the smoke from an incense stick, then through a candle flame and finally sprinkle it with pure water.

You can do the same with your guardians. As you do so, visualise strong stone walls from the earth, powerful winds, fierce flames and rushing torrents of water providing a barrier between your home and all negative influences.

Making a Protective Kitchen Shrine

The god of the kitchen is still a feature in Oriental homes. And the kitchen still serves as a focus for the natural protective energies that were in earlier times believed to reside in natural foods symbolising Mother Earth.

To make a kitchen shrine:

* Near your stove, place a protective domestic symbol such as a china thimble, a corn dolly or knot (a symbol of domestic happiness, traditionally made from the last sheaf of corn to be cut at Lammas, 31 July–1/2 August), a tiny china teapot or house, and a pot or two of protective herbs such as basil (which also keeps flies away), clover, heather, peppermint, sage and vervain, or a dish of spice such as cinnamon.
* Light a small night light in a pottery dish just before you begin cooking.
* When you have cooked your evening meal, place a tiny quantity in a small covered container, or a few raw ingredients (such as raisins or a spoonful of honey) in a shallow dish as an offering near your night light.

* If this seems wasteful drop a small coin in a dish each time you cook a main meal and, when it is full, give the money to a charity.

Gradually your kitchen shrine will accumulate happy positive domestic vibrations.

Finally, place a protective crystal under the doormat at the kitchen door to the garden, if you have one, and at the front door or any external door to absorb any negative energies brought in from the outside world.

Witch Bottles

Like the bottles in fairy stories that capture a harmful spirit or genie, witch bottles are a traditional form of protection against negative influences, although they are symbols of positive power rather than having any connection with spirits or ghosts. They are often found in the walls of old houses, where they were placed during the building as a protective barrier against malevolent influences, both earthly and otherworldly. Witch bottles were large dark glass containers, with sharp metal objects inside, such as nails and pins.

Stoneware bottles were also used. You can often obtain a cider flagon or buy an old glazed flagon with a stopper from an antique stall. These are called Bellarmine jars and used to be found in East Anglia in the UK and throughout Germany and Holland.

Witch bottles are easily made, although it is preferable to add red wine and dried rosemary rather than following the ancient practice of urinating in the bottle.

Any glass jar or bottle will suffice. If you can find one of dark red or green, so much the better. Old glass bottles can be bought at antique markets if you want to follow the old ways.

To make it into a witch bottle:

* Fill with a dark liquid.
* Into the liquid drop iron nails and screws, some bent into the shape of lucky horseshoes.
* Add a pinch of sea salt for protection and cork your bottle firmly or screw the lid tightly.
* Seal with red wax.

* Originally the witch bottles, like fertility bottles, would be buried under the doorstep or outside the threshold when a new family moved into a house or a major change, such as the birth of the first child, occurred.
* If you do not want to undertake major excavations, bury it deep in a sealed container in a flower bed near the front of your house or, if you have a doorstep sunk into the earth, place it under that.
* Otherwise, store it as near to the front of the house as you can, perhaps in the front eaves of an attic. In an apartment you could erect a very high shelf near the entrance.

Shadow Magic

Children often fear shadows, although they may enjoy making rabbits against the wall by torchlight at night. However you can use shadow magic as a protective device.

In myth, witches would call upon stone lions, bats and owls to go forth and hunt their enemies on full moon nights and then shadows would loom large against the golden orb. Such an incantation of vengeance would be counter-productive, even if it were possible, but the huge shadows cast by even quite small models of animals, birds or statues, such as Shakti, the benevolent aspect of the Hindu Mother Goddess, can offer watchfulness through the night.

I use a pottery cat. (Cats were sacred to the Egyptian goddess Bast around 3000 BC. She was the special protectress of pregnant women and mothers.)

I have had many bad experiences in my attic bedroom of a woman with long hair, whose face I cannot see, who sits spinning. She seems quite malevolent and I think is a projection of my own fears and doubts, which can be as terrifying as external threats. I light candles on my dressing table, where the cat sits at an angle so that her shadow looms large on the wall, and ask the cat to protect my boundaries.

As you leave your home each morning, draw a protective circle of light around it to protect it from harm and intrusion. I have heard of two women in Florida who are convinced that such protective incantations shielded their homes from the effects of a major hurricane when others around were damaged.

19

Salt Magic

Salt rituals are among the oldest forms of magic and can be used not only for psychic protection but in money-making visualisation and in healing. Salt has always been central to religious and magical practices because it was the one absolutely pure substance. It was regarded as precious because it was the main means of preserving food through the long winter months for early settlers around the globe. The Westernised name comes from Salus, Roman Goddess of Health, whom the Greeks called Hygeia.

The Greeks and Romans mixed salt with their sacrificial cakes and threw salt on sacrificial fires. Salt was also used in ceremonies of sacrifice by the Jews. In Christian belief, salt and water were considered potent in restoring health and in exorcism.

Because of its preservative quality, salt became a religious symbol of purity and incorruptibility. In earlier times salt was placed in coffins as protection against the Devil. In lands populated by the Celts a plate holding a pinch of salt and a pinch of earth was laid upon the breast of the newly deceased to represent the mortal, corruptible body and the immortal, incorruptible soul.

Salt was also used with holy water to ward off evil and increase physical strength as well as fertility. It is still used in the preparation of holy water. Medieval alchemists regarded salt as one of the three major essences that made up life, together with mercury (quicksilver) and sulphur.

When brewing mash for animals, a handful of salt was sprinkled on top to keep witches from poisoning the food. Salt was also used as an early antiseptic. In honour of Salus, nursemaids would put a pinch of salt into the mouths of newborn infants and salt was put into the first pail of milk from a cow which had just calved.

Salt Rituals

You can use ordinary table salt but sea salt is more traditional. Keep your ritual salt separate, in a small, wide-necked glass jar with a lid or stopper, and have a tiny deep dish made of silver or unglazed pottery for your rituals.

In magic, salt traditionally represents the Earth element and so has a powerful earthing energy. Ancient rituals blessed salt in the name of the prevalent deity. Some modern practitioners find it alien, when asking blessings, to use the traditional names of pagan goddesses, such as Brigid; Triple Goddess; Maiden, Mother and Crone of the Celts; Diana of the Classical tradition; or Isis, Mother Goddess of the Ancient Egyptians. You may wish to use terms like 'Goddess Mother', 'Father God', 'Mother/Father God' or 'Power of Light, Love and Goodness'. You may find it easier to visualise a golden light around your salt, rather than using specific names, as you ask for blessing.

Alternatively, leave your jar in the sunlight and moonlight for twenty-four hours, on a window ledge, surrounded by small white clear quartz crystals. When you wish to use the salt, take a small quantity from your jar, using a silver spoon or pottery spoon, and place it in your special dish.

Raise your dish in both hands and, facing North, turn your body clockwise through the four compass points. As you face each direction, say something like: 'May there be blessings on this element of salt as I use it for positive action. May all dark thoughts and intents, my own or those of others, dissipate and be replaced by only good intentions, light and love.'

Protective Rituals Using Salt

In magic, salt was traditionally scattered around thresholds and in protective circles against all evil influences. Spilled salt would be cast over the left shoulder into the 'eye of the Devil' or evil spirits, who were believed from Roman times onwards to lurk on the left or 'sinister' side. The belief in spilling salt came from the idea that accidentally tipping such a sacred substance would invite retribution. In Leonardo da Vinci's painting *The Last Supper*, the upturned salt cellar reflects the belief that such an action represented a breaking of trust and friendship.

Modern ritual no longer concentrates on casting out demons or dark spirits, our ancestors' explanation for human malice and negativity. However, we are all aware that our own negative feelings can at times cast a dark shadow over our homes, or that others may feel hostility towards us, and that these bad feelings can be released either intentionally or unintentionally.

A Simple Domestic Salt Ritual

This can be used either for a particular room or for a whole apartment or house. Mix a few pinches of ritual sea salt with pure spring water in your special dish. You can buy a sparkling bottled water, or purify some tap water by placing it in a clear glass container in sunlight and moonlight for twenty-four hours.

Sprinkle a few drops of salt water in the four corners of the room and place a small outward-facing mirror or hang a clear quartz crystal at each window to reflect back negative feelings from outside. If you want to protect the whole house, mix a larger quantity of salt water in a larger metal or unglazed pottery bowl. Place the large container of salt water in the room which you feel symbolises the 'heart' of the house – this may be the kitchen, the lounge or perhaps the dining room – and leave it for 12 hours.

A More Complex Salt Ritual for Protection

If you feel a room is especially dark or gloomy, or you have inexplicable night terrors, place a small quantity of sea salt or a coarse-grained salt in a small dish on a table in the centre of the room. Because salt represents the Earth element it grounds your room in calm, benign influences. Pass over the dish a lighted incense stick or oil burner, with a protective fragrance such as lemon or peppermint, to allow the Air element to blow away negativity.

Pass a lighted candle of protective pink or purple over the salt for the Fire element, seeing the light spreading outward in spirals. Blow out the candle, sending the light to every corner of the room. Finally, sprinkle a few drops of rose water, or a few drops of any floral oil such as geranium or jasmine, for the Water element, and let the healing waters restore love and harmony to the room. Leave tiny drawstring bags of salt or twists of salt in silver foil in each corner for a few days and you will feel the atmosphere lighten.

Salt and Money Rituals

Because salt was so highly prized in Ancient Rome, imperial soldiers were sometimes paid in salt – hence the expression 'worth his salt'. Salt was traditionally traded for treasures and the Celts would barter their salt for rich artefacts for their burial mounds. Salt became associated with material prosperity and thus forms a focus for spells for necessary material possessions.

However, money rituals of any kind rarely work if the practitioner has only a vague desire for money or unrealistic expectations. Magic works on needs. The ritual is only the first part and those dreamy souls who practise magic, and then wait for pennies to fall from heaven, rapidly become disillusioned.

A Salt Ritual for Prosperity

Carry out this ritual when the crescent moon is first visible.

* Form a heap of salt on a table in a cone shape – 4 or 5 tablespoons will suffice.
* Ring it with small shiny coins of your local currency, beginning at the 12 o'clock position and moving clockwise until you have completed the circle. Make sure each coin touches the one on either side so that the circle is unbroken.
* Light golden candles outside the coins at the four compass points and visualise the cone of salt being transformed into a heap of shining golden coins, rising higher and wider until it spills over the floor and covers it.
* Leaving the coins in a circle, spoon or scoop the salt into a clear glass container without a top.
* Let the candles burn away naturally and, when they have gone out, remove your coins from the circle anti-clockwise, beginning at the 12 o'clock position so that the first coin you placed is the last to be removed. Put them in an uncovered box.
* Position both the glass container and the box on a window ledge and keep them uncovered for the intervening days and nights until the full moon first appears in the sky.
* When you wake the next morning, dissolve the salt in water in the glass container and pour it away, seeing your money-making plans flowing forward. Spend the coins on a present for someone or a small item to improve the home.
* Spend the rest of the month, until the next crescent moon,

putting your plans into practice. If necessary, repeat the ritual and keep the impetus in the real world going throughout the next month. If your plans are long-term you may need to carry out the ritual for several months. You will find that, if you persist, your efforts in the real world will bear fruit.

Salt and Health

In Rome, rings dedicated to Salus were worn as a talisman against ill-health. The ring was engraved with a five-pointed star surrounded by a coiled serpent, a symbol of healing.

Salt baths, highly valued for their restorative properties by our ancestors, can cleanse the skin and help with aches and pains, fluid retention, tiredness, arthritis, muscle strain, stiffness and the fatigue that occurs after influenza. Sea salt (½–1 cup), added to your bath water, brings physical relief and relaxation. Soak in the mixture for twenty minutes. Rinse your skin with fresh water afterwards and you will feel both refreshed and relaxed.

The psychic and spiritual effects of salt baths are no less potent. Home-made bath salts are gentler on the skin than commercial ones and can provide, both in their making and usage, a powerful focus for magical energies. As you mix your bath salts, you can endow them with your dreams, psychic insights and the focus of your desires.

A basic bath salt is very easy to make and you can add colours and fragrances to empower them for love, heightened psychic awareness or harmony.

There are two basic recipes that are equally effective. The first offers harmony and the integration of the unconscious and

The talisman of healing

conscious worlds; while you create the mixture, your unconscious mind surfaces, as your hands move mechanically, stirring and pouring. This channel offers access not only to your own inner wisdom but also to the unconscious wisdom of mankind in all times and places, past, present and perhaps future.

To use one of these bath salts:

* Wear something soft and flowing so that you can slip easily into your bath. Take your time stirring the ingredients, lighting a pink or purple candle, and burning a relaxing fragrance such as lavender or white musk. You may find that you enter a half-dream state.
* Use a smooth wooden bowl made from one of the magical trees – oak, hazel or rowan – and either a wooden spoon or a pestle. Do not consciously think of any special questions but see light pouring from around and within you into the salts, enriching and at the same time integrating all the different strands of your being.
* Fill the bath, letting the sound of the water carry you further from the real world. Light gentle pastel candles around the bathroom.
* Mix the salts into the water with your hands, then lie in the infused water. You may move backwards in time or see other realms in your mind's eye, either as complete pictures or flashes of colour and scents of trees and flowers growing in far-off places.
* You may wish to place a favourite crystal, a rose quartz or amethyst, in the water.
* Let the water cool naturally, rinse your body under a warm shower and wrap yourself warmly in a towelling robe.
* Blow out the candles, sending light to any who need it.

A Basic Spiritual Harmony/ Psychic Awareness Bath Essence

Mix together:

    1 tablespoon bicarbonate of soda
    5 drops essential oil such as lavender
    juice of 1 lemon or a few drops of lemon essential oil
    1 teaspoon carrier oil such as sweet almond or wheatgerm
    110 g (4 oz) or ½ cup of sea salt

Bath Salts for Love, Reconciliation, Psychic Dreams and Success

By varying the colour and fragrance of bath salts, you can endow them with particular energies. You may wish to make up a large quantity of the basic salts and then add colour and oils as you need them. However the mixing is such a potent time that it is best to do it just before your bath in order to endow the salt with the particular focus.

The basic ingredients are sea salt or table salt, baking powder (bicarbonate of soda) and Epsom salts (magnesium sulphate), all of which can be bought from a chemist or supermarket.

You should use:

> 3 parts Epsom salts
> 2 parts baking soda
> 1 part sea salt or table salt

For an average bath tub, 1 1/2 tablespoons, 1 tablespoon and 1/2 tablespoon of each should be sufficient. Test with your hands to make sure that the water feels soft and not abrasive. Mix together to form a base for your fragrant salts. As you do so, see brilliant white light endowing the mixture with pure energy and spirituality.

Use a natural food colouring, mixing it in with a wooden spoon, drop by drop, until you have the right colour, seeing a shaft of the appropriate coloured light, carrying whatever strengths you need. The salts should be slightly moist. As you see the colour entering the salts, visualise whatever is your current need and desire. Let the vision become more brightly coloured:

Pink is for tranquillity, friendship and reconciliation.

Purple is for psychic insight and psychic dreams.

Blue is for learning and professional success.

Green is for love, emotions and children.

Yellow is for learning and communication on all planes.

Orange is for health and individuality.

Red is for passion and issues of survival.

Oils for Happiness

Finally, add the essential oils, drop by drop, and mix with a spoon until all the ingredients are moist. Do not use more than 10 drops oil to 1/2 cup bath salts. Many people find that 6 drops is enough but be guided by your own instincts. Below I have suggested three mixtures and have listed some essential oils that are good mixers, safe and associated with various energies. If you are pregnant or in poor health, you should always check with a doctor, chemist or registered homeopath before using any unfamiliar product. As a rule, do not use more than three essential oils (four maximum if they are all the same kind, e.g. floral). Experiment to find the best mixers. Do not use them directly on your skin, with the exception of lavender, and then only in moderation. Do not use metal bowls for mixing essential oils.

A bath for psychic protection might include:

> 3 drops sandalwood
> 2 drops pine
> 1 drop lavender

A bath for increased psychic awareness might include:

> 3 drops lavender
> 2 drops peppermint
> 1 drop lemon

A bath for love might include:

> 3 drops rose or rose geranium
> 2 drops ylang ylang
> 1 drop neroli

Choose one of the oils only for the bath, depending on your needs. Follow any instructions on the label:

For healing: use 5 drops of either eucalyptus, lavender, rosemary (not in pregnancy), sandalwood or tea tree.

For learning: use 5 drops of either bergamot, lemon (use in moderation and store in a cool, dark place), lemongrass, peppermint (do not use immediately before sleep) or white thyme (use in moderation and not in pregnancy).

For love: use 5–6 drops of either jasmine, neroli, rose, rose geranium or ylang ylang.

For psychic dreams and insights: use 5–6 drops of either jasmine, lavender, rose or neroli.

For success: use 5 drops of either camomile, frankincense, orange or patchouli.

Section Six

Magic Alphabets and Charms

20

Runic Writing

Rune means 'secret' or 'hidden', from the ancient Northern European word *ru*. Runes were angular markings made by the Germanic peoples (the English, German and Scandinavian tribes who shared a common heritage and language which gradually split into different dialects). These marks, made on stone, metal and wood, were used on inscriptions, monuments and for magical divinatory purposes.

The runic symbols were more than just an alphabet. Each symbolised a whole concept, much like a Tarot card. The first pre-runic symbols, which formed the basis for later runes, were very simple and date from the Bronze Age and early Iron Age. The runic systems that remain today date from the second or third centuries BC, when the Germanic peoples came into contact with the alphabet of the Etruscans who traded across Europe as far as the Baltic.

Magical alphabets, such as the runes, derive their power partly from their secrecy (that which is not named in the common tongue). Each rune also has a meaning hidden in itself, a power that has been lost in modern scripts. For example, A is a sound or letter which has no symbolism in itself, whereas its runic equivalent *Aesc* means the ash tree, a symbol of strength, endurance and wisdom:

Therefore every time you write your name or a wish in runic letters, you are adding the potency of each letter meaning, not in a frightening way but as a focus for your own power.

I have listed the meaning of the symbol by each letter so that you can see how what you write can focus different energies. For example, you might use a fire rune, such as Nyd, which is N, or the protective rune sound NG/Ing whose symbol appeared on houses throughout Europe and Scandinavia until the sixteenth century, and even later in country places.

Because modern scripts came relatively late to the runic world, there are disagreements over correspondences. Indeed, every book you read offers a slightly different version. I have used a middle-of-the-road system, based on the Anglo-Saxon runes, as this gives a greater variety of letters.

The runic alphabet

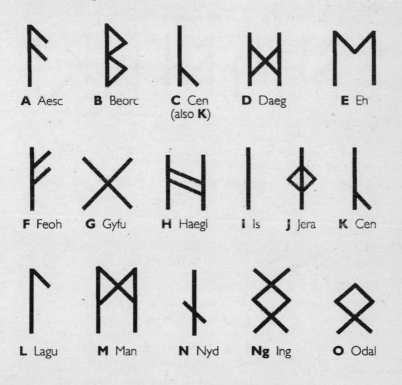

A Aesc   **B** Beorc   **C** Cen   **D** Daeg   **E** Eh
                           (also **K**)

F Feoh   **G** Gyfu   **H** Haegl   **I** Is   **J** Jera   **K** Cen

L Lagu   **M** Man   **N** Nyd   **Ng** Ing   **O** Odal

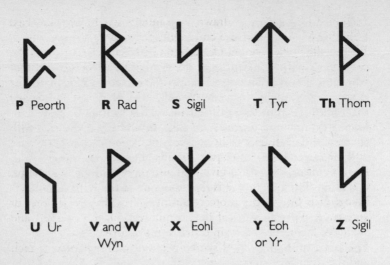

P Peorth	**R** Rad	**S** Sigil	**T** Tyr	**Th** Thom

U Ur	**V** and **W** Wyn	**X** Eohl	**Y** Eoh or Yr	**Z** Sigil

For example, my name, Cassandra, would be spelled:

Practise writing your name and simple messages. Because the system isn't sufficiently complex to match English spellings with all their variations you may compromise. What matters is the essence of the message. A simple message, scratched with feeling on a pebble and cast into the turning tide, needs no spell-check.

Aesc A is the ash tree, symbol of strength, endurance and wisdom, for the world tree Yggdrasil (which supported the nine worlds of Norse cosmology) was made of ash.

Beorc B is the birch, symbol of the Mother Goddess. Because of its association with the birch trees that covered Norway after the last Ice Age, it represents rebirth and new beginnings.

Cen C and **Ch K** is the torch, one of the fire runes, that was used to light the dark halls of the Vikings during the long winter nights. So it has come to represent the inner voice and flame.

Daeg D is the dawn, the awakening and enlightenment, the light at the end of the tunnel, and is named after Daeg (son of Nott, Goddess of Night), whose radiance was so dazzling that the gods fashioned him a chariot drawn by a pure white horse, Skin-Faxi ('Shining Mane'), who also emanated sparkling light.

Eh E is the horse, symbol of harmony between rider and man. So beloved were warriors' horses that they were given elaborate burials when they died. Odin the Viking Father God (Woden to the Anglo-Saxons) had an eight-legged steed, Sleipnir, who had magical runes engraved on his teeth.

Feoh F represented the cattle that the travelling peoples took with them on their conquests, and so this rune came to represent wealth and the price that must be paid for any choice.

Gyfu G means the gift or giving. It also represented relationships, especially sexual ones, and is therefore one of the fertility runes.

Haegl H is one of the protective runes. This was the mother or core rune, representative of the cosmic seed or grain of life, and stood for facing hardships in order to move forward.

Is I is the rune of ice, and symbolises waiting for the ice to melt and the right moment to come.

Jera or **Ger J** is the harvest, one of the fertility runes, and stands for the natural progression of life which must be followed and the effort that must be made to reap rewards.

Lagu L, the lake or waters, is the rune of emotions and intuition.

Man M is the rune of human life and mortality and speaks of realism and the need to fulfil one's own destiny.

Ing makes the sound 'ng' on the end of a word. Ing was the old fertility god who died each autumn to be reborn the next year. Ing was also deity of household protection.

Nyd N is another fire rune and comes from the old nyd fires that were kindled by rubbing wood together and used to light the festival fires. It represents needs that must be met from within ourselves rather than by looking to others.

Odal O is the homestead, which was very precious to wandering peoples. It is used to represent all domestic issues and is a protective rune of the home.

Peorth P, the rune or lot cup, was used for gambling and divination for they were one and the same. The fall of the runes from the lot cup could express the will of the gods and foretell the outcome of every venture. This rune therefore represents fate, in the sense that we all have a unique destiny to fulfil, and so is the essential self.

Rad R is the wheel – the turning sun wheel, the wheel on the chariot of the old fertility god Ing, or the wheel on wagons travelling to distant lands. It stands for change and action.

Sigil S and **Z** is the rune of the sun and represents energy, light and limitless possibility.

Tyr T is the star, the spirit warrior, the god of war who sacrificed his sword arm to save the other gods. His letter therefore represents altruism and sacrifice for a long-term goal.

Thorn, which makes the sound 'th' or 'the', is a rune of strength and protection. It is the mighty hammer of Thor, the God of Thunder, and so represents might in the defence of others.

Ur U was the aurochs, the mighty horned cattle that roamed the plains of Northern Europe until the early seventeenth century. Vikings wore the horns on their helmets in order to transfer the power of the aurochs to themselves. This rune letter therefore represents primal strength and survival.

Wyn V and **W** is the rune of pure joy and happiness, not through others but through the achievement of one's dreams and unique life path.

Eohl X is the eel grass that was harsh to the touch but provided shelter, bedding and food for animals and so was of use once the initial pain was over. It has come to represent the need to grasp the nettle and show courage in a crisis, which will then lead to better things.

Yr or **Eoh Y** is the yew tree, the tree of endings, and therefore represents the need to move on to the next stage in life or a relationship.

21

Hieroglyphics

Possibly the most beautiful form of magic writing is the hiero-glyphics used by the Ancient Egyptians. The script was, the Egyptians believed, given to them by the lunar god Thoth, master of languages and writing. His control over the hieroglyphs and divine words increased his magical energies. Indeed, hieroglyphic writing was considered so important that it was used only by the elite. The hieroglyphs were used to record the deeds of kings and to inscribe magic spells on the tombs of the great in order that they might safely reach the after-life. The words themselves were considered to have great power and were inscribed on amulets which were sold to the ordinary people.

Because only an elite learned this intricate script, it eventually died out and the secrets of the 'sacred writing', as the Greeks called it, were not rediscovered until the last century.

There are three types of hieroglyphics:

* Those that represent a sound, like the letters of our own alphabet. For example, ⌇ , a snake, is equivalent to our 'J' sound, as in 'John' or 'edge'. However, one complication is that the Egyptian scribes used very few vowels. So the sentence: 'Polly put the kettle on' would be rendered as 'Plly pt th kttl n'; rather like the speedwriting form of shorthand.

* Those that represent the sound or meaning of the word. For example, *nefer* ☥ , which looks like a primitive guitar, means 'beautiful'. But it can also be used as part of another word to represent the three consonants 'n', 'f' and 'r'. Jennifer

could thus be written ⟍⟋ᛞ (Jnfr).

* Finally, there are the 'determinatives' which tell the reader what sort of word the symbols represent. For example, the symbols 𓀀, 'a man', or 𓁐, 'kneeling woman', might be added to the end of a name to indicate the sex of the person named.

   ⊙, which means both 'sun' and 'day', can also be tacked on to a word (but not pronounced) to give the sense of time.

Ancient Egyptian hieroglyphics are very complicated. There are more than 700 of them, and it would take a far larger and more scholarly book than this to begin to explain their intricacies. But, thanks to the efforts of many scholars over the years, it is possible to write wishes and intentions in a form of hieroglyphic writing, using the table on p. 233, that corresponds to the original, although inevitably much simplified.

The Magic of Names

For the Ancient Egyptians, a man or woman lived as long as his or her name was written or spoken. For example, when Queen Hatshepsut died in 1470 BC, her stepson, as an act of vengeance, had her name chiselled off all her temples. Thereafter she effectively disappeared from history. In Egyptian tradition, writing your name in hieroglyphics was therefore an act of asserting your power and worth.

My name, Cassandra, can be written: KASSANDRA

Hieroglyphs could be written from either right to left or left to right. The rule is that you read into the face of the animal or objects depicted. So my name might be inscribed by a mason as:

Usually names were enclosed in a frame which we call a cartouche.

They could also be written vertically:

Cartouches

Using the alphabet provided, try writing your own name, remembering to leave out the vowels. Mark thus becomes Mrk and Helen, Hln. For C, as in Celia, use an S. An X can be represented by a KS. And F can be used instead of V.

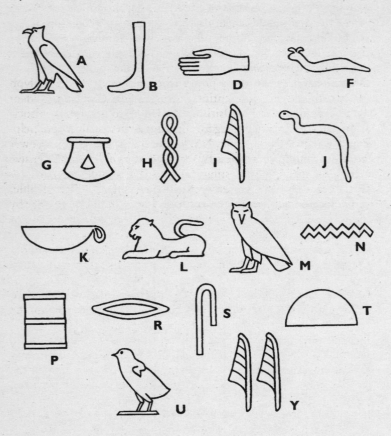

The hieroglyphic alphabet

Once you are happy with your name, try writing a wish or an intention. You may decide to write it first in English, omitting the vowels, until you become more practised. Unlike the runic alphabet, each letter is not necessarily a word of power by itself.

However, because hieroglyphics were considered magical and each letter does have an associated object or animal, you can, if you wish, create your own associations. I have suggested a few, based on Ancient Egyptian ideas. While most of the alphabet letters are not strictly power words, making associations may help to strengthen their potency for you.

A is the vulture, a power word representing the protective power of Isis the divine mother, in death as well as life. Therefore it is a symbol of protection from a powerful external force.

B is the leg. Not a power word, but you could associate it with swiftness of purpose.

D is the hand. Again not a power word, although the hieroglyph for two fingers is, representing Horus, a Sun God and God of Time, helping his father Osiris up the ladder to heaven. By association you could therefore regard the hand as an instrument of help.

F and **V** represent the viper. Unlike the snake, this is not a power word but could nevertheless be regarded as swift, sharp, defensive action, for the viper only stings humans if it is under attack.

G, the stand, is not a power word either. A different hieroglyphic, the pillow, had the sacred power meaning of uplifting and so, by indirect association, the stand could be interpreted as lifting up or supporting someone in time of need.

H, the rope, is not a power word, but vaguely resembles the amulet for the ladder and so could be regarded in the rising up rather than binding aspect.

I and **Y**, the single and double reeds respectively, were used to make papyrus for recording wisdom and so could perhaps be regarded as a symbol of knowledge and learning.

J is the serpent. Isis was regarded as the Snake Goddess and a serpent's head amulet was placed on dead bodies to prevent snakebite in the after-life. A serpent rod was also used to open the mouth to free the soul. So again, by association, the serpent is a symbol of freedom.

K or hard **C**, as in cat, is the basket. Not a power word but it could mean sustenance or gift. The alternative, the stair, could be a symbol of ambition or the desire for elevation or advancement in the worldly sense.

L, the lion, has for the modern world such an association with courage and nobility that this would be an obvious meaning. Plutarch reports that the lion was worshipped by the Egyptians who decorated their doorways with open lion mouths, as guardians to represent the rising of the Nile (because the river began to rise when the sun was in Leo).

M, the owl, has traditionally been associated with wisdom, but it is also a bird of warning, so the meaning might be to listen to your own inner warnings and wisdom.

N, water, is associated with the life-giving fertility of the Nile and so could legitimately be regarded as fertility.

P, the stool, could be seen as a respite, a resting place, and so might suggest temporary sanctuary.

Q is the hill, which could suggest a higher or different viewpoint.

R, the mouth, was vital after death so that the deceased person might utter the words of power that would enable him or her to gain entry to the next world (the ceremony of opening the mouth symbolically was therefore very important after death). Thus the mouth could represent the power to communicate clearly.

S or soft **C**, as in Celia, was the first letter of the word *seneb*, which means 'health' and was often used on its own in inscriptions to stand for the whole world.

T, loaf, regarded in all ancient societies as the staff of life, could represent the fulfilment of basic needs.

W, the chick, a symbol of young life, could be seen as innocence, enthusiasm and new beginnings.

22

*Talismans
And Amulets*

Most of us have a good luck charm – it might be a lucky penny or a favourite item of clothing. Martin Bell, the BBC television reporter, revealed that he would never go into a war zone without his 'lucky' white suit and green socks. And the late Lord Harvey of Prestbury, formerly Conservative MP for Macclesfield, always carried a wishbone wrapped in red, white and blue ribbons on polling day. 'I can't say if it worked but I increased my majority eight times,' he said.

The charm might not even be an object. In *Once There Was a War*, John Steinbeck writes of an English bomber squadron that had a goat as its mascot and came to believe in it as their good luck charm. When the squadron had to change its base quickly and left the goat behind, the men insisted that a special transport plane be sent to bring back its 'luck'.

When people talk about talismans they often mean amulets. An amulet is anything carried as a charm against illness or witchcraft. But a talisman can also be engraved with magical symbols or words, and it attracts good fortune as well as averting bad luck.

Coins were traditionally believed to be lucky because they were originally engraved with the image of a god, and then royalty who were supposed to have magical powers. The magic works because, the more you wear your lucky charm and good luck follows (partly because you feel more confident), the more the powers of success are concentrated in the symbol.

Brian Slade, President of the Isle of Sheppey Archaeological Society, described how a coin was used in a healing miracle:

The year was 1485 and a very young girl was playing in front of the gatehouse leading to Minster Abbey on the Isle of Sheppey, Kent. A heavily laden cart approached the gate. Its wheels were heavy, thick, solid oak, banded with iron, with sharpened metal spokes protruding to get a grip on the muddy ground. The little girl slipped and fell under one of the wheels. The Latin document recording the incident described her as being '*quastum in modum fere placentre planum*', squashed nigh 'as flat as a pancake', possibly the earliest reference in literature to this saying. It appeared that she was indeed dead.

The villagers gathered around the child's body and began to pray for her soul. Some, it is stated, prayed that she might be brought back to life by a miracle, but none happened.

At the time it was believed that, if a sick or injured person could be touched by royalty, he or she would recover. However, there was no royal personage at Minster who might touch the child. One of the women praying suddenly recalled that the image of royalty was in her purse. She took out a very thin silver penny with the image of Henry VI on it. She chose this king because he had been a very holy king – one who, it is documented, would have preferred to have been a monk or priest. He had died fourteen years earlier and miracles had been performed at his tomb.

Bending down, the woman touched the girl's body with the King Henry VI coin, hoping that the image might have the same healing power as the king it represented. Suddenly the child moved a little, moaned and recovered, as if by magic. What is even more miraculous, the child spoke, it is said for the first time in her life, for she had been dumb from birth. The name of the woman was Anne Plott, daughter of Thomas Plott. The 1485 report describes how the woman, after touching the girl's body with the coin, bent it (the coin, unlike modern ones, was of wafer-thin silver), so that it might never be spent on an unholy purpose.

One of the most common forms of amulet worn by modern women is the charm bracelet (although this item has dropped out of fashion). Does it bring good luck? It certainly did in 1934 for Charles B. Darrow, who invented a board game and used the charms from his wife's bracelet as pieces in the prototype. The game was Monopoly, the world's biggest-selling copyrighted game. It proved such a hit that the charms – the iron, the dog and the top hat – were never changed. However, a special edition has been brought out in which the charms have been replaced with *Star Wars* characters. Will this break the charm of the game?

Certain things have universal good luck meanings, such as the rabbit's foot, four-leaf clover and horseshoe. In olden times, country folk would fill a little red bag with a pinch of salt, a piece of cloth, a tiny lump of coal, a silver heart or silk cut into the shape of a heart, a silver sixpence and a piece of bread. The bag would be sewn up in red thread or tied with a red drawstring thread and these words chanted nine times:

> *This bag I sew [or carry] for me*
> *And also for my family,*
> *Let it keep through every day,*
> *Trouble, ills and strife away,*
> *Flags, flax, food and Frey*

The last line referred to flagstones for a home, flax for clothing, food, and Frey was the old God of Fertility in northern parts. However, you can put almost anything in your lucky bag that has special significance for you. The tradition spanned many cultures – for example, the Native American Indian and African medicine bag. The medicine (which simply means healing) bundle held an assortment of objects with magical and healing powers and these bundles were possessed by all tribes. Some contained only a few objects while others could contain over a hundred, including charms, herbs, hooves and feathers. The contents were often dictated by dreams and visions. The bundles would be opened before a special event or ritual as a symbol of the releasing of the power.

Medicine bags can also form a powerful focus for both attracting and banishing magic. They operate on the principle of sympathetic magic, by using a symbol of substance with the magical qualities of whatever you wish to attract.

Making Your Lucky Bag or Medicine Pouch

First find a small bag or pouch, made from any natural fabric. In it place about six objects that are talismans or amulets for you. They may be small treasures, such as charms that you have had from childhood, a little silver horseshoe from your wedding, a favourite crystal or stone you found on the beach on a specially happy holiday, a pressed flower given by a lover, or a small china animal of the kind that has seemed important to you.

If you have a stone, shell or crystal you might carve on it in one of the magical alphabets either your initials or a word of power, such as 'win', 'love' or 'success'.

If you have had a run of bad luck or just left an unhappy relationship, then make yourself a special good luck bag, with a small golden object for the power, energy and confidence of the sun; a silver charm or object for the intuitive wisdom of the moon; and a piece of copper or a copper coin for Venus, love and money. You could include a clear quartz crystal. These were regarded in earlier cultures as pure creative energy, and were called, in Japan and China, the essence of the dragon. Also add a small dark crystal such as a smoky quartz or obsidian (Apache Tear) for protection; and something living such as a pressed flower or a twig from a magical tree like hazel, hawthorn or rowan. In addition you may wish to choose something personal, perhaps from your childhood, that symbolises the essential you.

Mark your medicine bag or pouch with a personal symbol of power, either embroidered or written in gold or silver.

Natural Talismans

Lucky Heather

White heather rather than purple is considered the most lucky, perhaps because it is quite rare in the wild. It is said that, if a person comes upon white heather growing naturally, then he or she can pick it and any wish that is made will come true. Heather was associated with the Celts. In Celtic legend, when Oscar, son of Ossian (the renowned Irish bard and warrior hero of the third century), lay dying on the battlefield at Ulster, slain by Cairbar, he sent his true love Malvina a sprig of purple heather. As she heard the message of love carried by a faithful messenger, her tears fell on the flower, which turned pure white. Since that time white heather has represented eternal love.

Four-Leafed Clover or Shamrock

Clover is said to protect humans from fairy and witch spells and was traditionally worn in buttonholes. Clover under the pillow gives dreams of future lovers. The rarer four-leafed clover is especially lucky. In Sussex it is said: 'The first leaf is for fame, the second for wealth, the third a glorious lover and the fourth for health.'

A four-leafed clover is said to give its owner the ability to see fairies. One worn in the right shoe by a young unmarried woman on a journey was said to ensure that the first young man she met would become her husband.

Finding a four-leafed clover is said to bring good fortune very soon. Indeed, before you reach home, you should find a treasure. In Ireland finding a four-leafed shamrock is said to bring luck in gambling, racing and attracting the opposite sex. But you must always carry it with you and never show it to another person.

Making Talismans

Natural talismans, or amulets made from wood, stone or clay found naturally if possible, or crystals marked with your name or words of power or healing, are more powerful than any you can buy. Making your own endows the amulet with your essential self. You need a flat surface on which to burn, write or paint the signs. You can buy a pyrography set from an art shop or use the blade of an awl or screwdriver heated in the flame of a gas cooker. Alternatively, write your symbols using a permanent pen.

Look for a stone with a natural hole (traditionally believed to be a window to another world) and hang this from a string for your dowsing work. Alternatively, you can find a stone on a beach or river bank, of a material that will not crack, and drill a small hole for a cord. Or you could buy a small silver clamp to hold the stone or a crystal on a chain. You can then carry the stone or crystal in a small pouch. Round wooden discs, cut from a tree branch or even an old broom handle, can also be made into talismans. You can burn or chisel into the wood and then fill in the outline with paint.

Decide on a single word to represent your need or use the first letter of a whole sentence. Write this in your runic or Egyptian alphabet.

Magical Signs

Like secret alphabets, magical signs or symbols contain their own power and healing properties. Magical symbols date back to Palaeolithic times. The first Mother Goddess images were made as early as 20,000 years ago, in areas stretching from the Pyrenees to Siberia, and magical signs of the protection and fertility of the mother have consistently appeared throughout different religious and magical traditions – spirals, crescent moons, eggs and zigzags, to name a few. From these simple beginnings, magical and religious symbols of all kinds have been formed.

In Neolithic times and later, zigzags were painted on jugs to represent the Goddess renewing life with falling rain. Indeed, the hieroglyph for the Egyptian Sky Goddess, Nut, is a jug.

Bees and butterflies are also associated with early Mother Goddess magic. The butterfly is an image of regeneration which is linked with St Teresa of Avila. But it has a much longer history, having been found as a symbol of regeneration on Neolithic vases from the fifth millennium BC. The bee was another image that survived from these early times and reappeared in Christianity. The hive was likened to the womb of the mother. The followers of the Greek Corn and Mother Goddess Demeter were called *melissae* (Latin for 'bees'), and beeswax candles were used in both pagan and Christian religion, bees becoming a special symbol of the Virgin Mary.

The crescent moon talisman, which appears in pagan art, has also been recognised within the Christian faith and is shown in fifteenth-century paintings of the Virgin Mary. The first lunar discs engraved on mammoth teeth appeared as early as 2000 BC.

The spiral, associated with the womb and new life, was a very early charm for fertility and joy. And modern spiral talismans and amulets centre on shells for added potency. Ammonite fossils can be bought easily or found on beaches and represent the spiral pathway to enlightenment. They are also closely associated with the male symbol, the snake, who, because he shed his skin, was traditionally linked with rebirth and regeneration. (However, even the snake was originally a feminine symbol.)

Remains from seventh-century Northumberland reveal St Hilda's charms: ammonites on which snake heads are carved. It is said that they are the fossilised bodies of the original snakes that St Hilda cast over the cliff edge when she expelled the serpents from her Abbey.

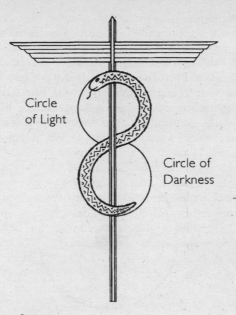

Circle
of Light

Circle of
Darkness

The caduceus of Hermes

Symbols of male power and courage developed with the advent of
the hunter-hero, a god of the early Bronze Age, and even before,
with the serpent, branching antlers, sprouting leaves and hunting
slaves. The double entwined snake of the Classical Hermes and
Mercury's caduceus (often shown as a living growing staff) is a
symbol both of healing and of powerful communication. The
snake forms two circles: the interlinked cycles of good and evil; life
and death; light and darkness. The wings on the caduceus are for
wisdom.

The ouroboros

Medieval alchemists saw the ouroboros, the snake swallowing its own tail, as a symbol of endless, unbroken cycles of time, birth and rebirth.

However, the simplest magical symbols are geometrical. One of the most common is the circle with the dot inside it, which is used as the astrological sign for the sun. The circle represents spirit and the whole cosmos, everything that is. The dot is the seed of new life, the limitless given form. This is a potent symbol of ambition, career, success, energy, action and making dreams come true.

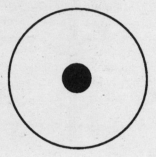

The sun symbol

The four-armed diagonal cross within the circle is the sign for the Earth. You also see this on hot cross buns, an example of a pre-Christian symbol entering Christianity. The idea was that, as you ate the food, you acquired the energies and fertility of the Earth. This is still the astrological sign for the planet Earth. It stands for fertility and money, for practical achievement and domestic harmony.

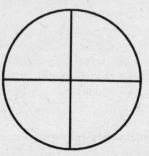

The Earth symbol

The Tau Cross, the T, is another ancient magical symbol representing the ladder from Heaven to Earth. Often a snake was entwined around the cross to show that wisdom can be obtained by anyone attempting the upward journey to the spiritual realm. Use it for any higher spiritual or psychic aims, altruism and sacrifice.

The Tau cross

The Ancient Egyptian ankh places a circle on top of the Tau Cross. It was a symbol of initiation and wisdom, representing the world of spirit, and was also used by women as an amulet against childlessness. Every Egyptian deity was portrayed carrying an ankh. The ankh still appears throughout the Western world as a symbol of immortality. Use it as a symbol of life and wisdom.

The ankh

The Seal of Solomon is important because it is based on the sacred triangle, representing the number three which is associated with many religions and cultures: the Triple Goddess; the Holy Trinity of Father, Son and Holy Spirit; and the concepts of mind, body and spirit. The two triangles of the Seal are the triangle of the Water element descending and the triangle of Fire ascending. The mingling of these elements also forms the triangles of Air and Earth. The triangles of the four elements, Earth, Air, Fire and Water, fuse into the middle quintessential shape of five; and the six eternal points give the magical seven spaces, seven being a sacred number of perfection.

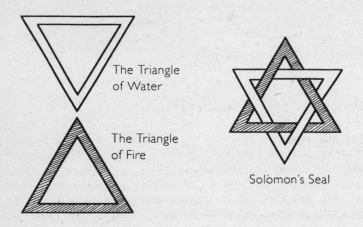

The Triangle of Water

The Triangle of Fire

Solomon's Seal

The making of Solomon's Seal

The pentagram is a five-pointed star representing Earth, Air, Fire and Water, with the fifth (uppermost) point representing spirit or Akasha or ether (the combination of the other four making a greater perfection). It both symbolises achievement and protects bodily health, especially when marked with the signs of the stars. The single point is displayed uppermost in all forms of positive magic. This is a sign of rising energies. Downward points were once regarded as evil and still represent wasted potential.

There are two ways of drawing the pentagram, a creative one and a banishing one for protective power. On your amulet you should draw a creative one, unless you are using it specifically for protection. They look the same to other people but you know the way you have drawn them.

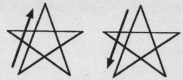

To draw the creative pentagram begin at the bottom and work up. For banishing, start at the top and work down

The pentagram and how to draw it

Dedicating Your Talisman or Amulet

You may choose to dedicate your talismans, as you did with your ritual magic tools (see p. 175), or take them to a sacred place – an old stone circle, standing stone or the place where they were found. Scatter some earth or sand across them, hold them up to the wind and then to the sun, and finally sprinkle a little water over them, as you do so endowing them with the purpose for which you have created them, whether it is for protection, success, love or happiness.

If you are using a crystal, wash it under running water for a few minutes and then leave it in water that has been charged by a favourite crystal you have owned for some time. Because crystals do pick up feelings and emotions from anyone who touches them, you want to start with your amulet crystal only charged with your own positivity.

Wear or carry your amulet constantly so that it becomes part of you. If bad things or negative emotions occur, as they do for anyone, hold your amulet and see light and power enabling you to overcome the hurdle. When good things occur, see the sun going back into your talisman and amulet and recharging it. If you can share your good fortune, then there are more good vibrations to fill the cosmos when you need them (think of this as a kind of cosmic savings bank).

Losing Your Luck and Regaining It

Once you have created your talisman, what do you do if it goes missing at a crisis point in your life? Such things happen all too frequently.

In the 1996 Miss World contest held in India, eighteen-year-old Miss Tahiti, Hinerava Hiro, virtually threw in the towel a week before the final because she had lost her lucky jewellery: 'Women in Tahiti wear jewellery of black pearls because they bring luck. I will not have luck on my side because I lost my pearl necklace,' she told reporters. The contest's organisers had misplaced one of her bags containing the costly necklace. She did not win. Was it because she had lost her luck or lost her confidence?

The first thing to do if your charm goes missing is not to panic. Remember that the charm itself is only a scale model of the real thing and provides a focus for your own innate abilities and powers. You can recreate it and use it just as effectively with whichever of the following methods seems best to you:

* Draw it on a piece of card or paper which you can carry with you. As you draw it, imagine the power flowing from the lost object, wherever it is, through you and into the symbol on the paper. Remember the hopes and fears that were associated with the lost object and the success that you had with it and allow the symbol to concentrate and amplify your energies.
* Acquire a piece of clear crystal. Stare into its depths, visualising the image of the lost talisman inside the crystal. Again, focus your internal energy into the symbol.

Section Seven

Other Dimensions

23

Ghosts and How to See Them

Most people have either seen a ghost or sensed a presence or know someone in their immediate family or circle of friends who has witnessed an apparition, heard inexplicable footsteps or smelled a deceased grandmother's perfume. Many of these experiences are entirely spontaneous but it is possible to be more in tune with presences from another dimension. The psychic arts described in earlier chapters – clairaudience, clairvoyance and clairsentience – will already have raised your awareness of this. Even if you have not seen a ghost before, or not since childhood, you will find it possible to tune into atmospheres and feelings from those who have died.

Ghostly experiences are of two main kinds. The first involves familiar friendly presences of deceased mothers, grandmothers, fathers and children. You may see a full apparition or have a sudden sense of being loved and watched over by someone who is no longer alive. Such experiences are very common but are often dismissed by psychologists and scientists as wishful thinking or just part of the grieving process. Countless people have told me that they have seen deceased loved ones looking quite alive, who communicated their enduring love and sometimes gave important advice. Contrary to expert opinion, the majority of these cases are totally positive and can help a grieving relative to accept the earthly loss. This might explain why deceased relatives are frequently seen sitting in a favourite chair at a family gathering. I used to believe that these appearances were 'all in the mind' but, over the years, I have come to accept that the essential person may indeed survive death. This has been demonstrated by cases such of that of Tracie, recounted in the Introduction, whose deceased mother warned her of an impending accident and so prevented a disaster.

I met Connor, who is a cameraman with an Irish television station, when I went to Avebury Stones in Wiltshire to make a programme for RTE. He told me:

> My mother died two years ago. She was one of four sisters and was especially close to her sister Marie who took her death very hard. Not long after Mother died, Marie was in her kitchen, making a cup of tea. When she looked up, she saw my mother sitting in a chair smiling at her. My mother looked much younger and really well. Then my mother disappeared.
>
> Every year the sisters would get together for a special treat. The year after my mother died was the first occasion they had not all met. In the restaurant, Marie looked up and saw my mother sitting at one of the other tables, again smiling. The others did not see her but Marie felt that all was well and enjoyed the rest of the day, knowing the sisters were together as usual. My mother appeared to Marie two or three times after that, until Marie told her, 'Look, you can go on now. I shall be fine. Don't wait here. I don't need you to be around any more.'
>
> Marie never saw my mother after that.

Although this sort of experience cannot be repeated in a laboratory, it makes perfect sense in human terms and helped Marie through the grieving process. One explanation is that the essential, etheric person that we are all said to possess (see p. 124) can survive death and still has bonds of love with those left behind. Alternatively, the power of family routine may be so strong that an imprint of a deceased person remains and can be triggered by surviving members of the family carrying out that routine activity at the customary time.

The second source of ghostly presence is when the apparition is attached to a particular place. Frequently these hauntings occur in an ordinary house where a previous owner died, after living in the dwelling for many years, perhaps establishing a very definite routine. In such cases, it is the house that holds the impression of the deceased person. This is borne out by the fact that a young child will often describe a domestic ghost in detail and verification will then be obtained from an elderly neighbour.

Mary, who lives in Norfolk, described a friend's daughter's experience:

Angela, who was five, talked frequently about an old man in her bedroom. When the family were going to move house, the old man appeared on the stairs to the child's mother and said, 'Don't move because I love children.'

I was intrigued and, after enquiries, discovered that an old man who had lived in the house some years before had died on the stairs. Two weeks later the house was unexpectedly sold and the little girl did not mention the old man again.

Gilbert Attard, a French parapsychologist who has studied the geophysical aspects of the paranormal for twenty years, offers a scientific explanation for phantoms.

If someone dies in a closed space: what would happen at the moment of death? Science has demonstrated that at that moment everyone releases a radiation or electromagnetic field which is directly linked, qualitatively and quantitatively, to the individual's chemical structure.

We can say that at the moment of death the magnetic field will imprint itself on the surrounding matter. An old Provençal tradition says that in a room where death has occurred all containers should be emptied of water, as the water will be contaminated.

Physics gives us an answer. We know that matter is composed of neutrons and protons which are in perfect equilibrium with their surrounding electrons. Biologists say that at the destruction of cells all the genetic material disperses, causing the release of a great quantity of energy which can resonate with the energies which compose other bodies, living or otherwise. I tend to compare this to nuclear fission which releases a great quantity of energy which becomes residual radioactivity.

At the moment of death everyone gives off a magnetic field, intensified by emotion, which can penetrate the surrounding matter and modify the biochemical functions of molecules. The result will be to impregnate the matter with the magnetic field of the deceased. This field is also charged with the emotion felt at the time.

This force, says M. Attard, could explain why clocks often stop at the moment of their owner's death. But his theory does not entirely explain the continuing communication between a presence and those who move into his or her home. Erica, from Pennsylvania, described her family's domestic phantom:

When I was in fifth grade at school we rented an old house from an elderly gentleman. His children were all adults, his wife was dead and the house was too big for him. He told my parents to feel free to paint and decorate anything that they wanted, but not to cover up the mural that he had painted for his wife in the basement. It was a hideous representation of his wife's home town in Italy. My mother taught ceramics classes in the basement and it was my favourite place to roller skate, so we were both down there a lot of the time. After a while, however, strange happenings began down there.

At first we noticed that one of the chairs from around the table always seemed to move in front of the mural, but each of us assumed that it was the other one of us that had put it there. Then there was the perfume. Suddenly the entire room would fill with this rose-scented perfume which was overwhelming at times. It only happened when I was alone down there and I really didn't want to tell my mom because I figured that she would just blame it on my imagination. I became so nervous I would not go down alone, although I felt safe with my mom.

One day when we were together the water went on full blast and the chair swung out from the table and scooted across the floor to the mural and the room filled with the perfume. My mother looked at me and I looked at her and we both ran up the stairs as fast as we could.

When we calmed down we shared our stories. My mother had experienced the same things as I had. Unfortunately for my mom, she taught her class down there and it was unavoidable. One evening after everyone had left and my mom was cleaning up (I was there, so she wouldn't be alone in the basement) the episode repeated itself and in the midst of it I was touched on the shoulder and the ghost said, 'Don't move my chair.'

That chair was never moved again. When we were moving out we mentioned it to the landlord and his reply was, 'My wife started that about a week after she died.'

Communicating with Ghosts

* If you do sense a presence or see an apparition, treat the encounter as you would any other communication on an earthly plane, maintaining the same politeness and respect for privacy. It is a privilege to see, hear or sense a ghost and you are in his or her home. To the ghost, you are the visitor or perhaps, if their world is still in motion, you are the apparition. (A woman who saw a Victorian ghost in the Assembly Rooms in Norwich appeared to startle the phantom.)
* If the ghost is set on a particular path, do not try to chase him or her. Follow discreetly and see where the phantom disappears, often through a wall. If you examine the wall carefully afterwards, you may see traces of an old door at the spot. Apparitions tend not to be aware of changes to their original home.
* Note any details of their appearance and clothing which may give clues to their age and identity. Study a map of the place and ask about the history if you are in a stately home or ruined abbey.
* Do not worry if you cannot match your phantom to a great lord or lady, or even to the ghosts recorded at the place. You may well have seen a servant whose dress was rather indeterminate. The majority of ghosts are ordinary people who lived out their lives within the walls.

Finding Ghosts

You are unlikely to see a phantom on a ghost-hunting weekend or at a famous haunted castle or palace, although some people *do* encounter apparitions on a Bank Holiday weekend in the Tower of London.

* Choose a less popular location, perhaps an industrial museum or a manor house, preferably one that is inhabited so that is still a focus of domestic life.
* Visit in the early evening, just before closing, on an autumn day; or in the morning, as the property opens in the spring.

These are times of the year when life is at a change point and so the dimensions move close. When it is quiet and the atmosphere fresh and unhurried, you are more likely to see or sense something.

* Choose a property or place that you can visit without a guide so that you can wander slowly, pause in alcoves with window seats, and let the atmosphere envelop you.

* If you cannot see or sense anything, study a picture of a former member of the family in the house or grounds and try to find their favourite spot.

* Choose a portrait of someone with whom you share emotional links. Perhaps you are both mothers of young children. Or, if you choose a servant holding a horse in a picture, you may see in his eyes a love of animals that you share. Read or ask about the person and you may find that, although separated by centuries and perhaps wealth and social class, you can identify with his or her joys and sorrows. The more you identify with the chosen character, the greater the bond and the easier it is to bridge the ages.

* Stand in the spot, or one like it, with your eyes closed, and recreate the painting in your mind's eye. Build up, especially, the image of the person you saw in the portrait, beginning with a vivid colour on a dress or tunic and expanding outwards until you are within the picture.

* When you open your eyes, you may see the person or someone else from the same time, perhaps a shadowy form, an outline or a mist.

* Extend a positive thought across the ages and you may find the picture clears slightly. Let it go when it begins to fade and spend a few moments allowing yourself to return naturally to the present.

Being Close to a Deceased Relative

As a general rule it is not advisable to try to call a deceased person back to you, since we do not understand the nature of the after-life or how it is that loved ones seem able to return at certain times and in certain ways. When the time is right, or you are sad or worried, you may find yourself seeing a strong picture of the deceased person or hearing in your mind a special phrase that he or she used as an endearment.

At the same time you might spontaneously detect a faint perfume or see a shadowy form and feel yourself enveloped in love. It has been described as being cuddled in a blanket of caring. However, some people do write to me in a state of distress because they have not seen or even dreamed of a loved one who has died. My son Jack, who is twelve, has a theory that when you die, you check in at heaven and can then pop back to see the family and perhaps say goodbye if the parting was sudden. After that the deceased visit as they might do if they were living abroad – on major family occasions or at times of crisis.

Jack's theory seems to be borne out by the many accounts I have heard of a relative returning a few days after death in a very vivid dream or a clear apparition and subsequent visits being less clear and frequent. But it may be that some people are too tired at first or too confused to reassure grieving relatives. Just as at a boarding school, new children settle in at different speeds. Some children phone home straightaway, while others wait weeks before getting in touch.

Of course these are only metaphors, couched in the everyday terms through which we inevitably view the after-life.

However, if you do want to feel close to a deceased relative, there are several steps you can take:

* Choose a place where you were happy together (rather than the cemetery) and visit at a time of year or a particular date that had significance for you both. This is a more positive setting than the anniversary of the death, although many apparitions of family members are seen spontaneously on such anniversaries.
* Go with a sympathetic friend or family member who also knew the deceased person and 'recall' the person by talking about previous happy occasions, the minor disasters that occurred, and the jokes and eccentricities of the loved one in order to recreate the whole picture.
* Wear or carry a memento if possible, use a favourite perfume or carry a pouch of tobacco smoked by the relation, and wear his or her favourite colour. If you have photographs taken at the place, bring them along. Visit a favourite tea shop and order a familiar meal. Slowly you will become aware of the

presence of the person, perhaps a shadow, a faint laugh or just a vivid picture in your mind's eye that seems achingly real. Do not dismiss these inner visions as mere imagination. You may hear the familiar voice in your ear or half-see out of the corner of your eye a fleeting familiar action.

* Place a little of the perfume on your pillow and you may dream a positive, happy contact. If not, be patient, for, in time, you will receive a hint, perhaps more, that death is not the end.

* Do not be afraid to talk to the dead person when you are alone. Many people do this and it is not a sign of madness but part of the gradual loosening of the physical bonds that, with a married couple, may have lasted more than half a lifetime. Make sure you have plenty of earthly contact and you will find that the conversations will diminish or even cease of their own accord, except in times of stress or sadness. However you may always want to say goodnight and you may hear in your mind's ear, or externally, your words returned.

* Finally, if you do get an opportunity to talk to a ghost, whether a family member or a stranger, he or she may look quite ordinary and three-dimensional. It is only when the person disappears into thin air that you may notice a slight chill in the air and feel the hairs rising on your neck.

Margaret was watching television in her caravan on her daughter's remote farm when she became aware that a woman was standing beside her, also watching the television intently. It was 11.15 at night and Margaret was very cross that someone had come into her caravan uninvited so late.

'What are you doing?' she asked crossly. 'It is very late to come visiting.'

The woman, who looked quite solid and was wearing ordinary clothes, dissolved into a mist and Margaret says she will always regret that she didn't chat to her phantom who just popped in to see a favourite show. The apparition never returned.

24

Mediumship

Mediums are men and women who have the ability (using clairaudience, clairsentience and clairvoyance, and sometimes all three) to contact people who have died and to communicate advice and sometimes warnings. Some also communicate with beings who, it is believed, are more spiritually evolved and may never have lived in earthly form. The most successful mediums, such as the late Doris Stokes, appear on television, radio and at huge venues such as Wembley Stadium where they may give mass demonstrations.

Other mediums operated through Spiritualist associations and Spiritualist churches, carrying out platform work in churches, halls or small theatres, and also give private readings to supplement their income. Many of these give platform demonstrations for expenses only. Mediumship is not, despite popular opinion, a lucrative profession for the majority of those called to it.

Some mediums, however, work entirely independently of any organisation, seeing clients at home and often helping people for nothing, dispensing tea and earthly wisdom along with clairvoyance. As in every world, there are also some charlatans who prey on people who may have just lost a partner or parent and be desperate for contact.

I used to advise people to seek a medium only through a Spiritualist church or organisation. However, during the last two years, I have discovered a wealth of mediumistic talent and compassion outside the official organisations and would now advise that, if you do want to consult a medium, you should ask friends and acquaintances. Personal recommendation is the best way of finding a reliable medium as, although many genuine clairvoyants and mediums do advertise in newspapers, it is hard to distinguish them from the frauds who use this method to attract the unwary.

How Mediumship Works

Mediums learn to tune into other dimensions so that they can seek contact with a deceased relative on behalf of a living family member, although their requests for such contact will not always be granted. A medium should not be judged good or bad according to their ability to communicate with a person on the other side. The deceased person may not wish to talk or may be unable to talk.

One of the problems of platform mediumship and private sittings, both for those seeking help and those would like to become mediums, is that sometimes only a single vital piece of proof may be given. If there is a half-hour session, the medium may feel obliged to provide more so as not to disappoint a sitter. Such expectations can be counter-productive in terms of quality, but the more mediums are exposed to media contact, the more the instant entertainment factor predominates.

Mediumship is, for many practitioners, a religion and calling and some Spiritualist services begin with prayers to God. All mediums believe in Spirit, a divine power that guides them, although in modern times, as with other religions, the strict tenets of Spiritualism are not followed to the letter by younger members who may believe in a more abstract power – of light and positive energy.

Good mediums often pick up information about people they meet in daily life, because their psychic awareness is highly developed. However, on a conscious level, most mediums live entirely in the everyday world, concerned with families, mortgages or rent, and shopping, just like anyone else. This is right, as it provides the earthing and commonsense elements that prevent psychic activity usurping the material world and, ironically, becoming less focused.

The majority of professional mediums remain fully conscious during a sitting or public demonstration and many also carry out healing work using their spirit guides. Few now use *planchettes* (a kind of heart-shaped ouija board with a pencil attached to write down spirit messages) or rely on the old methods of table tapping for 'yes' and 'no', or holding seances where spirits are called down for enthusiastic amateurs.

Physical mediums assume the face and sometimes the voice of a deceased person, or even take on the form of the person or a spirit guide in a mist or ectoplasm, a white malleable substance that can emanate from a medium during a trance. However, full physical mediumship is becoming more unusual, partly because this branch of mediumship became unfairly tainted by a certain amount of fraud, often precisely because the medium felt obliged to create an effect on demand that would only normally appear spontaneously.

Despite some suspicion among the general public about mediums, since the First World War, when so many young men lost their lives, there has been great demand for their services. Mediumship was not legal until the repeal of the Witchcraft Act of 1735 in 1951, and in 1944 a medium, Helen Duncan, was imprisoned on a charge of 'pretending to conjure up spirits'. In parts of the United States mediums and clairvoyants are still not allowed to practise.

Trance Mediums

Mediums usually have spirit guides through which they communicate with other dimensions and some mediums fall into a deep trance. The medium's voice changes into that of his or her guide, who may be a Native American chief or a Chinese sage – or some other archetype of wisdom. In an opening address, the guide may offer advice on the state of the world (a form of channelling). This can be very disconcerting, especially for younger people, although trance mediumship does produce remarkable results. And physical mediumship most often takes place in this trance state.

How to Become a Medium

It is said that mediums are born, not made, and some mediums will have experienced psychic phenomena from early childhood onwards. For others it is a gift that does not emerge until adulthood, perhaps triggered by a bereavement or serious illness.

The majority of people reading this book will have natural

mediumistic abilities, triggered by visits to ancient places or psychometry. But few will choose to develop this ability formally, as it does require a willingness to learn a structured approach to communicating with other dimensions and a commitment to a long and sometimes slow process of working within a psychic development group (see Chapter 29).

Because mediumship involves probing a world that is scarcely understood even by the most dedicated Spiritualist, it is not an art to learn with enthusiastic friends by summoning spirits into a candle flame or holding a seance to attract entities from another world. If we accept that there are good spirits then there will inevitably also be negative influences from beyond. I know of individuals and psychic development groups who have strayed into the business of spirit contact and rescue and found themselves haunted by terrifying malevolent presences, whether from a psychic or psychological source.

For those who become mediums there is an irresistible urge to develop their abilities. If you regularly see presences and hear voices, especially if you detect presences around total strangers, you may find that joining a psychic development group channels these powers in a positive way and could even launch you into a new career.

Formal Training

To develop formal mediumistic skills, you should begin by joining a psychic development circle with experienced mediums, under the auspices of a Spiritualist church or other organisations. There is really no alternative, unless you know of a wise and gifted medium who will help you in a private circle with two or three friends. Beware of organisations or individuals who ask for large sums of money in return for passing on their expertise. If they offer accreditation, or promise that you can become a medium in a few weeks or even months, check with one of the associations listed under Useful Addresses, especially if you see the advertisement in a newspaper. Even if you later leave the Spiritualist organisation, this initial support and safety net is vital; residential courses through genuine organisations will not cost much more than a holiday in a reasonable quality hotel. If you want to join one of these organisations:

* The first step is to find a Spiritualist church or Spiritualist association that seems welcoming. Try several in your area. Contact the President in advance. He or she will usually be wise, encouraging of newcomers, and glad to answer any questions. Someone will probably greet you at your first meeting.

* Do not be discouraged if you come up against back-biting, gossip or cliques. All churches, of whatever denomination, are run by real people, not saints, and you will find disagreements and pettiness that seem alien to the ideas you are seeking. Any organisation is only as good as its members. All of them contain at least some honest, kind people. By joining and persevering, you may help to create a better Spiritualist movement.

* Go first to an evening of clairvoyance and, rather than being eager to receive a message yourself, concentrate on the medium and how he or she works. When the medium offers a description of a person, try to share the vision and expand the details in your mind's ear or eye. Mediums tend to have one psychic sense that is better developed than the others.

* Tuning into the visions and voices heard by an experienced practitioner is an excellent introduction to mediumship. Afterwards, if you picked up any extra details, listen to the general chatter and, over the usual tea and biscuits, ask tactful questions to ascertain if you were correct.

* Attend a Spiritualist church regularly and talk especially to the older people who may be experienced platform mediums themselves. Most experienced Spiritualists love to share their knowledge and, if you can chat to the medium, he or she may give insights into their own reactions as spirits came through.

* Keep a notebook and, when you get home, note the methods used by visiting mediums and the response from the congregation to different techniques.

* Listen carefully to the announcements and scan the notice-boards for any open circle meetings where you will have a chance, with perhaps half a dozen others, to try out mediumship in a relaxed, controlled environment.

* At open circles, do not feel obliged to speak if you see or sense nothing about the other people in your group or if you do not receive any images or words from the spirits that others in the group identify.

* At first you may see animals, smell perfume or hear singing

and see only hazy impressions or lights. This is normal and it may be several weeks or even months before you fine-tune your mediumistic senses.

* Equally, if you do feel moved to speak, do not be afraid to do so for fear of being 'wrong'. There is inevitably in every circle, open or closed, the self-designated star who speaks with confidence, though not necessarily from the soul. Your own halting visions may be more genuine, and a good medium never pushes in a circle. Each time you do identify a person, name or piece of information clairvoyantly your confidence will increase. It is like learning to drive on a simulator. Eventually you have to take control of a real car and you will grate the odd gear, psychic as well as physical, before the process becomes automatic.

* Visit the bookstall, where there are often books to borrow as well as buy, and take out a subscription to a psychic and Spiritualist paper such as *Psychic News* (owned by the Spiritualist National Union) or *Two Worlds*. In these you will find courses, lectures, demonstrations and meetings advertised. Colleges, such as the Arthur Findlay in Essex and the College of Psychic Studies in London, run many excellent courses to aid mediumistic development. Addresses for these colleges are given in the back of the book, as are those of similar organisations in the US, Australia and New Zealand. Larger Spiritualist churches may also run a range of activities.

* It is traditional to wait to be invited to join a closed psychic development circle. But, if you are keen, you may find that it is possible to enter one quite quickly if you approach the President of the church and ask for guidance.

* Only a small proportion of mediums who sit in circles go on to do platform work at other churches or enter the wider arena of television or radio mediumship, which can be very hazardous and a great strain spiritually and physically.

* However, there are usually opportunities for you to accompany an experienced medium who is appearing at another Spiritualist church and perhaps either work alongside him or her on the platform or try going solo for a few minutes with the experienced medium there to help. Congregations tend to be very sympathetic to a trainee medium and their positive feelings will help to strengthen your own links with the spirit world. If you remember that you are there to help, not to

perform, you will find that you are just as much at home with
fifty people as with a single sitter.

* Begin with sittings for friends and acquaintances. There is
never any shortage of volunteers when you are not charging.
Explain that you will only pass on what you actually hear or
see, even if this is only a single phrase or image.
* Progress to sitting for strangers, perhaps recommended by
your local Spiritualist church. I used to believe it was wrong
to charge for psychic readings or mediumship but if you
charge for your time, rather than for your performance, then
you will feel less pressurised and will thus avoid blocking your
natural gift with anxiety.

Spirit Rescue

Some mediums use clairvoyance to see restless spirits and to guide
them into the next world. Sometimes what seems to be a polter-
geist or malevolent force can, by 'clear-seeing', be understood as a
lost child or former resident of a house. Margaret, a medium in her
seventies, explained how her clairvoyant gifts helped two unhappy
children:

> I was called to a house on the South Coast because a little boy
> had not been able to sleep at night since the family had moved
> there, some months before. The child woke screaming and
> crying every night but was unable to say why. I sat in the little
> boy's bedroom for a while and then went through to the
> bathroom where I saw another small spirit boy in the bath. He
> had drowned. I told him to come with me and I would look
> after him. I drove away and stopped the car in the countryside.
> I could feel him bouncing up and down on my lap the whole
> time. Then I saw a small light in the sky and asked the child if
> he could see it. He could and it became larger. I said that if he
> went towards the light he would see someone he knew who
> would take care of him. The infant moved closer to the light
> and I told him if he opened his arms the person would reach
> out for him. He said he could see someone, but smiled and
> was gone.
>
> I did not contact the family but, a few weeks later, my

husband started talking to Jim, a man he knew slightly in the local pub. Noel, the father of the little boy who could not sleep, came into the pub and greeted Jim who commented how much better Noel was looking. Noel, who did not know my husband, said that his young son had started sleeping through the night and at last the family were getting some rest.

Noel explained, rather shamefacedly, that his son had imagined there was a ghost but now said it was gone. Jim told Noel that it was not surprising the boy had been scared. Some time before Noel came to the area the house had been owned by a family who had an autistic son. The little boy had drowned in the bath.

Very experienced mediums are, they believe, able to help troubled spirits. When you have been practising for some time, you may be asked to join a circle for rescue work and in time you may be asked to go to the homes of those who have troubled spirits. If you can identify the spirit and his or her reason for remaining there, the family may accept the presence. Once acknowledged and explained, the phantom is frequently persuaded either to depart spontaneously or at least to co-exist peacefully with the family.

However exorcisms are not advisable. An unhappy essence should not be banished to outer darkness but encouraged to move on to the next level, which can be very difficult if the presence is attached to his or her home or even to an animal in the house that may resemble a former well-loved pet. Rather, the house and spirit should be offered healing and prayer. Always err on the side of caution, enclose yourself in protective light, and if in doubt ask for outside help.

Every diocese has an official exorcist who can be called on to help with really malevolent entities. It is important for conventional churches, mediums and healers to work together and conventional churches are increasingly recognising that there are many paths to God or Good.

Psychic Art

Psychic art is another form of mediumship. The psychic artist may produced amazing likenesses of deceased relatives of the sitter who are unknown to the artist. They may also draw or paint figures known to neither artist nor sitter who are subsequently discovered to be long-lost relations of the sitter, perhaps ones he never knew he possessed.

David, who works as a college lecturer on the South Coast, told me that he and his wife Susan visited a local Spiritualist church where a psychic artist, who had never visited the area before, was appearing. The artist drew a choirboy in his teens for the couple. He said the boy had died a few years earlier from leukaemia and was linked with them. At first David did not recognise the likeness but suddenly realised it was a younger version of Paul, a close friend of his son, who had died from leukaemia some years before. The young man sang in the local choir before his death, although David and Sue had not known him then. Paul had a beautiful voice. David and his wife had found it very difficult to get over Paul's death, as he had been ill at the same time as their own son who had recovered. David realised that the portrait was saying that Paul was now young and well again, but they did not feel able to tell his parents.

Experimenting with Psychic Art

Once you begin developing mediumistic abilities, you may feel compelled to draw a figure, perhaps a spirit guide you can see next to the sitter or someone he or she once knew who has died who seems to be playing the role of a guardian angel. At such a time, you may discover that you have artistic skills you never knew you possessed. However, these tend to be limited to the production of psychic art and at other times you may still be unable to sketch an acceptable flower pot! The sitter may instantly recognise the person as a relative or spirit guide they know and you may also talk quite spontaneously in great detail about the subject's former life.

One medium, called Dorothy, began her psychic art as a little girl. She was always drawing people she could see around her – nuns, Native American Indians, Chinese sages, angels. When asked, she would say they were the people she could see around her. Once Dorothy started going to school other children would laugh at her pictures of spirit people and so she learned to say that she was just drawing pretend figures.

Beginning Psychic Art

Even if you are not developing mediumship in a formal way, you may find that psychic art can be a good way of identifying your own spirit guides and those of others:

* Begin with a friend and see, in your mind's eye, someone standing next to him or her. You may see the whole person or just one feature that will expand as you begin to draw.
* Some people do not see anyone next to the sitter. Only as the picture unfolds on the paper do the features emerge. This can even be an outline of light that you trace over.
* Use pen, paints or chalks and large sheets of paper. Let your pen or piece of chalk guide you.
* Begin with your usual writing hand, although psychic art occasionally comes through the other hand.
* As you begin to draw, you may find yourself knowing details about the life of the person whose image is appearing. Use a tape recorder or ask the sitter to jot down details.
* You may have drawn a spirit guide or a past life – you will soon learn to differentiate between past lives and spirits. If it is a past life, you may find yourself talking in the first person and seeing the past world through the eyes of the character you are drawing.
* If it is a spirit guide, the sitter may recognise the person from dreams or may have been aware of a particular affinity with the environment in which the spirit guide would have lived.
* If the person is not recognisable to the sitter, get him or her to take the picture home and ask elderly relatives if they know the figure. Sometimes it is someone who will be of significance in the future.
* If you develop a talent for drawing figures that seem to evoke no response in you, try working with a mediumistic friend who may be able to supply the missing information, usually clairaudiently. Psychic artists do sometimes work as one half of a mediumship partnership.

25

Spirit Guides

Who Are Spirit Guides?

Spirit guides and guardian angels seem to fulfil similar roles and may indeed be one and the same. The spirit guide is often viewed as an actual entity. For example, it may be a deceased wise grandmother who continues to watch over and advise a particular grandchild throughout adulthood. More often the person is an archetype of wisdom from a Native American tribe, China or Ancient Egypt, a Romany gypsy, a nun, monk or doctor from past ages. I heard of a woman whose guardian angel/spirit guide had the voice of a BBC announcer. One morning, as she lay in bed about to light her first cigarette of the day, he warned her not to do so or she would cause an explosion. When she got out of bed, she discovered that the kitchen was filled with gas that had leaked during the night.

Other people believe that their guide has never taken human form but is an evolved spirit on the astral plane who takes an interest in human affairs and seeks to guide them to a greater understanding of spiritual matters. It may be that during our lifetime we have several spirit guides, according to our age and level of development. Whether we view spirit guides as external projections of our own inner, more highly evolved selves or as actual angelic beings, their function is entirely positive and can lead us to greater spiritual insights. If you believe that the guide is part of an evolved self, then the wisdom may be coming from the collective human memory. However, some people are convinced that such knowledge is being transmitted by an older, wiser soul. Whatever the source of the knowledge of past, present and potential future, for many mediums, clairvoyants and healers their spiritual guides are an integral part of their work.

Do I Need a Spirit Guide?

There are those who never had an invisible friend as a child and who feel that the concept of a spirit guide is alien to their way of life and philosophy. This is no bar to psychic development. It is quite possible to practise mediumship on the basis that you are contacting the permanent core of a deceased person, using the trigger of a living relation to recreate what he or she would have said and done about a present dilemma or a future situation.

However, in my experience, the deeper you explore the psychic and spiritual world, the less you can easily explain by reference to the self alone. As I researched my book *Miracles*, I came upon evidence that suggested strongly to me that I had been mistaken in believing that human willpower and intuitive abilities accounted for all human experience, without any reference to a universal source of goodness (whatever name it is given).

Even if you do not accept the existence of angels/spirit guides, you may still find it helpful to visualise an evolved form as a focus for your spiritual, psychic and healing energies.

Childhood Spirit Guides

Children's imaginary friends may be spirit guides who help them cope with the world and then move on to other children. I came across a woman who as a child had an invisible friend who was called Jockson. Jockson came from Australia. Thirty years ago Carolyn was amazed to hear about a friend's daughter's invisible companion friend called Jackson who matched Jockson in every detail. Carolyn was not a Spiritualist and, while Spiritualists naturally accept this concept, many other children also talk about their 'angel friend'.

Nor do such friends necessarily disappear at school age. Many children are afraid to talk about these companions for fear of ridicule and some parents are afraid that invisible friends are a sign of psychological disturbance, although more than a fifth of children, especially intelligent ones, are reported as having such friends.

Lee, who is ten and lives in Lincolnshire, wrote to me:

One day when I was three years old I was playing in the kitchen with my big teddy bear. I suddenly turned around and saw a boy standing there. I felt really scared and started to scream. My mum tried to calm me down. She could see that I was staring at something. Although she could not see him, she could sense the boy was there.

The next time I saw my friend was when I was about four and a half. I was in the front room playing with my cars and suddenly felt that someone was watching me. I looked up and there was my friend. From that day we started to make friends. He was a lot kinder to me than any other friend, except that we did not fight like other friends. Since I met my friend we have moved to three different houses and we now live in a nice house in the country and it is lovely here. When I am feeling bored or lonely, I hope in my mind that my friend will come and usually he does.

When I am out on my own he often walks along with me. My mum usually knows when my friend is downstairs with me. Although she cannot see him, she senses him. He does not really like my telling anyone about him and so I do not use his name to anyone else. He is about ten or eleven and often tells me stories and lots of secrets, but I am allowed to share them.

When I tell people I have a special friend, I know that most of them do not believe me. I know he is real and so does my mother. He tells me funny jokes and really likes my new dog.

Adult Spirit Guides

Adult spirit guides often first appear during adolescence, in dreams or daytime visions. For clairvoyant and mediumistic work, this archetypal source of wisdom and goodness acts as a focus for psychic and healing energies. As a child, Lucille, a past-life therapist and clairvoyant, had a little Egyptian girl as her spirit guide. Recently Lucille has noticed her Egyptian friend, now also grown up, appearing in her dreams and past-life work. However, Lucille's special guide and helper is Karesia, a lady who wears a long blue cloak with a mantle and is very beautiful and gentle.

Lucille first saw Karesia in a dream playing a piano and the music went up into the air and formed pictures. Karesia gradually became a living entity and would assist Lucille in her past-life work and rock people in her cloak when they were unhappy, especially those who had suffered distressing childhoods. Client after client would spontaneously describe the blue lady who appeared in regressions and during healing.

A woman called Mandy who had been unhappy as a child and still had a traumatic life described Karesia: 'She is a beautiful lady. She is smiling at me. Now she is taking me up in her arms and wrapping her cloak around me. I am being rocked, as if I am in a small boat.'

Another client, Derek, an ambulance man who went back to a life as a Second World War pilot, also saw Karesia and described her as beautiful with long golden blonde hair down her back, and in her hand a silver flute. Karesia's skin was very soft and she told Derek that she could play many instruments.

Lucille has tried to unravel the identity of Karesia and once asked the 'blue lady' who she was. Karesia laughed and replied: 'We are very close. We always have been, from when we were in Atlantis together.'

Atlantis has been the focus of many psychic visions and there is a detailed description of the lost continent in Plato's *Timaeus*. The description was said to have been brought back from Egypt by the poet Solon. Plato wrote:

There was an island situated in front of the straits which are by you called the Pillars of Heracles; the island was larger than Libya and Asia put together, and was the way to other islands, and from these you might pass to the whole of the opposite continent which surrounded the true ocean; for this sea which is written the Straits of Heracles is only a harbour, having a narrow entrance, but that other is a real sea, and the surrounding land may be most truly called a boundless continent. Now in this island of Atlantis there was a great and wonderful empire which had rule over the whole island and several others, and other parts of the continent.

She was pre-eminent in courage and military skill, and was

the leader of the Hellenes. And when the rest fell off from her, she defeated and triumphed over the invaders, and preserved from slavery those who were not yet subjugated, and generously liberated all the rest of us who dwell within the pillars.

But afterwards there occurred violent earthquakes and floods: and in a single day and night of misfortune all your warlike men in a body sank into the earth, and the island of Atlantis in like manner disappeared in the depths of the sea.

Was Karesia a past-life link with Lucille who had gone on to become an evolved being on the astral plane? Or was Karesia a higher part of Lucille herself, a part that assumed a separate identity in healing and psychic work and was 'seen' by others as the evolved part of Lucille?

During adulthood, we may have a series of spirit guides who draw near at different stages. You may already know your spirit guide or guides, however you interpret their source. By far the majority of people sense them around before falling asleep, as shadowy forms or as inner voices and visions. There may be one predominant image, for example a monk, and you may find yourself drawn to cloisters or old abbeys or be fascinated by illuminated manuscripts.

If you do not sense such a figure but would like to communicate with a more evolved self or being, you can build up a picture of your 'idealised persona'.

Identifying Your Spirit Guide

In Native North American tribes, identifying one's totem or idealised power creature was one of the first initiation rights for both men and women on reaching adolescence. It is interesting that in the developed Western world we often adopt Native North American chiefs themselves as spirit guides, although they tended to look to nature for their inspiration.

At the age of thirteen, Native North American boys would be taken to the forest and left alone to fast for several days. The first animal, bird or reptile they met or which acted in a significant or unusual way – perhaps a deer coming very close or an eagle circling above several times – would be taken as a personal totem.

Sometimes the creature would appear to speak to the boy, who was in a semi-hypnotic state induced by hunger and perhaps lack of sleep (for the boys would often be woken regularly by adult males camping some way off or made to perform arduous tasks). Thus, names such as Lame Deer or Running Bear would replace their childhood names. Girls too would be taken to a safe place where such 'fasting totem visions' might occur.

Children and adolescents in the West frequently have animal invisible friends but, because of cultural conditioning, these young people tend to focus on a human form for their 'power person'. To identify your spirit guide:

* Visualise whoever is for you the wisest, most noble person, past or present, who could serve as a focus.
* Find out as much as you can about your guide's culture. Read any literature, visit museums or even theme parks where your 'totem figure' is featured.
* Gradually isolate your unique persona, concentrating in your mind's eye on each feature and the details of your guide's dress. 'Hear' a voice, with its special accent, emphasis on certain words, and idiosyncrasies of speech. How, it is often asked, can a Chinese sage speak French or Boston American? One answer would be that any experience is interpreted through our own framework of experience, just as a small child will see an essence in the form of an angel complete with golden wings.
* When you go to sleep, hold the image of your spirit guide in your mind's eye as you drift into dreams. As you wake, draw the image close in your semi-conscious awareness. Gradually the figure will begin to speak and to act as a guide through your dreams, and eventually start to appear occasionally in your waking world. Whether this is your own inner voice speaking or some benign force, you will gradually discover, through dialogue, wise counsel and knowledge you could not access on a conscious level. If you begin developing mediumship skills, you may be aware of this figure standing beside you, whether in your mind's eye or externally, and the appearance may herald clairvoyant or clairaudient knowledge.
* Should any negative figures or words appear, enclose the vision in a cloud of soft pink mist and see it rising away towards a soft blue lake of healing sleep.

26

Discovering
Past Worlds

Have we lived before? Can we learn to look back at our past lives? Pam, who lives in County Durham, wrote to me describing her young son's spontaneous past-life recall:

> We were travelling to Sunderland one day in June 1996. We were just coming into a small village called Ryhope on the outskirts of Sunderland when our son Adam, who was in the back seat of the car, sat forward. He pointed to a spot just before a bridge we were about to go under, saying he had died over there. My husband Eddie and I looked at each other and I asked Adam to repeat what he had said. Again Adam told us that he had died over there and again pointed beside the bridge.
>
> A bit further along the road, Adam pointed to the same spot from a different direction and repeated that he had been killed at the place. As Adam was only three and a half, it was a shock for us. I asked how he had died. Adam told me that he had been in a plane and that it had crashed. There had been a man pressing on his chest and then there was water on his face. He kept saying that it was not an accident but that he had died on purpose. We let the matter rest for a couple of weeks.
>
> When we questioned Adam again, he repeated to us about the plane which was a quiet one, not a fast one like a jet, flying round and round. Then it crashed and he was dead. Again, we let things lie for a while.
>
> One day when my dad called round we just happened to mention what Adam had said about the plane crash. My father sat there and did not seem to believe what we were saying.

Then he told us that a plane had crashed at that spot during the Second World War. I wanted to find out more. I telephoned the Sunderland Air Museum and asked them about the crash. The curator told me that it was a British plane and the only person who had been killed was the pilot. His name was Cyril Joe Barton and a book had been written about him, as he was a hero because he had lost his own life avoiding crashing on the town of Ryhope. I managed to get hold of the book. As I read it, so many of the things confirmed the details Adam was gradually unfolding.

Cyril Joe Barton had been on a mission over Nuremberg when his plane had been attacked. It was badly damaged and all the communications systems were destroyed. Cyril gave a signal to the crew but three of them misunderstood and baled out, one of them being the navigator. He decided to try to make it back to England with the rest. When Cyril arrived over the north-east coast, he was running out of fuel. As he swooped low over Ryhope he noticed all the houses. He circled round to avoid the houses and on the last turn he came down.

The plane smashed in half. The half containing the crew landed in a soft dung heap which saved their lives, but Cyril landed beside the railway lines and was killed. Locals tried to revive him but he did not regain consciousness. Cyril Joe Barton was later awarded the VC.

About a month before Christmas, Adam suddenly took the book from my desk and said that the photo of the man on the front was him before he died. He had not shown any interest in the book before. When we sat down with Adam and asked him questions about events described in the book, he was able to point out the plane that he was flying and, though many of Cyril's friends and family were pictured, Adam always pointed out Cyril among them, even at different ages, and insisted that it was him.

For about three weeks, Adam carried the book around, saying that it was his book about him and he would not let anyone touch it or put it away. He kept showing me the flight of the plane on the maps that are shown. While I have been writing this account, Adam has come up to me and said that when he gets a big lad, he wants to fly planes again and showed me how he marched when he lived before.

Ever since Adam has been able to talk he has told us about

planes crashing, and every time we have mentioned going on holiday in a plane Adam has refused because he says planes crash and he has shown us this by moving his hands and making the sounds. Every now and then he will come out with some new detail and I go straight to the book to check and he is usually right.

Reincarnation

Adam's experience would appear to confirm that, in certain circumstances, reincarnation can occur. Reincarnation, the belief that the soul returns to a new body after death, is accepted by about two-thirds of the world's population, mainly in the East, and is thousands of years old. Such philosophies see our lives as a progression – learning lessons we need to learn or righting mistakes we made in past lives. A noble creature may take human form in a new life, while someone evil may descend to a lower species. The ultimate aim is to escape from the cycle of birth and rebirth to perfect enlightenment and total union with the cosmos. Another view is that we return to a kind of cosmic melting pot, to be reborn, perhaps as a different life form, irrespective of our behaviour.

The Western tradition of reincarnation is less well documented. Some Ancient Greek philosophers, such as Pythagoras, were influenced by ideas of reincarnation. Early Christian Gnostic (shamanistic and psychic) sects also believed in rebirth, perhaps having inherited the idea from Ancient Egypt. In the twelfth and thirteenth centuries the persecuted Cathars in France subscribed to the view that we are all reborn many times. Belief in reincarnation re-emerged with the spiritists (Spiritualists) in France in the 1850s and this influenced the Theosophists in England, a group founded by Madame Blavatsky, a Russian trance medium, in 1875. The Theosophical Movement reintroduced the idea of reincarnation to Western society. Nowadays, with the growing interest in Eastern religions, reincarnation is more widely known, if not accepted, in the West.

Psychologists and psychotherapists suggest that past-life recall is a channel through which our secondary or inner personalities can develop by means of creative interplay with a therapist. The idea of the Collective Unconscious or Great Memory (put forward by

Jung) would explain past lives as tapping into a particular archetypal symbol with which our present situation shares some characteristics. Whether we accept that we had specific past lives that can be recalled or whether we tap into another life (real or symbolic), regression can help to use the wisdom of the more distant past to heal our own recent past sorrows and to move forward; by re-experiencing emotions through a past-life scenario we are able to receive information from the great pool of wisdom shared by all human beings, past and present.

By far the majority of past-life experiences are spontaneous, many being recalled by children under the age of seven. The most successful recent research has been among children who suddenly begin to talk about a past-life – sometimes, like Adam, quite unprompted and with detail far beyond the knowledge of their years. I once encountered Dom, who was two and a half when he climbed on an adult visitor's motor bike, revved it up and announced quite calmly, 'I know how to do this. I was a biker. I was killed in a crash.'

In a similar case, described to me by psychic researcher Joe Cooper, an eighteen-month-old child seated on a motor bike by an adult suddenly announced, 'When I was seventeen I was killed on a motor bike.' At the time the infant could hardly say more than single words, and he could never be persuaded to repeat the statement. Such early 'memories' seem to fade and, although there are tantalising cases of adult spontaneous regression, many in later life are elicited by past-life recall.

Exploring Past Lives

If you want to visit a past-life therapist, the organisations under Useful Addresses will provide lists of reputable therapists. However the majority of practitioners use hypnotherapy and you may not want to hand over control in this way, even to an experienced hypnotherapist. Furthermore, some people feel that any past lives they may access will be unconsciously directed by a particular therapist. Or they may be disappointed by the results because the life recalled is very mundane or only a few details emerge. (However, the latter problem may have more to do with the ordinariness of the vast majority of lives in whatever age.)

The spectacular cases reported in the media in reality form only a tiny, non-representative proportion of past-life recall experiences. I recently regressed Annie who talked of walking along a long flat country road in France, living on a farm with her granny and making bread. Annie said, although her life was hard, looking after the animals on the farm, she was quite contented. The group of people who were watching were disappointed that the picture was not more exotic. I regretted the fact that no dramatic events unfolded (mainly to increase my own psychic credibility), but Annie's past-life visions left her feeling very happy and relaxed. And I suspect that if I am regressed in 200 years' time to my present life, my visions will alternate between sitting at the word processor and washing up!

Practising Regression

You do not need to enter a deep trance state to recall a past life. You should simply be in a relaxed state so that your conscious mind is not pushing you along a particular track and you are not so anxious that you see nothing.

It is best to begin regression work with another person so that there is direct input and you can relax, knowing that the other party will guide you back quickly to the present. You need no special expertise to work together. Indeed, if you begin past-life exploration at the same time, you can explore the past together at a gentle pace.

Take it in turns to be the regressionist and the regressed (although, if you are close, you may find that you can see and even play a part in each other's visions). Some people are convinced that we are with the same set of people through many lifetimes, albeit in different relationships. And past-life work often indicates the strength of these links. Where a shared clairvoyant or telepathic link ends and true regression begins matters less than whether the experience is pleasurable and perhaps offers hints for solving present crises or overcoming fears and worries.

All psychic work begins with the imagination and ends – who knows where? If you find yourself creating a scenario, go with it and it may lead you into another world ...

How to Prepare for Past-Life Work

* If possible, try to withdraw from the modern world for two or three hours before a regression, avoiding television, computers, even the telephone. You can carry out past-life recall anywhere but the evening is especially magical, and you can go to bed afterwards and perhaps continue your visions in your sleep.

* When it is dark, light some candles rather than switching on lights.

* Prepare yourself by having a warm bath with a few drops of essential oil – lemon grass for spiritual awareness, or sandalwood for spiritual harmony – and wear comfortable clothes so that you feel relaxed. Take the phone off the hook so you will not be disturbed. Use an incense such as frankincense or rosemary, which have protective properties as well as increasing spiritual awareness.

* If you are working alone, ring yourself with pink, purple and white crystals, or place one at your head or foot, and sit in a comfortable chair or lie on a couch or bed. You can use pink-tinged and white pebbles if you have no small crystals. Or you may have a favourite large crystal that you could hold.

* Let a friend sit in a chair close to your head and lie on the couch or bed, holding between your hands either a large stone with a naturally formed hole in it or a crystal for past-life awareness, such as a piece of amber or polished jet (fossilised natural substances that are millions of years old and carry within them the wisdom of millennia). You can use such a focus when you are alone or hold your special wish crystal that contains the energies of angels or spirit guides or the evolved wisdom of your higher self.

* If you are alone, use a favourite tape of music or structured fantasy that you have found helpful for meditation work or allow your friend to guide you, using some of the ideas suggested below. At first people tend to rush through the stages, especially if guiding someone else, but allow for a three- or four-minute silence between each stage.

* Rather than concentrating on relaxing the different parts of your body, which may be counter-productive in triggering visions, close your eyes and count backwards, either from 100

to 0, or through the alphabet, watching the numbers and letters scatter like stars through the darkness.

* In the jewelled darkness, create an ongoing scene, either travelling above or beyond the earth, upwards towards a particularly brilliant star on a rainbow-coloured magic carpet or down a softly lit tunnel, carried on cotton wool clouds to a point of light. Travel across a sea with gentle waves towards the sunset or down a winding, tree-lined river on a boat through a rainbow waterfall, or on a carousel that turns and stops in a clearing in a beautiful forest.

* Visualise someone benign waiting for you – a guardian angel or your ideal or higher self who may be dressed in a guise that suggests wisdom and spirituality.

* Follow him or her along a path until you reach buildings.

* Choose a gate or door that you want to enter. If it does not seem right, carry on until you see the right natural entry point for you. If in doubt, follow a bird, butterfly or small animal that in myth represents helpful and protective instincts.

* See yourself first as a child in whatever setting is around you, unless this image does not feel right. There is no rule that says you have to begin as a child. You may not want to begin in childhood if you are not comfortable with your present childhood memories.

* Look at your feet, your clothes, your hair, your skin, your face, in a mirror or pool if there is one. Are you hot, cold, happy, sad? Can you gain any clues from the type of clothes you are wearing? Is there a uniform, or any insignia you could check afterwards? Are your hands smooth and chubby or worn with work?

* Next observe your surroundings. What are the buildings made of? Is it a town or a rural place? Are there woods or mountains? Are you near the sea or a big river? Are there any features that will help you identify time and climate? Is there a home that is yours? Can you enter it? What is it like inside? Is there distinctive furniture or coverings? What sounds can you hear? What odours or fragrances can you sense? Can you touch anything?

* Are there any people around? Are you a stranger or do the people you see relate to you? Are you a servant, part of an organisation? Do you work with them, live with them? Can you identify a time or place from the activities you see around

you? Is there any conversation you can share or overhear? Does one person seem important to you? If so, is he or she familiar?

* When you are ready to return or sense impending difficulties, look around and you will see your guide waiting. Follow him or her back to the doorway or gateway and then retrace your path to the carousel or the boat and continue until you reach the entry point, the bright star or tunnel.
* You may not want to rush straight back into life, so sit quietly for a while and perhaps make yourself a warm drink. If you have been working with a friend, talk over your experiences and see what moments you shared. One regression in an evening is enough, so arrange another day very soon for the other person to be regressed.
* Rest or spend your pre-sleep time listening to soothing music or watching the night sky if it is clear.

Natural Triggers of Past-Life Recall

If you experience no past-life sensations in an artificial setting, try visiting an ancient site, castle or industrial museum created from genuine buildings to which you feel attracted, sitting quietly in the sunshine and concentrating on a particular spot on a wall on which light is reflected. If there is nowhere in your immediate area that appeals take a map of an 80-kilometre (50-mile) radius around your home and, with your eyes closed, choose a location with a pin. Then phone the local tourist office to find a historical site close to the spot you picked. When you arrive, you will be surprised to find that you feel instantly at home and may instinctively know your way round.

To make the most of this technique:

* Begin your past-life recall early in your visit before your conscious impressions impinge on your psychic awareness.
* Create a picture frame of light and gradually expand it in your mind's eye so that you are inside the frame.
* Walk towards a distant figure and, as you do, see the castle, abbey or cottage filled with life and people.
* Now look down at your feet and see what shoes you are

wearing. Move upwards and find a reflective surface so that you can see your own features.

* Follow someone who is dressed similarly and enter into his or her routine.
* You may be recognised and greeted. If so, try to learn something about your life.
* Go beyond the immediate environs into the town or countryside and look for clues as to the era in which you find yourself.
* When you are ready, retrace your steps and stand within the frame of light, letting it recede and diminish.
* Walk quietly around the site and see whether you recognise any places you visited in your past-life recall.
* Look especially at old paintings and photographs which may seem vaguely familiar. You may recognise faces and places from your regression.
* Find out what was happening at the approximate time to which you returned.
* After a while, you will find yourself linking into other times and places, even if you did not have a specific life there. Psychometry, clairvoyance and past-life recall are all aspects of psychic awareness and, as you become more practised, the different strands will move closer together and give you more frequent and detailed experiences.

Section Eight

Healing

27

Healing

The Power of Healing

Healing is a natural ability which we all possess. Medicine is gradually learning more about the complex relationship between mind, body and spirit and about the power of the immune system to fight disease. Whether spiritual healing channels healing rays from a divine source, or awakens the natural power of the body and mind to heal itself of illnesses diagnosed as terminal, matters less than the fact that quite spectacular cases of healing do take place. Dr James Le Fanu, a GP who has studied both physical and spiritual phenomena extensively, has commented on the 'hidden and mysterious ways in which the body heals itself'.

Under Useful Addresses you will find a list of organisations that will train you to become a healer. If you do want to become a professional healer, although few charge for more than expenses, you should undergo instruction with an accredited healer.

However, the majority of healing work is carried out by individuals for themselves and for close family or friends, channelled through the deep bonds of affection that enable family members to send love and sometimes healing energies to absent relations or partners who are in distress. Pat told me, for example, that she was suddenly moved to pray for her absent husband as he was involved in a serious car crash 40 miles away.

Of all the healing methods, crystal healing is the most direct and can easily be learned for self-healing and for helping friends and family. Whether using crystals or any other form of healing, however, there are no guarantees of success. For every person who is spontaneously cured there are 10,000 more whose pain may be relieved a little. Someone with a serious illness may simply feel more comfortable or at peace after healing, and then go on to die. This should not be regarded as failure. Many spiritual healers add the words 'if it is God's will', which is not a get-out clause but an acknowledgement that sometimes the good and noble die and even little children cannot always be saved. Indeed I have come across the story of a skilled healer, Margaret, who found that, while she seemed able to heal other children, she was unable to heal her own son Robbie who died from a brain tumour. However Robbie did remain active, playing football almost until the end, and felt a wonderful warmth when his mother put her hands around his head.

Crystal Pendulum Healing

From the earliest times, gems and crystals (either crushed into powders and used as ointments or even swallowed or applied as magical remedies) have been used against the ills of mankind. The living energies of crystals focus the healing energies from the earth and amplify our inner healing powers.

Rose quartz, amethyst and clear crystal quartz seem naturally tuned for healing work. I suggested in Chapter 10 that you might like to include a healing stone among your personal crystals. Other stones associated with healing include agate, amber, bloodstone, jade, jasper, lapis lazuli and sodalite. You can use your divinatory crystals but you may prefer to keep one or two special healing crystals that you regularly energise and cleanse.

A pair of matching, smooth, rounded rose quartz crystals can be used for contact healing, or a smoky quartz can be used for removing negative energies and a clear crystal quartz of the same shape and size for replacing them with positive powers.

Charging and Cleansing Healing Crystals

The simplest yet most effective method is to hold a clear crystal pendulum over the stone or stones to be energised and pass the pendulum over them in slow clockwise circles nine times. With each sweep, see the glowing energies emanating from the pendulum.

To cleanse your crystals, pass the pendulum slowly anti-clockwise over the crystal or crystals nine times, seeing dark misty negative powers rising upwards and being absorbed by the pendulum.

Keep your pendulum well charged and positive by holding it under cold clear running water and then leaving it in water steeped with rose petals, over which a cleansing and empowering incense, such as pine, and a white candle flame have been passed.

Beginning Crystal Healing

Crystal healing is very instinctive. You will find that some books recommend a certain kind of crystal for a certain condition, but this may not be right for you. Experiment with different kinds of crystals and find which works best. A clear crystal quartz will energise and clear blockages and a dark crystal will help to remove pain and act as a harmoniser.

Holding Your Crystals in Healing

Since the right hand is controlled by the left side of the brain and controls assertive energies, it is said that you should hold your energising crystals in your right hand for healing. Use clockwise movements with your crystal or crystal pendulum to input healing powers.

If you use a crystal or pendulum for removing pain or calming, the left hand is controlled by the right, 'feeling' side of the brain and so you should use your left hand with an anti-clockwise movement to draw out pain.

Crystal Chakra Healing

In Chapter 1, I introduced the idea of Chakra Magic (p. 19). As well as psychic and physical functions, chakras are also linked with the health of different parts of our bodies. Where a chakra becomes blocked, physical symptoms, pain or tension can indicate a 'dis-ease'.

Many people find it helpful to link particular crystals or colours with those symbolic energy centres in order to balance certain deficiencies or blockages in the physical and psychic body.

The chakras are linked to each other and to the body through spiralling energy lines. The three main energy channels are: the *sushumna*, the central channel that begins at the base of the spine and rises to an area at the base of the brain; the *ida* and the *pingala* which also extend from the base of the spine to the brow and end at the left and right nostrils. They criss-cross the sushumna in a spiral like a caduceus (the twined snakes on Mercury's staff).

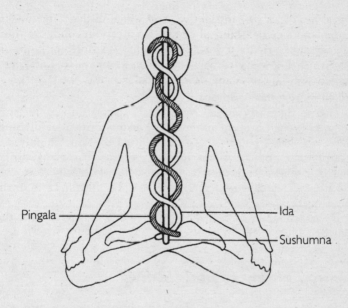

The paths of energy

As these channels operate on a psychic level, they do not follow definite paths. For this reason I have not given a diagram of the meridians since they are unique to each person. You may find that you use different routes to each chakra at different times, according to the current dominant energy.

Tracing the Energy Lines

When the chakras are balanced and healthy their colours are clear and luminous and they rotate smoothly. But when they are blocked they become cloudy or sluggish, making that sphere of our body feel wrong or our whole functioning slow and difficult. You can see the chakras in your mind's eye or use a crystal pendulum or a clear quartz crystal to trace your energy lines intuitively.

If you aren't familiar with chakras, begin at the base of your spine and trace an energy path through your body to your head. Do this by passing a clear crystal quartz over the front of your body slowly or getting a friend to pass a pendulum upwards, if you find it difficult yourself. If you already follow the tradition of chakras, still let your crystal guide you and, rather than concentrating on specific chakra energies, experiment with this more generalised method to tune into your own instinctive knowledge, which can enrich more formal methods.

The pendulum or crystal may spiral at spots throughout your body, as though it is encountering a small whirlpool. This could well be a chakra point. The chakras listed overleaf are only one interpretation; other systems involve more or fewer, so you may find that your energy centres do not coincide exactly. However the strongest circling will probably take place in the areas of the main organs.

If the pendulum or crystal feels heavy or seems to vibrate, this may be a blockage point.

General Chakra Crystal Healing

If you have a pain at one of the blockage points, rotate your pendulum or a dark crystal anti-clockwise to clear the blockage. See the pain or discomfort rising as a dark mist or a grey piece of wood, tugging until it is free. Cast it mentally into the cosmos to form a star and be healed.

Hold your pendulum or a clear quartz crystal and rotate it clockwise to replace the pain with healing energies or crystal movement, seeing pure white sky energies pouring through the crystal into the body.

Chakra Healing Using Specific Chakra Crystals

Once you have traced a blockage with your pendulum or quartz crystal to the area of a specific chakra, you can hold the appropriate coloured crystal over it. If you simply wish to promote general well-being, hold each coloured crystal over its appropriate chakra or lie with your crystals in place at all the suggested chakra points.

The Root or Base Chakra

This is situated in the base of the spine, seat of the *kundalini* or basic energy source. It is linked with your legs, feet and skeleton, and the large intestine. For disorders in any of these organs, use earthy red opaque stones such as red jasper or red tiger's eye or one of the banded red/brown agates, brown tiger's eye and black obsidian (Apache Tear) or any dark reddish-brown to black pebble.

Run your chosen root chakra crystal from the base of your spine and over your whole skeletal form. Feel the lines of energy and the pull of the earth of which we are all part. Crystal work can emphasise well-being as well as seeking out ills.

But perhaps your bones ache? Or you suffer from irritable bowel syndrome or pains in your legs and feet? If it's a pain, perhaps it's a blockage and so you may need some gentle energy to draw out the pain. This may also help if you tend to have to dash to the loo when you get stressed. And for panic attacks (which are rooted in getting your fight/flight mechanisms attached to the wrong cause), clearing your root chakra may help. Visualise the gentle earth and deep volcanic fire warming and soothing your pains away.

The Sacral Chakra

This is situated near the genitals and is said to govern physical pleasure, sexuality and the blood. The womb, reproductive system, kidneys, circulation and bladder all come within its sphere. Use orange crystals, such as carnelian or amber, jasper, banded orange agate, or the orange sandstone pebbles you can find for free.

Pass your crystal over your reproductive system and, even if you are no longer fertile, feel the life force. Trace your veins and sense the blood flowing through you. The sacral chakra is ruled by the moon so do not feel the solidity of the root chakra but your flexibility and the life force flowing.

Problems with PMT, menstruation, pregnancy and childbirth, and for men impotence, prostate troubles, premature ejaculation and other psychosexual ills, can all benefit from contact with sacral crystals. So, too, can circulation problems, cuts, anaemia and any blood-related difficulties. Often, creative crystals can be of greatest use in enabling the blood, fertility and creative sexuality to flow and so you may like to use clockwise movements freely. In today's society we get very worried about our physical nature and can get all kinds of blockages imposed on us by other people. Of course we should seek medical help, but in many areas psycho-physical and psycho-psychic pressures can interfere with natural functions.

If you have a cut or a problem with heavy menstruation, use your orange crystal to slow the flow of blood by leaving it on the affected chakra area for a few minutes.

The Solar Plexus Chakra

This lies just above the navel. Its body parts include the liver, the spleen, stomach and small intestine. It is said to absorb the life force from living food such as fruit, vegetables and seeds.

Solar plexus crystals include citrine, golden amber, yellow jasper, soft yellow moonstone and yellow calcite. Run a solar plexus crystal over your stomach (seat of the gut feelings which are such a good guide in life) and think of the centre of your being absorbing and filtering not only food but impressions from all the senses, including your sixth sense, and from people.

When things are wrong in this area we can suffer from ulcers, indigestion, a yellowy skin and feelings of nausea. Eating disorders, such as anorexia and bulimia, also have their seat here when the balance of eating is upset and food (which is necessary for strength and growth) becomes attached to an emotional trigger.

Yellow crystals can be used to calm this chakra when we are feeling churned up by life. No chakra acts in isolation and we all know that stress can upset our stomachs or cause those tension knots that make us writhe with pain. See this chakra bathed in gentle golden light, like early morning sunlight after rain.

The Heart Chakra

This chakra lies in the centre of the chest and radiates over the heart, lungs, breasts and also the hands and arms we use to hold and touch those we love. Heart chakra crystals include pink and green stones of all kinds, from brilliant green malachite or deep green aventurine to softer jade, amazonite and moss agate. Pink stones of this chakra include bright rhodonite or rhodochrosite, healing rose quartz (my favourite stone) and pink kunzite. Pink stones are also associated with the skin and a receptive pink stone, especially rose quartz, is excellent for rashes and skin irritations.

Pass a heart chakra stone around your heart, chest, breast and arms and feel the power of unconditional love flowing within you, without any guilt or recriminations.

Chesty coughs that go on and on without any apparent organic cause, a susceptibility to bronchitis and asthma, as well as irregular heart movements and hyperventilation, can all reside here. If it's a problem caused by emotion or an over-reaction physically in the form of an allergy then your green or pink crystal can be passed anti-clockwise to draw out the trouble.

It also helps to add a sacral red or orange crystal (also directed clockwise) over the heart chakra to get the blood circulating round your body and restore the colour to your cheeks. Some people who suffer permanently cold fingers, even in summer, say this helps.

The Throat Chakra

This was once described as the vehicle for speaking the truth that is in your heart. As well as the throat and speech organs, the throat chakra also controls the neck and shoulders and the passages that run up to the ears.

Throat chakra crystals include lapis lazuli, turquoise, aquamarine and blue lace agate and, as the gateway between the head and body, this is a vital chakra for free communication so that the energies can link with higher spiritual functions.

Run a throat chakra around your throat, neck and shoulders and you may well instantly trace any lines of tension. Feel the healing blue (traditionally one of the most healing colours) soothing and clearing, and you may hear the words you need to say.

If things are wrong in this area you may suffer from sore throats, colds, swollen glands and thyroid problems. I often get a cold or become hoarse before an important broadcast so I know stress is a vital factor in this area. Use a blue throat chakra crystal, such as blue lace agate or a soft aquamarine, to relieve sore throats and painful glands or lessen the effects of a cold. Or you can apply it in an anti-clockwise circle, if that is how your receptive energies work, over aching tense shoulders or neck muscles and feel the knots melt.

The Brow Chakra

This is just above the bridge of the nose and controls the eyes, ears, and both hemispheres of the brain, as well as the psychic functions attributed to the Third Eye. Its colour is indigo, merging from a true navy blue to soft purple. The best crystals are a soft amethyst, sodalite and peacock's eye (bornite).

Hold your crystal between your eyes. You may see soft rainbow colours or hear faint sounds, even music, but any flashes you get are already within your psyche and can only illuminate your world.

When this chakra isn't functioning properly you may experience a lot of headaches, nightmares, noises in your ears or temporary blurring of vision with no organic cause. If you can't sleep or feel afraid then use a brow chakra crystal, such as a pale amethyst or purple fluorite, to soothe your anxieties. Or if you have a headache, rub your amethyst, dipped in cold water, anti-clockwise across your temples and between your eyes to draw out the pain.

You can also sharpen your intuition by rubbing the brow crystal clockwise and letting the sensations come.

The Crown Chakra

This is at the crown of the head and its function is the coming together of all the energies to create something different and greater. So it rules the whole brain, body and psyche; our growth and our well-being, physical, mental and spiritual.

The best crystal for connecting with this chakra is perhaps clear quartz, a brilliant purple sugilite or a rich deep violet and white banded amethyst.

When this chakra is blocked, your whole body is out of sorts. You are likely to feel tired but unable to relax, worried but unable to focus your actions. You may suffer a series of minor accidents and have a permanent cold. You may feel alienated from friends and family but be unable to feel happy alone.

Your Chakra Crystals

Over time you may build up a special set of chakra crystals, one for each chakra. Each night you can arrange them in a formation of the seven chakras by your bedside, visualising the different coloured energies pouring into you, removing blockages, restoring the balance between mind, body and spirit, and giving you power to face the new day.

If any chakra seems particularly important or an area of your physical well-being needs attention, you can light a candle in the colour of the associated chakra and pass the appropriate crystal through the flame for Fire. Next, light an incense for health and renewed vigour, such as lemon, pine or cedar, and pass the crystal through it to symbolise Air. Sprinkle pure Water, in which a clear crystal quartz has been kept for twenty-four hours, and sea salt for Earth and place your crystal near a vase of greenery or flowers in your bedroom while you sleep.

In the morning, carry out the same ceremony outdoors, and then hold or pass the crystal over the appropriate chakra and feel the blockage clearing and the energy pouring in. Take the crystal with you and hold it over the chakra at noon and again at dusk.

Crystal Healing Using Tiny Crystals

I recently went to visit a very gifted Irish healer called Mary Maddison. She demonstrated a technique using tiny crystals which I have modified to fit in with my own research into crystal healing. I am very grateful to her for teaching me more about crystal healing in one evening than I could have learned from a dozen books.

To use this method:

* Take a china bowl, sufficiently deep and wide to put your feet in and move them comfortably. Fill the bowl with tiny polished crystals.
* You will need several hundred, but you can buy these tiny shards in mixed quantities quite cheaply as they are too small to sell individually. Ask your local mineral store or New Age shop if you can have a discount for buying in bulk.
* Charge the crystals by passing a crystal pendulum clockwise over the bowl nine times.
* Place your bare feet in the crystals and close your eyes.
* The crystals may feel warm or cold and you will feel energies flowing or even prickling throughout your body. Wriggle your toes and let the crystals 'climb your legs', so that the energies of the different crystals flow and refresh you.

* After about fifteen minutes, take your feet out of the bowl and see how many of the crystals remain on your soles.
* The fewer crystals on your feet the less harmonious is your physical and mental well-being. More than ten crystals on each foot show your energies are flowing freely, especially if the crystals are well-distributed over the whole sole. If one foot is covered and not the other, it may be that your life is out of balance and one aspect of your life is predominating over the other. The left foot is controlled by the right side of the brain, where intuition and creativity reside. More crystals on this side might suggest that you are neglecting the practical aspects of your health and well-being and should check your diet and get plenty of exercise.
* The right foot is controlled by the left side of the brain, the seat of logic, assertiveness and rote learning. A predominance of crystals here suggests you may need to spend more time promoting your mental well-being.
* Shake the crystals on to a large piece of paper.
* Look first at the crystal colours, assuming that you have a fair selection of all colours.
* If all the colours are equal, you are well-balanced, relatively free from stress and your physical health is good.
* Colours that are missing may indicate an area that needs attention. If there are only one or two colours you need to look after your health generally and get plenty of rest. Check the crystal colours listed.

Remedying the Deficiencies

Take a larger crystal of the missing colour and sleep with it next to your bed for a few nights. Try to add that colour to your life, especially by eating foods or drinking beverages of the missing colours.

After use, cleanse your bowl of crystals by passing your pendulum over it nine times anti-clockwise, or until you feel the pendulum become heavy.

You can also plunge your hands into the crystals before an important meeting or examination or communication in which the written word is involved. Your thoughts will be clearer and more ordered and you will find that uncertainty fades away.

28

Absent and Contact Healing

The key to healing is love and compassion. One of the most gifted healers I have come across is Aunty Connie who lives in Camberley in Surrey. She treats the ailments of the pensioners who visit her to have their hair done. 'I give them a quick blast of healing for their bad backs or arthritis while they're sitting under the dryer,' she told me. 'But it is as important to listen to what they say, because healing is about what people feel, what their troubles are. If they can feel less alone, that they are important to someone even for a short time, then their physical troubles melt away.'

Connie's secret is that she cares for people. Because she is interested in them, she heals their spirits.

Being a healer involves far more than treating a specific ailment. Skilled healers frequently use clairvoyance and mediumistic abilities to uncover the root cause of a problem that may give rise to mental, physical and spiritual discomfort. Occasionally physical symptoms may have a purely psychic cause.

For instance, Pete, who lives in Milton Keynes, was godfather to a little girl called Katy and often went to stay with her family who were close friends. But every time he visited the family, he suffered what seemed to be asthma attacks and was unable to breathe. Sometimes Pete would be ill for days after he had stayed the weekend at Katy's house, although he had no trouble at other times. His mother wondered whether he was allergic to the pillows and suggested he took his own. Pete refused, saying she was fussing. The next time Pete visited Katy, he had no trouble. However, two days after Pete returned home he was so ill that his mother telephoned a healer late at night. The healer said at once that Pete had been staying at a house with children, but that another little girl had died in the house some time before. The little spirit child really liked Pete but was jealous that he paid attention to the other children. Pete checked the local history and found that a little girl had died in the house. He even managed to track her grave in the local churchyard. Pete went to the graveyard and sat by the child's grave, explaining that that she was making him very ill and asking her to stop. From that time, Pete had no more trouble.

Had Pete been cured by absent healing? Or was the psychic explanation enough to trigger a healing response from Pete's own immune system to whatever was making him ill in the house? Since a child had died in the house, the healer had used mediumship to suggest not only the cause but the cure. And, by visiting the grave, Pete seemed able to break the physical cycle.

Absent Healing at Home

Healing circles led by accredited healers frequently hold absent healing sessions in which prayers and healing are sent to those who need them. However it is quite possible to practise absent healing at home, using a candle flame and a large crystal as a focus. You can work alone or with a group of friends (see Chapter 29).

Have a special book or a section in your psychic notebook in which you can write the names of anyone in your immediate circle, relations or friends or even people you read about in the newspaper or hear of on radio or television who may be ill or suffering in some way. Remember your own needs as well.

Sit in a circle or, if you are alone, use a clear quartz crystal to draw a circle of golden light of both energy and protection around yourself. Ten o'clock at night is traditionally a healing hour, perhaps because the demands of the day are ended and the healing energies can work throughout the night, when people are most relaxed and receptive to spiritual benevolence. However, any time can be a healing time, although it is good to have a set time for your healing work, perhaps half an hour once a week.

* Set a small table in front of you or in the centre of your circle if you are working with friends.
* Light a pink, purple or pale blue candle and let its light shine

into the crystal, which could be your personal healing crystal of amethyst, rose quartz or cloudy crystal quartz. Brilliant clear crystal spheres were used in Oriental cultures for healing, harnessing the power of the sun. And crystal quartz, held up to sunlight, can be a focus of daytime healing work.

* Begin your healing work with some pranic breathing, drawing in healing blue and purple light, or visualise your chakras opening so that your inner fire merges with the pure white life force from beyond.

* Alternatively, sit quietly and let the benign forces of the universe move around you. Some people offer a prayer or look deep into the crystal and visualise the healing energies as golden beams swirling within the flickering candle light.

* Read aloud each name in your healing book, pausing between each name and seeing the healing rays passing outwards and upwards to the person whose name has been spoken. If you know the person, see him or her in your mind's eye, surrounded by golden light, warmed and energised. See dark strands of pain leaving the body in grey strands and being carried in anti-clockwise spirals to become sunbeams or being absorbed downwards into the healing womb of the earth.

* When you have finished, sit quietly once more, gazing into the crystal. Let your own anxieties and pains be absorbed within the crystal and see them being replaced by pure light.

* Finally blow out the candle, concentrating on a particular person who is most in your thoughts, or sending the love and light to those for whom you have asked for healing and to all who are angry or unhappy. Send a little of the love to yourself. If you wish, say a final prayer and uncast the glowing circle of light. If you have opened your chakras, close them again or see yourself enveloped in pink protective light so that the healing energies will not be buzzing in your head all night.

* Wrap your healing book in white silk or a light material and keep it in a special drawer. Wash your crystal under running water or leave it in water with another charged crystal.

* Have a drink or a light meal to ground yourself and spend a few minutes chatting to your friends about everyday matters, or carry out a light domestic task such as tidying up or watering your indoor plants.

Contact Healing

Contact healing for anyone outside close friends and family is fraught with difficulties and it is best, if you do want to help others in this way, to be trained by a recognised organisation where you will be gradually led through the different stages.

As with mediumship, there are gifted healers who work outside any organisation and have no formal training. However, there have been so many charlatans and people seeking gratification of their own desires by claiming to be healers teaching healing, often for a high fee, that you would be best advised to contact a recognised body, such as those listed under Useful Addresses. If you cannot find an organisation in your area, begin with your local Spiritualist church who may run classes with an accredited healer or can direct you to someone trustworthy and skilled.

Contact Healing Within the Family

Rubbing a child's hurt knee or holding a hand over a lover's aching brow are examples of spontaneous contact healing within the family. The most effective method of contact healing is to apply gentle pressure to the root of the pain.

In order to find the root of the problem:

* Using a crystal pendulum or pointed quartz crystal, begin at the place where the person complains that he or she feels pain or discomfort.
* Gently move the pendulum or crystal about 5 cm (2 inches) from the body, using small circular movements and following the energy flow, until you suddenly encounter a negative force which may be reflected as a heaviness or the pendulum swinging wildly. The patient may even give a small yelp of discomfort. This is the root and it may be nowhere near the site of the pain. For example, migraines can be linked to the stomach if there is a food allergy and an ache in the neck may be linked to holding the base of the spine in an awkward position, perhaps because of a leg pain.
* As you become more practised, you can visualise the root of the pain and will no longer need the outer confirmation of the pendulum.

* You can use either your hands or a pair of round, smooth, rose quartz crystals.
* First, gently apply some warmed oils to the afflicted area with your fingers, anti-clockwise to ease the tension. Gently massage the brow, wrists and back of the neck for a general malaise. For the body you can use grapeseed, sunflower or sweet almond carrier oils; and for the face, wheatgerm or sweet almond. As you massage, visualise the dark knot of pain or sorrow being unravelled and dissolved by the oils of golden fruits and wheat.
* Using your fingertips or your crystals, gently rub either side of the afflicted area, first clockwise to energise it; and then one stone clockwise and the other anti-clockwise, reversing the procedure so that both provide balanced energies.
* Before long your hands or the crystals will feel warm. Kirlian photography has captured sparks emanating from healers' hands and there may be a mild buzzing of electricity.
* When you have finished spend a few minutes quietly talking to the person who has received healing energies and, if you wish, offer a silent prayer for their recovery or at least relief from pain and peace of mind and spirit, if their body cannot be restored to health.
* Contact healing, for trained healers and family members alike, is tiring, so try to spend the rest of the day without undue stimulation.

Where healing differs from conventional massage or aromatherapy (although both can be healing arts) is that the movements and oils are channels for spiritual love and awareness – many healers say from a higher source of goodness and wisdom. As you work, your hands are agents for positive love and sympathy and this is the reason that relations can often be effective healers without any training. As with many spiritual arts, the power of one person's love and affection for another can transfer healing powers or, if you believe in God, act as a transmitter of divine love. Indeed, many healers first discovered their powers when they healed a husband, wife or child.

Sun Power Healing

To use this method:

* On a sunny day, hold a clear crystal sphere or large, clear, pointed crystal quartz or crystal pendulum to the sunlight to be warmed, but make sure that it is still cool enough to be held against the skin without discomfort. Sun power healing is especially effective outdoors, near a lake or river where the sunlight reflects off the water.
* As you hold it up, see all the restorative and energising powers of the sun's rays entering the crystal sphere or point.
* Ask the family member you wish to help to sit or lie in the warm sunlight.
* Hold the crystal sphere or point over the source of pain and gently touch the afflicted spot so that rainbows are reflected within the quartz. Place the quartz on the Third Eye on the brow if the person is depressed or anxious.
* Visualise crystal rainbows radiating throughout the person's being, filling any dark corners and melting any knots of pain or sorrow with brilliant warmth.
* When you have finished, place the crystal between you and hold it for a few minutes so that it can act as a transfer for love and friendship that will transform any harshness from the sun's rays into optimism.
* If the person is well enough, spend an hour outdoors in the sunlight together and place your crystal sphere in water to be warmed and charged once more by the power of the sun.

29

Forming a Psychic Development Group

For many people, psychic development is essentially a private path, although they will inevitably end up doing readings for friends. Other people decide to develop a specific psychic art, such as mediumship or healing, through accredited organisations.

Whether you hope to make a career in the psychic world or just want to develop your skills by trying new approaches and exchanging information, you may find it useful to organise an informal group of friends to meet regularly, perhaps once a week on the same night, in each other's houses.

Eventually you may want to advertise for others who are interested in developing their psychic awareness to come along. But you should not have more than seven or eight in all or the group can become fragmented. Until the group does have a strong identity, you may not wish to invite people to share what is inevitably a very personal experience involving trust between members. I have been to several groups and was happiest in a group of five people who became very close and were able to share personal hopes and dreams quite freely, knowing that there was real friendship and affection between us.

You can consider hiring a professional clairvoyant teacher. But this can be quite expensive since you may end up paying for two or three hours' time plus travelling expenses. Also, in my experience, a trained leader tends to give readings and perform and you may be shy of displaying your own lesser talents or disagreeing.

Organising the Group

Have a preliminary meeting in which you can plan for about six meetings ahead, deciding on the topics, the different venues and equipment you will need to buy.

You should each choose a topic that interests you and act as leader for that particular week. You can decide what equipment you need to buy at these planning meetings and one person can act as co-ordinator. You may wish to purchase equipment for your own week or everyone can bring the necessary items for themselves each week, with the person at whose house you are meeting providing basics such as matches and paper and supper afterwards. Another method is to decide on the topic and each agree to bring a certain item.

Starting a Magic Box

Start a box of basic scrying, divinatory and magical equipment that can be passed on to the person holding the next session. Buy candles (white, red, silver, gold, purple and green will suit most purposes), pens in different colours, some clear quartz and dark coloured crystals for healing work, inks, a selection of dried herbs, basic oils such as lavender, lemon and eucalyptus, and a series of tiny objects such as silk flowers, dolls, silver hearts and charms for ritual magical focuses. Keep an ongoing list, adding items as they need replacing, and decide on an urgent item that each group member can contribute every week.

Introducing a Topic

Prepare materials by photocopying or writing lists, such as astrological candle colours, to distribute. Read around your subject, especially seeing if you can find any associated legends or historical facts that will place the topic in context. There is a list of books at the end that I have found helpful in my own studies. Have a practice run-through of any practical activities you plan.

Check in advance that you have all the necessary equipment and ring other members to see if they have had any difficulties in obtaining anything.

Prepare the room with candles, crystals, a soft incense such as lilac or rose, and offer a low-alcohol wine or fruit cup (alcohol, like drugs, tends to give a false sense of power and confidence and blunts natural perceptions).

After a brief introduction, begin the practical work as soon as possible and have two or three suggested activities. This should fill about half the allotted time.

You may then want to spend time trying out ongoing skills, such as psychometry, talking about significant dreams and perhaps sitting quietly around a candle flame, practising visualisation or absent healing.

Suggested Activities

Candle Magic on the New Moon

Each month you could meet either on the night of the crescent moon or during the week of the new moon.

* Place some cushions in a circle on the floor and make sure you have plenty of matches, plus your list of the relevant candle colour correspondences, and a selection of coloured candles and candlesticks for those who forget or come along to the group for the first time. Choose one person to make sure that everyone has what he or she needs and to suggest at intervals the movement through the different stages.
* Light the room with a few silver candles for the moon.
* Provide a selection of different-coloured strips of paper on which to write wishes. Each person will need a candle in his or her astrological colour (see below), plus the appropriate candle colour for your wish (see the list on p. 86).
* If the candlestick base is not broad, you may need a dish or small tray under the wish candle to catch the ashes of the wish.
* Ask those who are coming to bring symbols to set around the candles, such as jewellery and coins for prosperity, flowers for love, fruit for health and golden objects or charms for success. Small silver objects symbolise the moon, for silver is both the

colour and metal of the moon. Candlesticks in a silver colour are also symbolic.

* Ring the two candles with any red, yellow and orange stones, plus any moonstones.
* Have small dishes of oils to dress the candles with oils of the moon, such as jasmine, clary sage, sandalwood, neroli and ylang ylang.
* Rub the oil into first your astrological candle and then your candle of need, from top to bottom anti-clockwise and bottom to top clockwise, visualising your need or wish.
* Take a strip of paper in the same colour as your candle of need and write on it your name and your wish, in a magical alphabet if you prefer.
* When everyone has written their wishes, sit quietly for a few minutes in the candlelight, visualising a happier future and tuning into the new moon energies, promising new beginnings.
* At a given signal, begin, one at a time round the circle, burning each wish. Light the paper from the astrological candle and burn it in the candle of need.
* As an individual's paper is burned in his or her own wish candle, send love and positive thoughts to carry the wish on its way.
* When all the wishes have been burned, leave the candles to burn away in a safe place while you have supper. Pleasure should be an important part of a psychic group, with plenty of laughter.

Zodiacal Candles

Aries (21 March–20 April): Red.
Taurus (21 April–21 May): Pink.
Gemini (22 May–21 June): Pale grey.
Cancer (22 June–22 July): Silver.
Leo (23 July–23 August): Gold.
Virgo (24 August–22 September): Green.
Libra (23 September–23 October): Blue.
Scorpio (24 October–22 November): Burgundy or indigo.
Sagittarius (23 November–21 December): Yellow or orange.
Capricorn (22 December–20 January): Brown or black.
Aquarius (21 January–20 February): Violet or dark blue.
Pisces (21 February–20 March): White.

Flower Psychometry

In Chapter 3, I described ways in which you can use flowers to learn about the past and the potential future of the person who owns the flower. Flower psychometry is very suitable for group work. Some confident clairvoyants will select and identify flowers from a whole tray of blooms in order to tell you about the owner.

To practise this skill:

* When you arrive at your group, place your flower (with a tag marked with a letter) on a tray by the door so that no one sees who has brought which flower.
* If your group is small, you can each bring a bunch of mixed flowers and let each person go separately into another room, tag just one, and place the whole bunch on the tray.
* Let everyone take a tagged flower by touch, with his or her eyes closed, and hold it for a few minutes to see what impressions are received. Meanings for the different parts of the flowers are given on p. 38.
* Begin each reading with a description of the flower and its tag letter so that the relevant information can be identified afterwards. Record the impression on tape; only when all the flowers have been read should the owners identify their own flowers.
* Once the initial reading has been made, let anyone in the group add their impressions about the flower. Pass the flower round, holding it in turn, and share any pictures or impressions you receive. Sometimes you can get surprising pictures from your own flower that can link with a distant relation or early event in your life or even that of an ancestor.
* Once the flowers have been identified, play back the tape and allow each owner to interpret the impressions.

You can also bring along an old family treasure or even a stone from an old site or beach, pass it round, and again share impressions.

Circle Dancing

Circle dancing not only raises Earth energies, but lets the mind fall free. Link hands around a candle in a darkened room and step-tread, reciting a sacred word such as 'OM' or 'Shalom' (peace), or chanting a simple phrase such as 'We are One' or 'This is the Way' – whatever seems appropriate.

In the summer you can go into the garden if it is large enough, or to a clearing in a forest in the early evening. You can circle a large oak or ash tree, coming together after each circle to touch the tree and absorb its powerful life force.

Sometimes circle dancing fails because the dances are so complex that anxiety about performance clouds the conscious mind and so is counter-productive. I once went circle dancing with a group who met in a church hall where ley lines cross. The initial, powerful vibrations could be felt through the floor, but the magic was totally ruined because some of the long-standing members insisted on practising quite complex dances and complaining if newcomers were making mistakes. Only at the end, in the final simple stepping dance around a candle, did the energies flow freely.

Avoiding Problems

There is no limit to the activities into which group members can lead the other participants – guided visualisation, astral projection, past and future life work – by adapting and extending the ideas contained within this book.

Everyone has psychic strengths and weaknesses and can both teach others and learn from them. You cannot be equally skilled in every method, but do not be discouraged or tempted to sit out of an activity if you find it difficult.

There are no rights or wrongs, only different levels and forms of experience. If one member of the group appears to dominate or display superior knowledge, try not to allow him or her to be the star but encourage each other to take turns and, if necessary, interrupt with humour. I once heard a former witch say she left her coven because every gathering was like a trade union meeting full of power politics. This can be avoided with tact and good humour, and a level of communication that rivals the deepest friendship can be obtained by sharing psychic awareness in a positive way.

Psychic Development

We have touched upon many psychic arts in this book. Some you will adopt, some you may develop through further reading and practice, and some will not be right for you.

You can use your increased psychic awareness in everyday situations, to communicate better in love and business, and to become more spiritually aware (able to tap into potential futures and take charge of your destiny). You may use your gifts for your own spiritual and psychic development, or help friends and sometimes perfect strangers by giving them readings and interpreting their dreams and other-dimensional experiences.

You may go on to become a professional clairvoyant, healer or medium, in spite of the intense and sometimes heartbreaking contact with people in need who are searching for answers and comfort. You will be rich only in thanks and the joy of serving others, unless you become one of the few media stars who reap riches of the earthly kind.

Once your psychic horizons and awareness have expanded, you will never again be able to ignore your inner voice. You will sometimes be sad, for your heightened sensitivity will make you more aware of the sorrows of others. Joy also will be more intense and you will see sunsets, rainbows, newborn babies and smiles as daily miracles. If you listen to your inner voice, and trust your visions, dreams and daydreams, you will not be less connected with reality but able to see beyond the surface clutter to the true meaning. Then you can make connections that harness logic in the service of inspiration.

Real magic is everywhere. It can be accessed via natural imagination and intuition, if we tune into the powers of the earth and sky and our own inner wisdom. Each of us has two million years of experience behind us, and many more aeons ahead, to help us make sense of the world. We are creatures of past, present and future, equally at home in any and all times.

Now the exciting part begins: making a little part of the universe your own.

Useful Addresses

Spiritualism

United Kingdom

Spiritualist Association of Great Britain, 33 Belgrave Square, London SW1 8QL. Tel: 020 7235 3351. www.charitiesdirect.com
The Arthur Findlay College, Stansted Hall, Stansted Mountfitchet, Essex, CM24 8UD. (This is also the address of the Spiritualists' National Union.)

Australia

Australian Spiritualist Association, PO Box 248, Canterbury 2193, New South Wales.
Canberra Spiritualist Association Inc., Griffin Centre, Civic, Canberra.

Spiritualist Churches in Australia
These represent a selection of those who are eager to offer help and mediumship:
Brisbane Spiritual Alliance Church, 208 Logan Rd, Burunda, Brisbane, Queensland.
Elizabeth Spiritualist Church, Corner of Hogarth and Goodman Roads, Elizabeth South 2011, South Australia.
Logan Spiritualist Church, 7–9 Mary Street, Kingston, Tasmania.
The Melville Spiritualist Centre, Winnacott Street, Perth, Western Australia.
Newcastle Church of United Spiritualism of Australia, 61 King Street, Newcastle, New South Wales.
The Valley Spiritualist Church, 8 Thorne Street, Windsor, Brisbane, Queensland.
Victorian Spiritualists' Union Inc, 71–73 A'Beckett Street, Melbourne 3000, Victoria.

Canada

Spiritualist Church of Canada, 1835 Lawrence Avenue East, Scarborough, MIR-2Y3, Ontario.
The Directory of Spiritualist Organizations in Canada is published by the Survival Research Institute of Canada. A copy can be obtained by sending 5 Canadian dollars or the equivalent to:
Walter J. Meyer zu Erpen, Survival Research Institute of Canada, PO Box 8697, Victoria, V8W-3S3, British Columbia.
(The organisation can also be contacted by e-mail at: gateway@nucleus.com.)

Spiritualist Churches in Canada

A small sample of those who actively welcome contact:
Community Spiritualist Church and Circle of Light, 245 East Broadway, Vancouver, V5T-1W4, British Columbia.
East Hamilton Spiritual Church, 83 Ottawa Street North, Hamilton, L8H-3Y9, Ontario.
The Gateway Spiritualist Centre, 1069d Kensington Road NW, Calgary, T2N-3R2, Alberta.
Toronto Spiritualist Temple, 706 College Street, Toronto, M6G-1C1, Ontario.
Winnipeg Spiritualist Church, 1551 Arlington Street, Winnipeg, R2X-1V2, Manitoba.

New Zealand

New Zealand has Spiritualist churches in Christchurch, Dunedin and Wellington:
The Spiritualist Church of New Zealand, 41 Glenroy Street, Woolston, Christchurch, South Island.
The Spiritualist Church of New Zealand, Corner of Rankeillor and Lorne Streets, South Dunedin, South Island.
The Spiritualist Church of New Zealand, Second Floor, 14–16 College St, Wellington, North Island.

United States

These represent a very small sample of the large number of associations in the US:
California State Spiritualists Association, 5537 Whitney Avenue, Carmichael, California 95608.
Connecticut State Spiritualist Awareness, 101 Leffingwell Avenue, Waterbury, Connecticut 06710.
Illinois State Spiritualist Association, 10913 S. Parnell, Chicago, Illinois 60628.
Indiana State Association of Spiritual Science, NSAC 1724 Marsha

Drive, Indianapolis, Indiana 46214.

Maine State Spiritualist Association, RR #2, Box 5055, Carmel, Maine 04419.

Ohio State Spiritualist Association, PO Box 253, Ashley, Ohio 43003. Tel: 614 747 2688.

San Rafael Serenity Spiritualist Association, 322 Upper Road, San Rafael, California 94903.

Texas Spiritualist Assocation, 5213 Chestnut Lane, Bellaire, Texas 77401.

Lucid Dreams

United Kingdom

Celia Green, Institute for Psychophysical Research, 118 Banbury Road, Oxford, OX2 6JU. www.oxfordshire.co.uk

United States

Lucidity Project, PO Box 2364, Stanford, California 94305.

Earth Energies

United Kingdom

Findhorn Foundation, The Park, Forres, Scotland, IV36 0TS. (Workshops and courses that teach about meditation, consciousness and nature spirits.)
British Society of Dowsers, Sycamore Barn, Hastingleigh, Ashford, Kent, TN25 5HW. (Lectures and courses on using dowsing to heal illness.)
The Ley Hunter magazine, PO Box 92, Penzance, Cornwall, TR18 2BX.
RILKO (Research into Lost Knowledge Organisation), 8 The Drive, New Southgate, London N11 2DY. (A Charity Trust that provides education, on ancient sites, geomancy and earth mysteries.)

United States

The American Society of Dowsers, Dowsers Hall, Danville, Vermont. Tel: 05828 0024.
USA Stonewatch (Earth Energies), 334 Brook Street, Noank, Connecticut 06340.

Auras

Auragraph Energy Research Centre, Box 8378, Wooloongabba, Queensland 4102, Australia. (Help and equipment to study the aura.)

Past Lives

United Kingdom

A list of UK past-life therapists can be obtained from:
Atlantis, 37 Bromley Road, St Anne's on Sea, Lancashire, FY8 1PQ.
Corporation of Advanced Hypnotherapy and Hypnohealing, PO Box 70, Southport, Lancashire, PR8 3JB.

United States

The Association for Past-Life Research and Therapies, PO Box 20151, Riverside, California 92516-0151.
Dr Roger Woolger, Laughing Bear Productions, 5 River Road, New Paltz, New York 12561. (For training seminars in past-life work.)
OOBES, Kenneth Ring, Department of Psychology, University of Connecticut, Storrs, Connecticut 06218.

Paganism

The Pagan Federation, BM Box 7097, London WC1N 3XX.

Parapsychology, Psychic Study Societies and Colleges

United Kingdom

ASSAP (Association for the Scientific Study of Anomalous Phenomena), Dr Hugh Pincott, St Aldhelm, 20 Paul Street, Frome, Somerset, BA11 IDX. Tel: 01373 451777. www.assap.org
The Churches Fellowship for Spiritual and Psychic Studies, The Rural Workshop, South Road, North Somercotes, Near Louth, Lincolnshire, LN11 7BT.
The College of Psychic Studies, 16 Queensberry Place, London SW7 2EB.
Fountain International, 35 Padacre Road, Torquay, Devon, TQ2 8PX. (An organisation that hopes to improve the world through meditation, crystals and spiritual awareness.)
The Ghost Club, Tom Perrott, 93 The Avenue, Muswell Hill, London N10 2QG. Tel: 020 8883 0191. (Founded 1862.)
Haunted Scotland, 35 South Dean Road, Kilmarnock, Ayrshire, KA3 7RD, Scotland. (This is a bi-monthly magazine produced by Mark and Hannah Fraser who will also help with any ghost sightings, problems with hauntings etc. They are always glad to receive accounts from anywhere in the world, but especially Scotland. Tel: 01563 539509.)
The Scottish Society for Psychical Research, Secretary and Newsletter

Editor, Daphne Plowman, 131 Stirling Drive, Bishopbriggs, Glasgow, G64 3AX. Tel: 0141 772 4588.

Ireland

Irish UFO/Paranormal Research Association, Box 3070, Whitehall, Dublin 9, Eire.

United States

American Society of Psychical Research, 5 West 73rd Street, New York, New York 10023.
Ghost Trackers Journal, Box 205, Oaklawn, Illinois 60454.
Parapsychology Foundation Counselling Bureau, 228 East 71st Street, New York, New York 10021.
Strange, PO Box 2246, Rockville, Maryland 20852. (Paranormal research organisation.)

Healing

United Kingdom

The Abbess Well and the Well of the Triple Goddess, Minster, Isle of Sheppey, Kent. (Healing water is available freely, although donations towards the upkeep and restoration of the Minster well are appreciated. The image of the Triple Goddess, which has been implicated in 'miracle births', can be seen by advance appointment. Contact Leon and Brenda Stamford. Tel: 01795 872882.)
British Alliance of Healing Associations, Mrs Jo Wallace, 3 Sandy Lane, Gisleham, Lowestoft, Suffolk, NR33 8EQ. Tel: 01502 74224.
Dr Bach Healing Centre (Bach Flower Remedies), Mount Vernon, Solwell, Wallingford, Oxfordshire, OX10 0PZ.
National Federation of Spiritual Healers, Old Manor Farm Studio, Church Street, Sunbury on Thames, Middlesex, TW16 6RG. Tel: 01932 783164.

Australia

Himalaya Centre, 12A and 12B Inglis Street, Diamond Creek, Melbourne, Victoria 3089. Tel: 03 9438 4194.
Mary MacKillop Sanctuary, 24 Bourne Gardens, Cook, Canberra 2614. Tel: 06 251 5655. (Counselling.)
The Pathway to Wellness Centre, 8/116 Curlewis Street, Bondi Beach, Sydney, New South Wales 2026. Tel: 02 306 819. Mobile: 0414 387 323.
Swedenborg Enquiry Centre, 1 Avon Road, North Ryde, NSW 2113. Tel:

02 9888 1066. E-mail: sllandec@ozemail.com.au.
The Women's Health Centre, 47 Cambridge Street, Rockhampton, Queensland 4700.

Canada

National Federation of Spiritual Healers (Canada), Toronto, Ontario. Tel: 416 284 4798. (Call for information.)

United States

World of Light, PO Box 425, Wappingers Falls, New York, New York 12590. Tel/Fax: 914 297 2867.

Specialist Shops

United Kingdom

Mandragora, Essex ..., Oxfordshire, OX9 3LS. Tel: 01844 260990. (For books, tapes, tarot decks, incense etc.)
Pentagram, Cheapside, Wakefield, WF1 2SD. Tel: 01924 298930. (For pagan, magical and occult supplies.)

Australia

The Rock Shop, Arcade 83, Shop 4, 8 Bongueville Road, Land Cove, Sydney, New South Wales 2026. Tel: 02 4284247.

New Zealand

Gem Rock and Minerals, 52 Upper Queen Street, Auckland. Tel: 09 774 974.

South Africa

Tapstone Mining Corporation CC (for crystals), Dido Valley Road, PO Box 20, Simonstown 7975. Tel: 021 86-2020.
Rock and Gem Shop, London Arcade, Durban. Tel: 304 9267

United States

The Crystal Cave, 415 Foothill Boulevard, Claremont, California 91711.
Magick Bookstore, 2306 Highland Avenue, National City, California 92050.
Eye of the Cat, 3314E Broadway, Longbeach, California 90803.

Further Reading

Bailey, Arthur, *Dowsing for Health*, Quantum, 1993.

Balfour, Michael, *Megalithic Mysteries*, Dragon's World, 1996.

Brewer's Concise Dictionary of Phrase and Fable, Helicon, 1992.

Campbell, Eileen and Brennan, J.H., *Dictionary of Mind, Body and Spirit*, Thorsons, 1994.

Cockell, Jenny, *Past Lives, Future Lives*, Piatkus, 1996.

Crowley, Vivianne, *Wicca, The Old Religion on the New Age*, Thorsons, 1989.

Cunningham, Scott, *The Complete Book of Oils, Incense and Brews*, Llewellyn, 1993.

Cunningham's Encyclopaedia of Crystal, Gem and Metal Magic, Llewellyn, 1991.

Cunningham's Encyclopaedia of Magical Herbs, Llewellyn, 1990.

Devereux, Paul, *Shamanism and the Mystery Lines*, Quantum, 1995.

Dunwich, Gerina, *Wiccacraft, The Modern Witches' Guide to Herbs, Magick and Dreams*, Carol Publishing, 1993.

Eason, Cassandra, *Crystal Divination for Today's Woman*, Foulsham, 1994.

Discover Your Past Lives, Quantum, 1996.

Encountering Ghosts, Blandford, 1997.

Every Woman a Witch, Quantum, 1996.

The Mammoth Book of Ancient Wisdom, Robinson, 1997.

Miracles, Piatkus, 1997.

Pendulum Divination for Today's Woman, Foulsham, 1994.

Furlong, David, *The Complete Healer*, Piatkus Books, 1996.

Graham, Helen, *Visualisation, An Introductory Guide*, Piatkus, 1996.

Green, Marian, *A Calendar of Festivals*, Element, 1991.
  The Elements of Natural Magic, Element, 1989.
Hamilton, Robert, *Earthdream*, Green Books, 1990.
Heselton, Philip, *The Elements of Earth Mysteries*, Element, 1991.
Hoffman, David, *The Complete Illustrated Holistic Herbal*, Element, 1996.
  The Elements of Herbalism, Element, 1990.
Holbeche, Soozi, *The Power of Gems and Crystals*, Piatkus, 1989.
Hole, Christina, *The Encyclopaedia of Superstitions*, Helicon, 1995.
Meadows, Kenneth, *Earth Medicine*, Element, 1989.
Ozaniec, Naomi, *The Elements of the Chakras*, Element, 1989.
Parker, Derek and Parker, Julia, *The Secret World of Your Dreams*, Piatkus, 1996.
Randles, Jenny, *The Paranormal Source Book*, Piatkus, 1996.
Snow, Chet B., *Dreams of the Future*, Thorsons, 1991.
Stein, Diane, *The Women's Book of Healing*, Llewellyn, 1990.
Thorson, Edred, *At the Well of Wyrd, a Handbook of Runic Divination*, Samuel Weiser Inc., 1988.
Williamson, Linda, *Contacting the Spirit World*, Piatkus, 1996.
Wilson, Colin, *The Atlas of Holy Places and Sacred Sites*, Dorling Kindersley, 1996.
  The Giant Book of the Supernatural, Parragon Books, 1995.

Index